Under Custer's Command

Potomac's
MEMORIES OF WAR
Series

Outstanding memoirs that illustrate the personal realities of war as experienced by combatants and civilians alike, in recent conflicts as well as those of the distant past. Other titles in the series:

Under Custer's Command

The Civil War Journal
of James Henry Avery

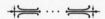

Compiled by Karla Jean Husby
Edited by Eric J. Wittenberg
Foreword by Gregory J. W. Urwin

POTOMAC BOOKS, INC.
Washington, D.C.

First Memories of War edition published in 2006

First paperback edition 2002
Copyright © 2000 by Karla Jean Husby and
Eric J. Wittenberg

Library of Congress Cataloging-in-Publication Data

Avery, James Henry, 1837–1902.
    Under Custer's command : the Civil War journal of James Henry Avery / compiled
by Karla Jean Husby ; edited by Eric J. Wittenberg ; forward by Gregory J. W. Urwin.—
1st ed.
      p. cm.
    Includes bibliographical references (p.) and index.
    1. Avery, James Henry, 1837–1902.   2. United States. Army. Michigan Cavalry
Brigade (1862–1865)   3. United States. Army. Michigan Cavalry Regiment, 5th
(1862–1865)   4. Custer, George Armstrong, 1839–1876.   5. Michigan—
History—Civil War, 1861–1865—Personal narratives.   6. United States—
History—Civil War, 1861–1865—Personal narratives.   7. Michigan—History—
Civil War, 1861–1865—Regimental histories.   8. United States—History—Civil
War, 1861–1865—Regimental histories.   9. United States—Civil War, 1861–1865—
Cavalry operations.   10. Soldiers—Michigan—Biography.   I. Husby, Karla Jean.
II. Wittenberg, Eric J., 1961–   III. Title.

E514.4 .A94   2000
973.7'474—dc21

                                                      00-056444

ISBN 1-57488-744-0   (paperback)

Printed in Canada

Potomac Books, Inc.
22841 Quicksilver Drive
Dulles, Virginia 20166

10 9 8 7 6 5 4 3 2 1

An attack of cavalry should be sudden, bold, and vigorous. The cavalry which arrives noiselessly but steadily near the enemy, and then, with one loud yell leaps upon him without a note of warning, and giving no time to form or consider anything but the immediate means of flight, pushing him vigorously every step with all the confidence of victory achieved, is the true cavalry; while a body of men equally patriotic, who halt at every picket and reconnoiter until the precious surprise is over, is not cavalry.

Maj. Gen. J. E. B. Stuart
General Order No. 26, Cavalry Tactics
July 30, 1863

Soldiering with the Michigan cavalry has been one continuous road of hard fighting. Both on foot with their carbines, and mounted, their sabres have carried terror in every charge.

New York *Herald*
1864

We have passed through days of carnage and have lost heavily. . . . We have been successful. . . . The Michigan Brigade has covered itself with undying glory.

Brig. Gen. George A. Custer
May 14, 1864

For all that this Brigade has accomplished all praise is due to Gen. Custer. So brave a man I never saw and as competent as brave. Under him a man is ashamed to be cowardly. Under *him* our men can achieve wonders.

Maj. James H. Kidd
6th Michigan Cavalry
June 3, 1864

*This book is dedicated to the
men of the Michigan Cavalry Brigade,
who followed its guidon into many an action.
It is also dedicated to the
memory of the men who wore both the
blue and the gray, and who
gave their lives for the last true
measure of their devotion.*

Contents

Contents

Maps

Foreword

UNDER THE BOLD AND AGGRESSIVE LEADERSHIP OF BRIGADIER GENERAL George Armstrong Custer, the Michigan Cavalry Brigade became the finest mounted unit of its size in the Union army. Indeed, it might be argued that Custer and his "Wolverines" were the first Yankee troopers to discredit the myth of Southern mounted supremacy when they stopped "Jeb" Stuart from turning the right flank of the embattled Army of the Potomac at Gettysburg on July 3, 1863. There is no doubt that someone from the Michigan Brigade mortally wounded Stuart at Yellow Tavern on May 11, 1864, the sharp fight that marked the Union cavalry's coming of age under Major General Philip H. Sheridan.

Despite its importance, the Michigan Brigade went many years without receiving the attention historians have accorded to other legendary Civil War brigades, such as the Iron Brigade, Irish Brigade, and Stonewall Brigade. For much of the past century, readers interested in a detailed account of the Michigan Brigade's service had only one place to go—the writings of Brevet Brigadier General James Harvey Kidd, who briefly commanded the Wolverines after Custer took charge of a division. Kidd's 1909 book, *Personal Recollections of a Cavalryman in Custer's Michigan Cavalry Brigade in the Civil War,* is an undoubted classic, but a military organization with the record of the Michigan Brigade deserves greater representation in the historical literature.

It is fitting that Kidd's preeminent biographer, Eric J. Wittenberg, should be responsible for getting another Wolverine into print. *Under Custer's Command: The Civil War Journal of James Henry Avery,* by Sergeant James H. Avery of the 5th Michigan Cavalry Regiment, will take its place with Kidd's memoirs as an indispensable reference on the exploits of the Michigan Brigade. That Avery represents a voice from the ranks makes the pairing even more ideal, as the plainspoken sergeant saw the Civil War from a different angle than did General Kidd.

Avery's *Under Custer's Command* is more than just a notable historical resource. It is even more than a good read. Anyone who picks up this book will feel as if he has sat down for a long, heart-to-heart talk with a Civil War veteran. Avery's words exude an unrehearsed candor and an unassailable authenticity. He wrote without fear or favor, addressing subjects that would have embarrassed his more image-conscious comrades. Amid these pages, tales of vice, cowardice, and desertion share space with feats of valor and self-sacrifice. Avery also disdained the pompous literary conventions that make so many Civil War memoirs seem dated and a trial to read. Anyone who wants to know what it was like to be a cavalryman in one of the hardest fighting units in the Union army will do well to start here. The experience will be both pleasurable and stimulating.

There are certain portions of Avery's narrative that should be of interest to serious students of the Civil War. His adoration of George Armstrong Custer was typical of the men who fought under the "Boy General" from 1863 to 1865. Avery sheds new light on the military career of Russell A. Alger, the 5th Michigan Cavalry's most famous colonel, who later became William McKinley's secretary of war. Avery also provides vivid descriptions of such battles as Gettysburg, Monterey Pass, Fourth Brandy Station, Buckland Mills, the Wilderness, Yellow Tavern, Hawes Shop, and Trevilian Station. Finally, Avery witnessed one of the most controversial incidents in Sheridan's Shenandoah Valley Campaign—the summary execution of seven Confederate guerrillas by Union cavalrymen at Front Royal, Virginia, on September 23, 1864. Avery's testimony will cause conscientious historians to revisit and reinterpret that tragic episode.

By publishing Avery's memoirs, Eric Wittenberg has raised his own stature as a historian of Civil War mounted operations. His informative introduction and the numerous notes he includes to illuminate Avery's text enhance the value of this book and should make it attractive to both professional historians and wider audiences. Although Sergeant Avery did not live to see it, he was fortunate to have his work fall into the hands of such a competent editor. And we are all fortunate that Sergeant Avery, like so many other Civil War soldiers, chose to record his experiences.

Gregory J. W. Urwin
Associate Professor of History
Temple University
Philadelphia, Pennsylvania

Preface

THIS BOOK IS THE RESULT OF AN UNUSUAL COLLABORATION. KARLA JEAN Husby is the great-great-granddaughter of James Henry Avery, known to his friends and family as Henry. Henry's journals and reminiscences have been in his family's possession since the turn of the century. For Karla, telling his story became a true labor of love. She spent several years pulling this narrative together, working hard to decipher the handwritten notations, to identify individuals, and to make some sense of her ancestor's story. She succeeded in putting together the pieces and developed the story into a cohesive narrative.

In doing so, Karla faced a daunting task. During the Civil War, Avery kept a daily diary of events, and in later years he put his notations to life in his personal journal. Unfortunately, over the years, some pages of his writings were lost. Through careful review of his war records and pension records, along with information obtained from her family's book of ancestors and other resources, Karla was able to fill in the missing facts, and his story was once again complete.

Once Karla had cobbled the story together, Eric J. Wittenberg got involved. Eric was asked to take the raw material developed by Karla and turn it into the final product that you see before you today. Drawing on his extensive knowledge of Union cavalry operations in the Civil War—and of the Michigan Cavalry Brigade in particular—he edited Karla's compilation and annotated it extensively. Drawing on Karla's research, he also wrote the introduction that follows, prepared the bibliography, compiled the listing of the campaigns of the 5th Michigan Cavalry, and selected the maps and illustrations that are scattered throughout this work. Thus the final product is a collaborative effort in the truest sense. Without the contributions of both Karla and Eric, this work would not have been completed.

Compiler's Acknowledgments

I WISH TO EXPRESS MY GRATITUDE TO GIFF RUFER OF EVERETT, WASHINGTON, for his encouragement and for loaning me his ten-volume set of *Miller's Photographic History of the Civil War.* I am also grateful to Kerry Chartkoff and Matt VanAcker of Michigan's "Save the Flags" for providing information and pictures. Likewise, I thank Patricia Bravender, the Grand Rapids, Michigan, Public Library historian, and the Marysville, Washington, branch of Sno-Isle Regional Library for their assistance in my research. Finally, I am grateful to the Oxford University Press, United Kingdom, O.W.L.S. Department, for its help in interpreting a problematic word.

I especially wish to thank my husband, Jerry C. Husby, for his love, compassion, understanding, and support while I researched and compiled Henry Avery's memoir. Likewise, I wish to express my gratitude to my brothers, Charles A. Ream and Ronald L. Ream, for their support and enthusiasm, without which I might not have been able to complete this task. I also owe a special thank-you to the loving memory of my grandmother, Lois Clay, from whom I inherited Henry Avery's memoirs. I send my love and appreciation to them for their support and affection as I struggled · ith this project.

I further wish to thank Don McKeon, Brassey's publisher, for the faith shown in me, for having the insight to bring Eric Wittenberg into this project—which has been greatly enhanced by his vast knowledge of the Civil War—and for making this work available to the public.

Karla Jean Husby
Marysville, Washington

Editor's Notes and Acknowledgments

ALL OF THE TEXT OF THE MEMOIR WAS WRITTEN BY HENRY AVERY AND COM-
piled by Karla Jean Husby. To maintain the historical integrity of the work, I
have retained Henry's misspellings, grammatical mistakes, and the other flaws
that dot the work. If a name was misspelled in the text, its correct spelling
appears in the annotations at the end of the book. Likewise, I have tried to
provide capsule biographies of most of the many soldiers mentioned by
Avery in his memoirs. Those capsule biographies also appear in the annotations. Unless otherwise noted, the source for those capsule biographies is the
official roster of soldiers published by the state of Michigan in the years just
after the Civil War.

I did some minor editing of the memoir, such as breaking up lengthy para-
graphs and breaking the narrative into chapters. For the most part, though,
the reader will not know where I have made changes, with the exception of
the chapter breaks. There are, however, a few places where the reader will
see material in brackets. Those instances represent places where I have
added some text to the narrative so as to connect things or to make sense of
the memoir. There are also several places where Avery withheld the names of
soldiers in order to protect their privacy. I have been unable to identify these
men. Those spots are so designated by (name withheld). I have tried to anno-
tate the work to provide the maximum amount of information and to steer
the reader to other sources that will allow him or her to seek additional information on the topics discussed by Avery, if the reader chooses to do so.

My introduction provides a biographical sketch of Henry Avery and gives
a brief historical sketch of the 5th Michigan Cavalry and of the legendary
Michigan Cavalry Brigade. Prof. Gregory J. W. Urwin of Temple University, a
leading Custer scholar and student of the exploits of the Michigan Cavalry
Brigade, has written the fine foreword.

As with every project of this nature, I have many people to thank, and I sin-
cerely hope that I will be forgiven if I neglect to mention someone who ten-
dered assistance in completing this project. I wish to thank my friend and

fellow cavalry historian, Greg Urwin of Philadelphia, for his insightful comments on this manuscript. I am also, as always, deeply indebted to Brian C. Pohanka, of Alexandria, Virginia, for his support and guidance and for taking the time to review this work. I am likewise grateful to Blake A. Magner for once again providing the fine maps that grace the pages of this book and for his helpful suggestions for editing Avery's memoirs, to Bryce A. Suderow for his assistance in locating and obtaining the illustrations that appear in this book, and to Sharon Bierman for her eagle eye and incessant nitpicking at the details.

Most of all, I wish to thank my much-loved and long-suffering wife, Susan, for her endless patience with my addiction to telling the stories of the horse soldiers of the Civil War. Without Susan's love and support, I would not be able to find the time and the freedom to tell the stories of these men who gave so much for their country.

Finally, I thank the editorial and production team at Brassey's for making the lengthy publication process as painless as possible. I hope that the public finds this work as intriguing as I do, and I hope that the reader finds the same merit in Henry Avery's story that I find.

Eric J. Wittenberg
Columbus, Ohio

Introduction

WITH THE COMING OF THE CIVIL WAR IN 1861, THE STATE OF MICHIGAN
had a total population of just under one million, of which almost ninety thousand men and boys volunteered to fight for the Union. Michigan's soldiers
made significant contributions to the Northern victory in the Civil War. Perhaps the most significant of those contributions was made by the Army of the
Potomac's Michigan Cavalry Brigade. There was perhaps no finer brigade of
volunteer cavalry to serve either the Union or the Confederacy during the
Civil War. Certainly no other brigade of horse soldiers was as famous or as
respected as were the men of Michigan, their distinctive red cravats flapping
proudly in the breeze as they went into many a battle.

The Michigan Cavalry Brigade consisted of four fine regiments of volunteer cavalry: the 1st, 5th, 6th, and 7th Regiments of Michigan Cavalry. This
brigade was organized in the early months of 1863 and served as a cohesive
unit for the balance of the Civil War. The Wolverines, as they proudly became
known, gained their greatest fame under the command of Brig. Gen. George
Armstrong Custer, the so-called Boy General with the Golden Locks. However, when the Michigan Brigade was formed in February 1863, Brig. Gen.
Joseph T. Copeland, a prominent judge and attorney from Pontiac, Michigan—the man responsible for raising and equipping the 5th Michigan
Cavalry—commanded the new brigade. Copeland, at age fifty, was much
older than the men he commanded and was probably not up to the rigors of
service in the field.

Consequently, in June 1863, on the eve of the great Battle of Gettysburg,
Copeland was relieved of command and was replaced by the twenty-three-

year-old Custer, who jumped in rank from lieutenant to brigadier general in a single day. Maj. Gen. Alfred Pleasonton, commander of the Army of the Potomac's Cavalry Corps, raved, "Custer is the best cavalry general in the world, and I have given him the best brigade to command."[1] Under Custer's leadership, the Wolverines became the most feared and effective Northern cavalry command. By May 1864, Custer would proudly claim, "We have passed through days of carnage and have lost heavily. . . . We have been successful. . . . The Michigan Brigade has covered itself with undying glory."[2] Another Union cavalry brigade commander, Brig. Gen. Wesley Merritt, told Custer, "The Michigan Brigade is at the top of the ladder."[3]

The Wolverines idolized George Custer and would have followed him to hell, had he asked them to do so. Maj. James H. Kidd, commanding officer of the 6th Michigan Cavalry, wrote to his father in June 1864, "For all that this Brigade has accomplished all praise is due to Gen. Custer. So brave a man I never saw and as competent as brave. Under him a man is ashamed to be cowardly. Under *him* our men can achieve wonders."[4] Pvt. William Kenfield of the 7th Michigan called Custer "the idol of his troopers and the terror of his foes." "Every man in his brigade worshipped him," noted Capt. Manning Birge of the 6th Michigan, "and would follow him through anything. They never went back on him nor he on them."[5] By the fall of 1864, even the Confederates reportedly had a healthy respect for the Michigan men. "They call his men the flying devils of Michigan," bragged Pvt. Joseph Jessup of the 5th Michigan.[6]

Later that fall, when Custer was promoted to division command, and Kidd, by then a colonel, took over as brigade commander, the men of the Michigan Brigade petitioned to be transferred to Custer's command, a request that was denied. Col. Peter Stagg of the 1st Michigan Cavalry, an extremely competent soldier, who received a brevet to brigadier general of volunteers for his gallant and meritorious service in the war, followed Kidd in command of the Michigan Brigade. Stagg led the brigade during the triumphant final campaign of the war, but the Wolverines are forever linked to the destiny of George Armstrong Custer.

[1] Gregory J. W. Urwin, "Come On You Wolverines!: Custer's Michigan Cavalry Brigade," *Military Images,* 7, no. 1 (July-August 1985): 9.

[2] Marguerite Merington, ed., *The Custer Story: The Life and Letters of General George A. Custer and His Wife Elizabeth* (New York: Devin-Adair Co., 1950), p. 97.

[3] Ibid.

[4] James H. Kidd to his father, 3 June 1864, James H. Kidd Papers, Bentley Historical Library, University of Michigan, Ann Arbor.

[5] Urwin, "Come On You Wolverines!" p. 11.

[6] Ibid., p. 15.

The 5th Michigan Cavalry was formed in the summer of 1862. That July, President Abraham Lincoln issued a call for three hundred thousand volunteers to serve three years "to bring this unnecessary and injurious civil war to a speedy and satisfactory conclusion." By that time, Michigan had already raised and sent three cavalry and sixteen infantry regiments, as well as eight batteries of light artillery, for the war effort and had a fourth cavalry regiment and another infantry regiment in the process of being raised. The new call for volunteers meant that Michigan's quota would be six new regiments of infantry and three more regiments of horse soldiers.[7] These new mounted units would be designated the 5th, 6th, and 7th Michigan Cavalry Regiments.

Copeland, then a colonel, was given the task of raising and organizing the 5th Michigan, then styled "Copeland's Mounted Rifles." One member of the regiment recalled that "on the 14th day of August, 1862, the Colonel very quietly went about the work of enlistment. From all parts of the lower peninsula the response came, full, hearty, and quick."[8] The new regiment would have a nucleus of officers who had experience in the 1st, 2d, or 3d Michigan Cavalry and would be armed with a powerful new weapon—the seven-shot Spencer repeating rifle. The Spencer was the first mass-production magazine-loading repeating weapon and had tremendous firepower. A soldier could get off nearly seven shots with it in a minute, while an especially adept infantryman could get off perhaps three shots per minute with his muzzle-loading musket.

By midsummer, the 5th Michigan Cavalry had been fully recruited, with eager young men arriving at the recruiting camp in Detroit in groups of fifty and sixty. By August 26, more than one thousand new horse soldiers were in training, and a few days later, another two hundred of them arrived. Copeland had to stop recruiting, and by mid-September, the training camp was home to "thirteen hundred men, some singing, some swearing, some hollering, some playing cards, and some dunning me for something to eat."[9]

The regiment would serve with great distinction throughout the balance of the Civil War. Out of the 260 regiments to serve in the Union cavalry, the 5th Michigan suffered the third highest number of men to die of battlefield causes.[10] The regiment's officer corps suffered especially heavy casualties,

---

[7] Edward G. Longacre, *Custer and His Wolverines: The Michigan Cavalry Brigade 1861–1865* (Conshohocken, Pa.: Combined Books, 1997), p. 81.

[8] James K. Lowden, "A Gallant Record: Michigan's 5th Cav. in the Latter Period of the War," the *National Tribune,* 16 July 1896.

[9] William H. Rockwell to his wife, 14 September 1862, W. H. Rockwell Letters, Waldo Library, Western Michigan University, Kalamazoo. Rockwell was a member of Avery's Company I.

[10] Lowden, "A Gallant Record."

losing ten of its commissioned officers, including Maj. Noah Ferry, whose brother Thomas was a United States senator from Michigan.

During its term of service, 1,866 men had enlisted in the regiment. A total of 101 of them were killed in action, and another 24 died of wounds over the course of the war. A further 69 unfortunates died while prisoners of war, and 109 men died of disease in the three years the regiment served. Finally, 196 men were discharged for disability, resulting either from combat wounds or sickness. Thus, of the 1,866 men who served, 303 never came home, representing 16 percent of the total regimental enrollment. When the men discharged for disability are added into this calculation, the regiment's total loss over the course of the war is a staggering 27 percent. Henry Avery was very lucky indeed not to have become one of those statistics. Despite the heavy losses, the regiment's Spencer rifles left an important mark on many a battlefield throughout the Civil War.

The author of this memoir, James Henry Avery, was born in Troy, Ohio, May 9, 1837, to James W. Avery and Ruhama Sutterlee Avery. A farmer, Avery moved to Michigan and married Ellen C. Dillenback on September 28, 1859, in Kent County, Michigan. When the Civil War began in April 1861, Henry and Ellen Avery were living in Hopkins, Michigan, with their first child, Augusta, born August 20, 1860.

Henry enthusiastically answered President Lincoln's call for volunteers. Reporting to Copeland's recruiting camp in Detroit, Henry Avery enlisted in Company I of the 5th Michigan Cavalry on August 14, 1862, and was mustered into service on September 3, 1862, at the age of twenty-four. The newly minted soldier stood 5 feet 10½ inches tall, and had a light complexion, with blue eyes and brown hair.[11]

Henry spent the fall of 1862 learning his new trade. When the regiment was transported to Washington, D.C., in the fall of 1862, Avery went along. He was promoted to corporal in January 1863, and to commissary sergeant in January 1864. Later in the war, he turned down a proffered promotion to first sergeant, as he enjoyed his role as commissary sergeant and did not relish the additional responsibilities the new position would subject him to. As commissary sergeant, Henry was responsible for seeing that his company's rations were properly maintained and distributed and that all got their fair share.

Although he was a commissary sergeant, Henry Avery saw plenty of combat during the course of the Civil War. When the 5th Michigan made a head-

---

[11] James Henry Avery consolidated service records, Regimental Descriptive Book, Company I, 5th Michigan Cavalry, The National Archives, Washington, D.C.

long charge into a Confederate wagon train at the Battle of Trevilian Station, Virginia, on June 11, 1864, Avery was cut off from his regiment. Along with twenty-seven other unfortunate comrades, Henry spent fourteen grueling days making his way back to the main body of the Army of the Potomac, safely returning to duty in July 1864.

Henry had health problems throughout the war and spent several stints in the hospital. In August and September 1863, he had an extended absence from his regiment, while he recuperated from a severe case of dysentery in a Union hospital located near Warrenton, Virginia. This illness plagued him for the rest of his life.[12] He fell seriously ill again in February 1865, and was hospitalized at the Michigan Cavalry Brigade's hospital in Winchester, Virginia. This time, the illness was serious enough that Henry Avery missed the end of the Civil War, instead spending the final days of the war in a sickbed. He was honorably discharged from service while still in the hospital at Frederick, Maryland, on June 23, 1865, and at the same time the rest of the company was mustered out.[13]

His military service finally over, Henry resumed farming in Hopkins, Michigan, returning home to his wife and young daughter. On September 29, 1865, his second daughter, Lucy, was born. Then on June 27, 1867, Ethel arrived. Orrin was born December 7, 1869; Ina was born on January 18, 1876; and Elizabeth arrived on February 25, 1878. Always proud of his military service, Henry Avery was a member of the largest veteran's organization, the Grand Army of the Republic, and was also a proud member of the Ancient Order of United Workmen, an early trade guild.[14]

In February 1880, Henry applied for a veteran's pension, claiming that the dysentery "finally resulted in chronic diarrhea inducing hemorrhoids or piles from which he has never recovered."[15] The pension was granted, but Henry's health continued to decline. Finally, on November 16, 1902, after an extended illness and complications brought on by his Civil War illness, Henry Avery died at the age of sixty-five. His widow, Ellen, received his pension of twenty-five dollars a month for the rest of her life.

James Henry Avery's funeral was held at the Church of Christ in Wayland, Michigan, on Tuesday, November 18, 1902. The service "was largely attended by many friends of this village and his old neighbors near Hilliards, where he

---

[12] James Henry Avery Pension File, Declaration for Original Invalid Pension, The National Archives, Washington, D.C.
[13] Ibid.; Avery's Combined Service Records.
[14] Wayland, Michigan *Saturday Globe,* 22 November 1902.
[15] Avery's Declaration for Original Invalid Pension.

had resided for many years." He was buried in the Ohio Corners Cemetery in Wayland, amid "the many and beautiful" floral offerings. Several days after his funeral, Ellen and his five surviving daughters, Lucy E. Bacon, Ethel B. Heniks, Augusta Lohman, Ina E. Smith, and Lizzie M. Clark, published a "Card of Thanks" in the local newspaper. They wrote, "We wish to express our most sincere thanks to the kind friends and neighbors who assisted us in the care and burial of our beloved husband and father."[16]

Ellen Avery watched another generation of promising young men go off to war when the United States entered World War I in 1917. She resided with her daughter Ethel Henika for the last years of her life, finally passing away on March 22, 1918, when she joined her beloved husband in death at the age of seventy-seven. Remembered fondly, Ellen was known as a woman who "had made many friends who will mourn the news of her death" and lived "a useful life in home and church."[17] She left behind twelve grandchildren and fifteen great-grandchildren—a fine legacy. One of those great-grandchildren, Dorothea Mae Lindell Ream, was the mother of Karla Jean Husby, the compiler of Henry Avery's memoirs.

The stories of the 5th Michigan Cavalry and of Sgt. James Henry Avery are forever intertwined. The two stories are, inevitably, inseparable. The pages that follow are the story of a young man's participation in the greatest adventure of his life.

[16] Wayland *Saturday Globe,* 22 November 1902.

[17] Wayland *Saturday Globe,* 24 March 1918.

1

A Soldier Goes to War

*"With the stiff upper lip that none know better than soldiers
how to put on, we were off . . . shouting the battle cry of
freedom."*

THE MICHIGAN CAVALRY BRIGADE, KNOWN TO THE WORLD AS ONE OF THE
best and most effective bodies of troops ever brought under the eye of the
best commander in the service; selected as it was from the best material, and
commanded by the best officers to be found; armed with the most approved
arms; never really beaten in battle, but always pushing the enemy, it gained a
renown equaled by few; excelled by none [that always made] a broad mark
of credit extended over the whole country!

But it is of one of its regiments principally, and one company in particular,
that this work is purposed to treat, but will bring in other regiments to support as occasion regards. In this work I shall give proper names and personal
adventures as nearly as my memory will admit, and shall endeavor to give
dates as near correct as possible; shall refer occasionally to Michigan in the
war, and such history as will help to give a detailed account of all moves as
seen by myself, or my companions, and from official reports.[1]

---

[1] At the conclusion of each action, campaign, or raid, a commanding officer was required to
compile a report of his unit's participation. Between 1884 and 1904, the War Department compiled the official reports into a 128-volume set known as *War of the Rebellion: Official Records
of the Union and Confederate Armies,* 128 volumes in 4 series (Washington, D.C.: U.S. Government Printing Office, 1884–1904). All further references to the *Official Records* shall be to the
"O.R.," and, unless otherwise noted, shall refer to Series 1.

I shall start with the enlistment of myself, and leave the cause of the war to others, as this is to be only a history of adventures, and scenes in camp and field of the company and regiment, with, as I said before, the support of the brigade.

In the summer of 1862, after the President had made the first call for three hundred thousand men, all was excitement, for it was then seen that a mighty struggle was to be undergone, to maintain our government, and it was the duty of every man who could bear arms to assist to the utmost of his ability, either in the field or at home, for we should have to depend in a large mea-sure on those at home for supplies. And all we asked was that our friends at home would see that our families did not suffer; and we would risk our lives at the front in the smoke of battle to save for them our glorious country; and as this was the feelings of the writer, we will take it also for the true feelings of all who enlisted. The Star Spangled Banner must and shall be saved, and again planted where it had been torn down by the hands of traitors.

The Star Spangled Banner, oh long may it wave, o'er the land of the free and the home of the brave.

It was in August, 1862, that I enlisted at a war meeting held in the congre-gational church, in the village of Wayland. There were several who enlisted at the same time; some for one regiment, and some for others. I enlisted for Berdan's Sharp Shooters,[2] as it may be here stated, the most of the company, of which I was afterward a member, were from the new country, in the county of Allegan, and were marksmen, who could, with a rifle, bring down a squirrel from the tops of the tallest trees, therefore, were to do good execution at fine shooting at long range.

After reporting at Allegan for duty, it was found that the regiment was full and we were not needed, therefore, returned home, but not to stay, as all were scattered in different parts of the army in a short time. I think it was on Sunday morning, a week or two later, that Judge W. B. Williams of Allegan[3]

---

[2] Col. Hiram Berdan was asked to form an elite unit of sharpshooters during the Civil War. Enough men demonstrated interest that two full regiments of sharpshooters were formed and equipped, with the designation of Berdan's Sharpshooters. To join the sharpshooters, a soldier was required to demonstrate prowess in marksmanship. To be eligible for membership, a man had to put ten consecutive shots within a combined distance of fifty inches from the bull's eye at a range of two hundred yards with rest and one hundred yards offhand. The soldiers wore special green uniforms and were usually armed with special Sharps .52-caliber rifles equipped with open sights. Membership was generally considered to be prestigious.

[3] Capt. William B. Williams of Allegan entered service in Company I, 5th Michigan Cavalry, at age thirty-six, at the time of the regiment's formation in the summer of 1862. He was commis-sioned captain on August 14, 1862, and served until the spring of 1863, when he resigned his commission on June 13. The reasons why he resigned his commission are unknown.

called on me, and wished me to join his company, of which he was captain, to go with the First Michigan Mounted Rifles, afterward, the Fifth Michigan Cavalry.

Of the men enlisting were Franklin Miller,[4] and Darwin E. Callaway,[5] along with myself. I will say here that Frank Miller was my companion through all, with a few exceptions, and came out without a scar. He was always a jolly, lighthearted fellow; and Callaway, who was quite a grumbler, was taken prisoner, and died in southern pens.

In Allegan, we joined a portion of the company with Geo. W. Lonsbury[6] as first sergeant, and after a meeting of the citizens of Allegan to present Captain Williams with a sword, we started at about nine o'clock, by stage, to Kalamazoo, where the regiment was being organized; and to make as good a feeling as possible, and cover up the grief of leaving home, a good deal of joking and laughing was indulged in, especially by one Mortimer Andrews,[7] who was the life of camp and march, nary a weary day after, in fact, he became so attached to the boys, and they to him, they always called him dad. One such a soldier would knock the blues out of a whole company and turn them into laughter. In this way, the first night after leaving home was passed off and morning found us in Detroit, where we marched to Banks Barracks[8] and assigned to our bunks by the quartermaster. We here formed the balance of the company which had preceded us, and a motley crew they appeared to be too; dressed in all styles of citizens dress and composed of all classes. Here too you could see the honest, quiet, brave, make up for a good soldier, and the smooth tongued, boasting blackly, who could do wonders in camp; but as afterward proved, as

---

[4] Pvt. Franklin Miller of Monterey, Michigan, enlisted in Company I, 5th Michigan Cavalry, on August 22, 1862, at age nineteen. He was promoted to corporal and served out his full term of service, being discharged at Fort Leavenworth, Kansas, on June 23, 1865.

[5] Thirty-year-old Pvt. Darwin E. Calloway of Hopkins, Michigan, enlisted in Company I, 5th Michigan Cavalry, on August 22, 1862. He was taken prisoner at the Fourth Battle of Brandy Station on October 11, 1863. Calloway died in captivity, either at Belle Isle, or, more likely, at the notorious Andersonville prison camp in Georgia.

[6] George W. Lonsbury of Saugatuck, Michigan, enlisted as first sergeant of Company I, 5th Michigan Cavalry, on August 12, 1862, at age thirty-three. He was commissioned second lieutenant in September 1863, as first lieutenant in July 1864, and as captain in November 1864. On March 12, 1865, he received a brevet to major, U.S. Volunteers, for gallant and meritorious service throughout the war. Maj. Lonsbury was mustered out at the conclusion of his term of service on June 19, 1865.

[7] Twenty-seven-year-old Mortimer Andrews of Allegan enlisted in Company I, 5th Michigan Cavalry, as the company farrier. He served his term of enlistment and was discharged on June 13, 1865.

[8] Banks Barracks was a training facility located in Detroit and maintained by the state of Michigan for the training of its recruits. It also served as the mustering point for the newly formed 5th Michigan Cavalry.

soon as gunpowder was on the breeze and touched his very sensitive nostril, away he would go to the rear and stop not until he was out of harms way. Here our bunks, or beds were one above another in four tiers, and room for two men in each. Thus one long board building accommodated the whole regiment of twelve hundred men, and was called Banks Barracks.

We were now drilled in guard mount and camp duty which is the first step to initiate us into the works of the army. We were at this time no more than an awkward squad, and many were the small fights caused by some remarks; which would afterward have been passed over, and what wonder, for here was the Yankee with supposed knowledge of every thing, the German whom you must not cross, the keen Frenchman, and the fiery Irishman, all strangers to one another like a lot of new horses together, if one got cross and kicked, others would kick, but soon get used to being together and then all right and good friends afterward. You might call your comrade hard names and he would laugh at you unless you call him a son of a _____, then the blood would fly.

The 30th of August 1862, the regiment was mustered into the service of the United States for three years, or during the war. The men were got into line and a horse brought out that would split a man that was not tough enough for a soldier, in going a few rods, each man was mounted without a saddle, the horse walked then trotted around a circle in front of the mustering officer and unless the parts fell off each side, he was passed, so far. Then he was taken to a tent and examined before a surgeon, being asked a few questions, draw up one leg and then the other, throw up first one arm then the other, if all right—pass this man.[9] Then you are tight, you cannot get away.

Thus the whole regiment were mustered in except a few who failed to pass. The next thing was to issue clothing to each man and in a few minutes an entire change was to be seen, a perfect, neat, tidy, regiment appeared on dress parade with new uniforms, black boots, white gloves and shiny buttons, you would hardly believe it to be the same lot of men. It was the pride of Detroit and the whole city, it would seem, turned out to view the parade each evening, nor was this the naive pride, as the history of the regiment afterward proved. All though some were mere boys, not over sixteen years, they made as good soldiers as men of thirty. On account of light-weight

[9] As Avery colorfully points out, the new recruits were given only the most cursory of medical examinations before they were sworn in and mustered as soldiers. This, of course, meant that a lot of physically infirm men managed to slip into the ranks of newly formed regiments. These men had to be culled out by a natural process of selection as the war proceeded.

proved to be better in respect to cavalrymen, as they were not so tiresome for a horse to carry, and do just as good service, generally stand more hardship than heavier men.

Now came company and regimental drill dismounted soon! All except a few were proficient in all the moves; then came the mounted drill, which being the same only mounted, was soon learned, and by the time we left the state were pretty well qualified to take the field, except the manual of arms, which came later while in camp at Washington.

Now this running the guard is very poor business, I should judge from the appearance of some of the men, especially after being on extra guard duty, but if you want to get into camp easily, bring a chick, or duck, as a bundle of feathers makes a pretty good pass; if there don't happen to be a supernumerary lieutenant[10] about, who wants to carry favor with the colonel! But it is bad business to go out and get drunk, for you are sure to get into trouble; I knew one man in Company G who was always getting out, getting drunk, and next in the guard house. I was with a patrol one night and we caught him, and started for camp, when passing a dark alley, he sprang away and led us a long chase, this time we lost him. I have since seen him in Washington get out, get drunk, and have a tare, then come to my tent (being acquainted with me), he would cry and promise to be a man, but whiskey was too strong for him to resist, he was otherwise a good soldier.

Now readers, you will perhaps agree with me that it took great moral courage to resist temptation to vice as much so as it took physical courage to meet the enemy in battle. I will show you by one circumstance that came under my own observation. We lost a man by sickness and his body was sent home, therefore, a guard under a lieutenant went as escort to the depot in Detroit. After delivering the coffin to the officials, the lieutenant led us to a hotel to rest and we were no sooner seated than a number of, I may say, devils in woman's garb, came into the rooms on purpose to rob the soldier, and ruin the man. And strong drink of various kinds was offered that they might the more easily accomplish their purpose. Now many were the times this would be tried, which proved to be the worst part of camp life, especially when near large towns, but the only way is to say "get behind me Satan" for you could not shun temptation. When on duty and many an officer as well as man, have been seen under the influence of drink, as I may further along note, but I will say right here for myself I had a wife and child at home besides my

---

[10] Avery refers to commissioned officers assigned to specific commands but not designated for service with specific companies.

own honor to guard and a will to say no. Therefore, I passed through the furnace without a burn. (When rum and temptation are thrown in our sight, we'll think of our nation and fight for the right.)

Soon after the clothing was issued, the company was sized off, and formed into squads with seven sergeants and eight corporals, of which I will here give the names in regular order. With the commissioned officers of the regiment and company:

Regimental:

Colonel Joseph T. Copeland; Lieutenant Colonel William D. Mann; Majors Freeman Norval,[11] Eboneezer Gould, Luther S. Trowbridge, Surgeon John P. Wilson, Ass't. Surgeon Addison R. Stone, Adjutant Richard Baylis, Quartermaster Arthur Edwards, Commissary Dwight A. Aiken, Chaplain Oliver Taylor.

Company I:

Captain William B. Williams, First Lieutenant George M. Dutcher, Second Lieutenant Charles H. Safford, Supernumerary Lieutenant Henry H. Finley.

Non-commissioned Officers:

First Sergeant George W. Lonsbury, Quartermaster Lawrence L. Crosby, Commissary Hannibal Hart, Duty Sergeants William C. Weeks, George W. Earle, Hiram R. Ellis, Martin Baldwin, William A. Piper.

Corporals:

William E. White, George H. Smith, Lewis Herner, David R. Taylor, George Kanouse, Robert Shriver, William H. Rockwell, Herman Garvelink.

Privates:

Avery, Henry (author)	Atkins, Samuel
Andrews, Austin	Batchelor, G. J.
Bliss, Henry G.	Burlingame, E. J.
Buchanan, Orris	Bennet, Caleb
Beaver, Charles	Burdick, Ruben
Collier, Daniel E.	Collier, Thomas
Cole, Gabriel	Clark, Samuel
Callaway, Darwin E.	Collins, James
Cole, Moses	Cummings, David
Cook, Henry	Cook, John

[11] Avery has misspelled this officer's name, which is actually Norvell.

Croff, Orlanda

Dallman, Henry

Dyre, Robert

Dyre, James

Drury, George

Dunn, William H.

Emmons, Abiul

Fox, Lafayette

Goodman, Wm.

Granger, Geo. C.

Hawks, Morgan B.

Hill, John

Kitcher, James

Miller, Franklin

Mann, Harvey W.

Munn, Geo. E.

Masson, Orlando

Murphy, John E.

Nolting, John

Pullman, Geo.

Rinehart, Jacob

Raab, Casper

Stuck, Abbert

Semon, D. H.

Slater, Nathan

Slaygal, Joseph C.

Thompson, M. C.

Warner, Henry

Wasson, Homer

Gardner, Geo. N.—Bugler

Miner, Jacob—Saddler

Chase, Elliot

Dalrymple, Benj. S.

Dyre, Russell

Dyre, Seth

Drury, William

Eaton, O. P.

Edwards, Wm.

Gavin, Cornelius

Goncher, Vernon C.

Hammond, Smith

Hicks, Geo.

Hodgetts, Geo.

Lane, Morgan

Miller, Godlep

Moses, Chas. E.

McWilliams, Wm.

Masson, Geo.

Newhoff, Wm.

Piper, G. A.

Powell, M. A.

Ross, Raphael

Renick, Albert

Slack, Anthony

Shupart, Geo.

Sanford, D. C.

Thompson, Geo.

Taylor, Chas.

Warner, E. A.

Bourman, Henry

Shaffer [Shaver], Samuel—Blacksmith

Andrews, Mortimer—Farrier

I will now try and give something of an idea of camp rations and mode of cooking. Each day two men were detailed for cooks, they were furnished with two large iron kettles and a large frying pan that would hold enough for the company. The cooking was done under sheds, in the rear of the barracks, and served on long tables to accommodate the whole company. The rations were boiled potatoes, boiled or fried meat, with often a pot of bean soup and coffee, the coffee was made in one of the kettles, and as different men were detailed each day, you may imagine that the cooking was not always the best. Our bread was sour bakers bread, generally rather stale. Some days the cooks would fry the bread in pork gravy, which made it more palatable, if not so healthy. The change of diet made a good many sick.

One day during the state fair held in Detroit, we were marched all day through the city, and getting in late, with no supper, the Col. ordered crackers and cheese for the whole regiment, which was a change that made us glad we were late. One duty in camp, known as police duty, was to clean the ground. Each man would be supplied with a brush of boughs of trees, and have to sweep the ground until not a particle of loose dirt could be found; then our horses were taken to water twice each day, down to the Detroit River, which all this taken together made the time pass off quickly. If we had a few minutes between, some would read, some play cards, and others, who thought more of home, spend their time writing letters to loved ones not to be forgotten. The bushels of letters were sent daily to friends who were anxiously awaiting news, expecting to hear that the regiment had been ordered to the front, but we were not to be sent off without again seeing home and friends; as we had been promised a furlough when mustered in and we got each a ten days furlough and left for home in detachments. One [detachment left camp] as soon as others returned, so as to have enough left to do camp duty.

I think it was in September that we left camp, Frank Miller, D. Callaway, Jim Kitcher[12] and myself, for Grand Rapids via the D&GH railroad. We arrived there about five o'clock in the morning, and as we were hungry, some wanted to stop in the city and get something to eat, but I told them to come with me, and led them out for my father-in-laws, which was about five miles out on the route we wanted to take, and arrived just after they had breakfast.

I think I had the best mother-in-law in the world, and knew she could cook better than our detailed cooks. She had seen us before we got to the house and had already started to get us something to eat. They were glad to see us and knew we were hungry, for soon we were called to the table which fairly groaned with a bounteous supply, and such biscuits, oh my! I have never forgotten them. I think they were the best I ever saw. I used to wish often after-

---

[12] Pvt. James Kitcher of Allegan enlisted in Company I, 5th Michigan Cavalry, on August 19, 1862, at age twenty-six. At some point, Kitcher was wounded in combat or fell ill, as he completed his term of service in the 2d Battalion, Veteran Reserve Corps. The Veteran Reserve Corps was a command composed of convalescent men whose terms of service had not expired, but who were typically physically unable to stand the rigors of normal service in the field. Kitcher received his discharge at Washington, D.C., on August 29, 1865.

wards, that we could have some when nothing but poor hardtack greeted our view, but those biscuits, they were the largest, lightest, nicest, sweetest, best I ever saw, and butter! Oh dear, I can't do justice to our appetites at that time, but let me say, it was the best thing during the war. After we had breakfast and rested, we started on our way toward Wayland. My brother-in-law was going part way with an ox team, and we rode until he got to the end of his journey, and then took it on fast across the fields for Hopkins, arriving at home just before dark. We found our friends all well and rather surprised to see us. You may think our ten days were spent pleasantly, and we left again for Detroit, and as we supposed, to go soon to the front. The parting kiss was given to our friends all around, the hand shaken with good wishes, and with the stiff upper lip that none know better than soldiers how to put on, we were off again, to gather from the east and gather from the west, shouting the battle cry of freedom.

We were quickly whirled along on our way to Detroit where when arriving in due time, we reported and took up our line of duty. I must mention here one source of amusement which furnished us with lots of fun; this was no less a personage than John Hill,[13] whom we called beauty from his queer, comical expressions of face. He would take a banjo, which he could play well, and getting on a dry goods box, would play and sing comic songs by the hour, to the amusement not only of our company but many of the regiment besides; and just here let me say that this same John Hill could take a Spencer or revolver and furnish just as good a time for the rebels to dance by, keeping time with "Hang Jeff Davis on a Sour Apple Tree."

On one occasion Governor Blair[14] made us a visit, and we expected to move at once to the front, as he had viewed the regiment and made some stirring remarks, but in a day or two, orders were issued that those who were voters might go home on a four day furlough to vote. This was a chance that all took who could, and you bet I was one of those who could vote, but finding my family in Grand Rapids and the time so short to go up to Hopkins, I did not bother with the voting, but Gov. Blair was re-elected all the same, for all Union men liked Mr. Blair, and he was a good war governor.

---

[13] Pvt. John Hill of Saugatuck enlisted in Company I, 5th Michigan Cavalry, on August 30, 1862, at age twenty-two. Hill was wounded in action in October 1863 and, after returning to action with the regiment, was taken prisoner on March 2, 1864, while participating in the infamous Kilpatrick-Dahlgren Raid on Richmond. He was released from captivity in October 1864 and was mustered out of the service at Fort Leavenworth, Kansas, on June 23, 1865—a young man who had sacrificed a great deal for his country.

[14] Gov. Austin Blair, war-time governor of Michigan.

Now as I find little more of interest in Detroit, I will just mention one time of guard duty, to show our friends what a soldier had to undergo. One night when I was on duty, there came up one of the tearing thunder storms with heavy rain, which drenched a man's clothing through, and compelled him to brace with all his might to stand at all. It then turned cold, as October storms often do, and left the poor boys who were exposed to it, wet and cold to go into guard quarters without a fire to warm by; for myself I fared better, for I was on guard behind a large building, with a friendly projecting roof, under which I could walk and keep out of the storm. The wind blew so hard that it tore down the adjutant's tent and scattered his papers all around. This being one of our first storms, we thought it pretty hard, but we got used to them later on.

Shortly after this, we left for the front, as orders had at last been received to that effect. A detail was made from each company of twenty-five men, under a lieutenant, the detail to include sergeants and corporals to assist the officers. And each man to take four horses and care for them on the route to Washington. Being among the number, I will give an account of that portion of the company which went with me. We cared for four horses and left the state, I think on November 2, 1862, two days before the balance of the regiment left over the same route. We occupied a coach attached to a heavy freight of stock cars, in which our horses were closely packed heads and tails. Our first supper on the train was taken about eight o'clock, at which we had our first taste of cold boiled pork and hard tack, and we did not relish either, but we were to learn afterward that this was good to what we should get sometimes. Our first stop was in Toledo, where we remained in the car for about two hours, and were served with hot coffee by the people. We were not subject to restraint, and some of the boys got off and committed some small depredations, such as taking lanterns off the trains standing by, and one soldier took a green hide and sold it. We were soon on the way again. With jokes and song we passed along and left Toledo far behind.

Our next stop was at Cleveland, where we unshipped our horses to feed and water, and it was the coldest place, I believe, we had seen, as the wind came off old Lake Erie, the last of which we were to see for years, and some never again. After feeding and reshipping, we were again off, slowly winding our way through Ohio, whose Union loving people were cheering us as we passed by. Ohio was doing well, but Michigan was even with her, and was excelled by none in sending troops. Our train moved so slowly that we could step off and on as we wished. A great liberty compared with the experience of the regiment to follow us, as we learned afterwards; the car doors of their train being guarded with sentinels to keep the boys in.

Somewhere on the road they passed us, so that when we got to Pittsburgh, where we again unloaded our stock to feed, and went to get supper in a large hall, we found our companions already there and waiting for us. We ate a good supper, during which two of the boys got to quarreling and whacked one another over the head with their tin plates, but they were to see the time that they could vent their spleen on the johnny rebs instead of each other. We of the horse guard had something else to attend to than quarreling, so we were off again to the shed where our animals were through eating and ready to be shipped, and we soon left the smoky city.

Leaving in the evening, morning found us at Altoona, on the top of the Allegheny Mountains, where we commenced the decent down the eastern slope, which is one of the most interesting scenes to be found. Here the great horseshoe bend,[15] where both ends of a long train will seem to nearly meet; there a high cliff, towering perhaps hundreds of feet above us, then a steep precipice far down which one might see glimpses of a shining river, peeping through the branches of trees, the tops of which were far below the observer; then here and there a clearing on the foot hills, with a pretty cottage nestled in a grove of trees. Our course next ran along the beautiful Monongahela with its bright sparkling water shining like silver; then by the broad Susquehanna; whose lake like expanse we could see gleaming with the rays of the morning sun. Passing brooks and rills, and vales and hills that lay in our course. We crossed the Susquehanna at Harrisburg. As we approached Baltimore we hoped to get a view of some of the work of the rebs, as we knew the track over which we were riding had been torn up in their raids not long before, and our interest was not abated until we reached the city, at which place we again fed our horses and gave them rest.

We were now in one of the hotbeds of secession, where the Sixth Mass. had met with opposition in passing through its streets,[16] and it seems the men must have been all patience, or blood would have run deep in the streets; but

---

[15] Avery refers to Horseshoe Bend, a major feature of the east-west railroad. The railroad curves around a mountain, making a 180-degree bend in the course of the railroad. Horseshoe Bend exists today.

[16] On April 19, 1861, the 6th Massachusetts Volunteer Infantry, one of the first Northern regiments sent to the defense of the national capital at Washington, D.C., arrived in Baltimore on a special train. There was no connection between the railroad the troops had taken from Massachusetts and the railroad they would use to complete their journey to the District of Columbia. Hence, the soldiers had to march through the streets of the rebellious city of Baltimore, their route lined with hostile crowds that grew large and unruly. A riot broke out, and 4 of the Bay Staters were killed, 36 wounded, and another 130 disappeared in the chaos. It was an ugly incident, one that foretold the brutal war that would follow. Bruce Catton, *The Coming Fury* (Garden City, N.Y.: Doubleday & Co., 1961), pp. 341–45.

forbearance was the order, and it was obeyed. No Southern army could boast such virtue. We found Baltimore a dirty, nasty town with a dark threatening aspect; but no indignity was offered us, for if there had been, the city would have suffered, as here we found our regiment again, and in no mood to be tampered with. Here we had our first experience with southern soil; a red, sticky clay, of which the southern people must be fond indeed. Sons of southern soil, mud sills of slavery, domineered over by aristocracy. Southern gentleman sap!

After feeding, we again cared for our horses, for the last time, and were on the rail again for Washington, at which point we arrived late at night, and went into camp as best we could until next day, when ground was assigned to us according to our position in the regiment. All then went to work to prepare winter quarters, and a camp of instruction, where we were to finish our education, preparatory to graduation in the field. Soon our tents were up and our horses provided with places in regular order, in front of our tents, separated by parade grounds.

It will now be necessary to divide the regiment into battalions, so that the reader, if he is acquainted with cavalry tactics, will be able to bear in mind the position in the regiment where my company, which was Company I, would be formed on all occasions, unless detached. The regiment was divided into three battalions, of four companies each, thus A, F, D, and I, First Battalion, and so on.[17] This brought Company A near the right center, or very near the objective point for artillery to aim at. But as companies always change off, and each takes the advance on a march, this would make some difference in position. We now began our work of drilling and fitting for the hard work to be done shortly in the field. The issuing of arms was the first thing, each man getting a Spencer rifle of seven shots, a Colt's revolver of five shots, and a sabre. This made each man almost an arsenal. Our rifles were found too long and heavy for cavalry and were changed for the Spencer carbine, a very nice, light arm.[18] These guns are what caused the Michigan Brigade to be called by the rebs "Kilpatrick's Seven Shooting Devils."[19] After they had a taste of our fire, they asked what kinds of guns we had, to load on Sunday and shoot all the week.

---

[17] To clarify, a battalion consisted of two squadrons. A squadron consisted of two companies. Majors usually commanded battalions, and captains usually commanded squadrons.

[18] Avery's description is a bit deceptive. The men of the Michigan Cavalry Brigade did not receive Spencer carbines until the winter and early spring of 1864. The men of the 5th Michigan continued to use the longer, heavier Spencer rifles until then.

[19] This refers to the Michigan Cavalry Brigade's assignment to the 3d Cavalry Division, commanded from June 1863 to April 1864 by Brig. Gen. Hugh Judson Kilpatrick.

During our stay near Washington, we could go out into the country with permission, but could not go into the city without a pass, as rebel spies and emissaries were plenty, and the city had to be well guarded. Sometimes, however, a pass would get a man into trouble as I know, for as myself and Frank had never been into the town, we asked Captain Williams for a pass to go down and get some stamps, and putting the pass, which he gave us, into my pocket, we were going along without thought of arrest, when we met the patrol. Halt! Order! Arms! was the command to the guard; your passes sir, to us. I pulled it out of my pocket, gave it to the sergeant who glanced it over. Full in guards, forward march; we were under arrest; the pass was dated wrong and we went to prison and were greeted with fresh fish, fresh fish from the rascals who ought never to see the outside of prison bars. We were taken to an upper room to await examination; during the day as I was looking out on the street, I saw a man from our regiment passing whom I hailed and told him to tell Captain Williams where we were, and in an hour or two, Lieutenant Dutcher's[20] white horse was seen coming and we were soon free to go to camp. This was our first and last experience in prison. Next day we got another pass and took a view of the city, week ending November 9, 1862.

As our camp was now well established on East Capitol Hill, Washington, our work was mostly drill and review, which was always the same day after day, but we took up everything we could to make the days pass off pleasantly, and agreeably. We used to ride out to the forts surrounding the city on the north and view the big guns that commanded the country for miles around. Jumping, wrestling, and pitching quoits, was indulged in by all. Here we will show, too, that life in camp was sometimes uncertain. One day Corporal Herner[21] was in Sergeant Baldwin's[22] tent talking some bantering talk, when Herner picked up a revolver and cocking it, pointed it at Baldwin's head saying "I will shoot you." Baldwin raised up his hand and pushed it away, which caused it to be discharged, the ball passing out the tent and piercing the

<hr/>

[20] Lt. George M. Dutcher of Saugatuck, who entered service in Company I of the 5th Michigan Cavalry at the time of its formation in August 1862. Dutcher was wounded in action at the Battle of Hanover, Pennsylvania, on June 30, 1863, but returned to action with the unit. He was commissioned captain on June 13, 1863, just before his wounding. He was honorably discharged for disability resulting from his combat wound in November 1863.

[21] This soldier does not appear in the regimental roster; however, his pension and service records at the National Archives confirm that he did indeed serve in Company I and that he was killed in action at the great cavalry fight at Yellow Tavern, June 11, 1864. See Lewis Herner Consolidated Service and Pension Files, The National Archives, Washington, D.C.

[22] Sgt. Martin Baldwin of Allegan enlisted as sergeant in Company I, 5th Michigan Cavalry, on August 21, 1862, at age thirty. He served his term of service and was discharged at Fort Leavenworth, Kansas, on June 23, 1865.

abdomen of Corporal Taylor,[23] who was leaning against a bale of hay, causing his death in a few days. Herner was never after the same appeasing man, and was killed later in battle. Thus, we lost a good man by carelessness.

After this a corporal had to be appointed to fill the vacancy, and Captain Williams selected your humble servant, who acted in that position until the following fall. I was often called upon to assist Sergeant Hart[24] in issuing rations, therefore getting used to that line of duty. Our tents were what are called A tents, and large enough to accommodate four men. E. A. Warner,[25] Harvey Mann,[26] Frank Miller and myself occupied one; our beds took up one half the room, and I agreed to build fires in our little sheet iron stove if they would let me have the fore side bed. Our cooking was not done now by detailed cooks, but the best cook in the mess was chosen for that duty. At that time, H. Mann was our best Bridget,[27] and his apple dumplings were splendid. During that winter we lived high, for we could buy anything we wanted extra.

---

[23] Cpl. David P. Taylor of Ganges enlisted as corporal in Company I, 5th Michigan Cavalry, on August 14, 1862, at age twenty-three. He died at Washington, D.C., on March 27, 1863, of wounds received by accidental discharge of a pistol and was buried in the Military Asylum Cemetery in the District of Columbia.

[24] Commissary Sergeant Hannibal Hart of Otsego enlisted in Company I, 5th Michigan Cavalry, on August 18, 1862. Hart was wounded in action in October 1863, and was honorably discharged because of disability on January 15, 1864.

[25] Pvt. Edward A. Warner of Hanover enlisted in Company I, 5th Michigan Cavalry, on August 20, 1862. Warner was honorably discharged at Fort Leavenworth, Kansas, on June 23, 1865.

[26] Pvt. Harvey W. Mann of Leighton enlisted in Company I, 5th Michigan Cavalry, on August 29, 1862, at age twenty-one. He was promoted to corporal and was killed in action at Shepherdstown, Virginia, on August 25, 1864.

[27] Avery refers to Mann being the best cook of the lot. Avery makes an allusion to cooking usually being considered women's work in the nineteenth century.

2

Chasing Mosby's Guerrillas

"The only way to succeed in cavalry is to work quickly, the more like lightning, the better, for this is the true mode of mounted fighting."

IN JANUARY, I THINK IT WAS, OUR REGIMENT WAS ORDERED OUT ON A SCOUT, so we packed up for our first raid into Virginia, and in early morning were on the march.[1] We crossed the Potomac at Chain Bridge,[2] and were on Virginia soil, and from there we took a route leading to Gainesville and Leesburg, going into camp the first night without seeing any rebs. This first night in the field we spent in fine style. The next day, after scouring the country all around and finding no enemy, we returned to camp. In February, we were ordered out again. This time a long, tedious march was made. We camped at Centreville on the first night. There had been a fall of snow, about six inches, after which

---

[1] Company I of the 5th Michigan actually did not take the field until February 8, 1863, as a result of bad weather. Then, they took off after the guerrillas of Capt. John Singleton Mosby, the legendary Gray Ghost of the Confederacy, who would give fits to the Union high command for the balance of the war. The Army of the Potomac's high command dedicated a vast amount of its resources to running down Mosby and his 43d Battalion of Virginia Cavalry. This particular mission was largely unsuccessful, as the Michigan men did not encounter any significant concentrations of guerrillas during a three-day mission. For Lt. Col. Freeman Norvell's account of the mission, see *O.R.*, vol. 20, part 2, pp. 60–61. Norvell, who was a drunkard, was cashiered from the army and sent home shortly thereafter for conduct unbecoming an officer.

[2] Chain Bridge was a major artery across the Potomac, connecting the Georgetown area to the Virginia side. It remains a major artery today.

a rain set in, and mud, water and snow was our bed; light and soft as feathers, but not nearly so warm. We would put down our saddles and try to sleep on them, but who could sleep in such a night; rain, rain, cold and wet, tired and sleepy. We wished the whole rebel army was near, so that our Fifth Michigan Cavalry could whip them, and end the war right there. But no, we were on the march again early, crossing the Bull Run battlefield where we could see such marks of war as bones, skulls, hands, feet, clothing—some blue and some gray, timber cut and torn by shot and shell, and buildings pounded down and perforated by solid shot. We stayed on this field the second night, and I slept with a large cannon ball under my head; a good pillow, was it not? But the novelty of the thing softened it somewhat.

Again morning found us on the march; passing to the east of Warrenton Junction we continued on south for two days, when we reached Burnside's army at Falmouth.[3] Going into camp there, we stayed a couple of days to rest and draw rations. Here we had a view of Fredericksburg, across the Rappahannock River, where a few weeks before, Burnside had met with defeat,[4] and where we were near the rebel army for the first time—indeed within range of their heavy guns. Here I saw Little Meg, big balloon, also the large telescope used to view the Johnnies with from afar, but they were sheltered for the time behind the hills. After recuperating our horses somewhat, we left again on our march back to Washington.

What we accomplished is known to the head officers, but not to me, except that we gained something of a knowledge of marching and camping out. On our way we passed near Mt. Vernon, the home and resting place of Washington. After a long, tiresome march, we again reached Washington, where we took up our old quarters for a short time, before going out for good. There was something to be learned from these marches that a soldier should notice, and that was to save his strength as much as possible, for it was often needed for the duty required, and for all night marches occasionally, but I have seen some men, when night came, and we were in camp, play cards nearly all night,

---

[3] After an aborted winter campaign through the muck of the Virginia countryside, Maj. Gen. Ambrose E. Burnside, the commander of the Army of the Potomac, retreated and went into winter camp at Falmouth, Virginia, on the northern bank of the Rappahannock River, across from Fredericksburg, approximately halfway between Richmond and Washington.

[4] On December 12 and 13, 1862, Burnside hurled the masses of the Army of the Potomac against nearly impregnable Confederate defenses on the high ridges overlooking the town of Fredericksburg. In an unequal contest, Burnside was thrashed, withdrawing on the second day with heavy losses. While watching the blueclad soldiers massing for an attack, Robert E. Lee, the Confederate commander, allegedly said, "It is well that war is so terrible, lest we grow too fond of it."

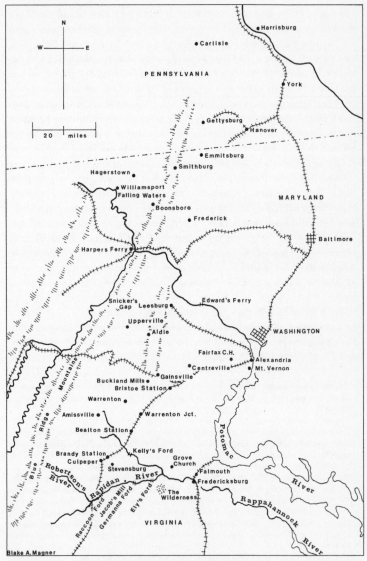

Virginia-Maryland-Pennsylvania Theater

and not be fit for duty next day; I had but little pity for such, and would put them on extra duty when I could, for they were robbing others of their rights.

One dark, rainy, windy night, Sergeant Hart and Crosby[5] were in our tent, and we were having a good time generally, when all of a sudden we heard the top of the drum, and made a rush for the parade ground, but alas, we had not heard the bugle call and were "pricked." For the benefit of those who do not know what pricked means, I will explain. When the roll is called, if a soldier is not present or accounted for, the sergeant puts a pin through his name, and he is marked for extra duty. But our excuse was a good one, so we got off, and this was the first and last time my name was pricked during the war.

Our next move was to break camp and take up our line of march across the long bridge for Fairfax Court House, where we went again into camp for picket duty at the front.[6] About this time the Fifth, Sixth and Seventh Regiments were organized into a brigade, and the First was afterward added.[7] The Fifth and Sixth each sent out a detachment to establish a post still farther out, beyond the reserve camp, and near the Chantita [Chantilly] farm. Here we had pleasant duty as it is not only pleasant, but healthy exercise to be mounted most of the time, riding around the country on a scout or even on post, which is sometimes tiresome and cold, as we found one night at least.

The 30th of March, 1863, the snow fell about twelve inches deep, but the next day took it all off and we had nice weather afterward.[8] Just imagine a very thick pine wood, with a hint of boughs in which huddled a half dozen men, and a huge fire in front. Now, this was comfort, but look outside and see the

---

[5] Quartermaster Sergeant Lawrence L. Crosby of Saugatuck, who enlisted at age twenty-seven. Crosby was later transferred to the Signal Corps in 1864 and was discharged in the summer of 1865 at the end of his term of service.

[6] The orders to march came on February 26, when the regiment was ordered to cross the Potomac and march to Fort Scott, where it joined the 6th and 7th Michigan Cavalry in a newly formed brigade commanded by Col. Sir Percy Wyndham, an English lord and notorious fop. Once the brigade came together, Wyndham led them on an expedition toward Fairfax, Virginia, intended to capture Mosby's guerrillas. This expedition was a failure.

[7] The four regiments of Michigan cavalry were formed into a brigade and assigned to an independent command of two brigades of cavalry assigned to the defenses of Washington, D.C. The Michigan Brigade was not a part of the Army of the Potomac's Cavalry Corps at this stage of the war but often acted in concert with it. Wyndham commanded this force for a time but was replaced in March 1863. Later, while en route to Gettysburg, the independent force of cavalry would be formally assigned to the Army of the Potomac, becoming the 3d Cavalry Division.

[8] Wyndham was relieved of command of the brigade in March when he was nearly captured by some of Mosby's guerrillas near Fairfax. The new commander of the cavalry forces was Brig. Gen. Julius Stahel, a Hungarian immigrant. Joseph T. Copeland, now a brigadier general of

heavy flakes of snow falling fast upon the pines and bending them nearly to the ground; the poor horses standing around, hitched to trees and shaking with cold and wet; then, again, see the sentinel sitting on his horse with his rubber blanket drawn tightly around him, now dozing, then suddenly starting at some slight noise, thus sitting for two long hours, which seem to him four, and asking himself what ails that relief, which the corporal has perhaps a little trouble to awake. Then on a pleasant night, but after a seeming long time, relief comes and the tired watcher takes his turn by the fire.

As Bushwhackers[9] were plenty, this was a good place for adventure, for often our pickets were fired upon in the stillness of night, causing the guards to be called out, every man in arms—in fact, we always slept with our guns in our hands, ready for instant use. But let me tell you, the guard is the most powerful man in the army, for he can bring the highest general to time, as he is not supposed to know or respect persons, especially in the night. I was taking out a relief, one dark, muddy night, when I heard the sound of horses splashing along. I sang out halt, and at the same time was challenged myself. I said advance and give countersign; the other party demanded the same, I told him I had the right of command as it was my picket ground, at the same time cocking my revolver and ordering him to advance. Frank, who was by my side, heard the click and also drew his revolver, quite a few seconds, the officer came paddling through the mud and advanced under my revolver. Giving the countersign, he proved to be a lieutenant from my own regiment; at the main camp, not with a patrol.

At one time there was a detachment from my company sent out five or six miles, and after they had gone, the officer in command of the camp sent for me and asked if I would undertake to escort a citizen outside the lines. I said yes, and he told me to pick a man to go with me. I of course took Frank, and we left camp and passed beyond our pickets, but no rebs troubled us and we came, after an hour or two, safely to our men who were at a farm house feeding their horses, and after being kindly treated and fed by the people, on the recommend of our charge, we left for camp with the company arriving safely without any adventure.

---

volunteers, commanded the Michigan Brigade. See *O.R.,* vol. 25, part 1, p. 80, for an account of this expedition. Mosby and his men evaded the dragnet of the frustrated Wolverines, prompting Maj. Noah Ferry of the 5th Michigan to write home, "had I been on trial in Michigan for whipping a lame idiot and stealing his dinner, I should not have been more mortified and ashamed then I was coming home yesterday." David M. Cooper, *Obituary Discourse on Occasion of the Death of Noah Henry Ferry* (New York: John F. Trow, 1863), p. 13.

[9] This probably refers to Mosby's command.

One early morning, the bushwhackers fired on our relief as it made the rounds, killing a horse and wounding a man; soon all were in the saddle and away; they would have captured some or all of them this time, but as soon as we came in sight of the rebs, Colonel Gray,[10] who was in command, had to maneuver the troops so long (instead of letting them go quickly) that they all got away. The only way to succeed in cavalry is to work quickly, the more like lightening, the better, for this is the true mode of mounted fighting; this was the secret of many of Custer's victories.[11]

Thus things stood up to June 16th, 1863, when we heard the bugle blow "Boots and Saddles," which caused a stir immediately, and we were soon in line and counted off in fours,[12] moving out of camp and down the road to Centreville and Warrenton,[13] beyond which, and to the north, we could hear the booming of cannon, and as we neared the mountains, the roar of guns became louder and faster.[14] We supposed we were on the way to take a part

[10] Col. George Gray of the 6th Michigan Cavalry, commanding this expedition.

[11] The Wolverines passed a quiet spring, picketing the Potomac River and fruitlessly chasing Mosby all over northern Virginia. They would not see active combat until the Gettysburg Campaign, June 9 to July 14, 1863.

[12] Cavalry usually marched in columns of four abreast.

[13] On 11 June, the 5th Michigan received a new commanding officer, who would lead the regiment until the fall of 1864. After a petition for appointment as colonel by Lt. George A. Custer was rejected by Gov. Blair, Lt. Col. Russell A. Alger was transferred from the 6th Michigan Cavalry and promoted to colonel so he could take command of the 5th Michigan. A lawyer by training, Alger was very well connected politically; during the McKinley administration in the 1890s, he would serve as secretary of war. Alger had a mixed record as a field commander during the Civil War. Alger seems to have been well liked by the men of the regiment; after the war, one of them wrote, "Let me offer this suggestion, that we owe very much of our good standing to the worthy and efficient who held the line, and especially to the man whom the State of Michigan delights to honor, the one the Grand Army reveres, and whose name is emblazoned in letters of gold on the heart of every one of Michigan's 5th Cavalry—the name of Russell Alexander Alger." J. K. Lowden, "A Gallant Record—Michigan's 5th Cav. in the Latter Period of the War," *National Tribune,* 30 July 1886. As we shall see, Avery had a good reason not to hold Alger in such high regard. Ironically, Custer became Alger's brigade commander just a few weeks later, much to the "Boy General's" amusement.

[14] The firing heard by the men of the 5th Michigan was a major cavalry fight occurring at Aldie, Virginia, on June 17, 1863. On June 9, the bulk of the Army of the Potomac's Cavalry Corps splashed across the Rappahannock River near Brandy Station and engaged the entire Confederate cavalry command in combat for nearly twelve hours. The Yankee troopers withdrew at the end of the day. The next day, the Confederates began moving north, beginning their second invasion of the North. On 17 June, Union cavalry, commanded by newly promoted Brig. Gen. Hugh Judson Kilpatrick, attacked Confederate cavalry posted strongly on high ground near Aldie. In a vicious battle, the Confederates defeated the Federal cavalry, nearly destroying the 1st Massachusetts Cavalry in the process. For a detailed study of this fight, see Robert F. O'Neill Jr., *The Cavalry Fights of Aldie, Middleburg, and Upperville: Small but Important Riots, June 10–27, 1863* (Lynchburg, Va.: H. E. Howard Co., 1993)—the best treatment of

in the heavy fight that was going on, but instead we were going to the left to keep the rebs from flanking Kilpatrick at Aldie, at which place he, that day, gave the enemy a good thrashing. One night out at Warrenton, and we were again on our way back to camp, where we arrived to find the whole of Hooker's Army from Falmouth[15] encamped to rest and then to move on across the Potomac, into Maryland; again chasing up Lee.

The next day,[16] we broke camp for good at this point, and took up the line of march toward the north, crossing the river next day at Edwards Ferry.[17] We were then in Maryland and fairly on the campaign, which was to be a very hard fought and victorious summer's work, and was to be ended by the heaviest battle of the war, Gettysburg, followed by several, lesser ones.

---

the important actions in the Loudoun Valley of Virginia. A young staff officer, Lt. George A. Custer, made a conspicuous charge at Aldie at great personal peril, catching the attention of Cavalry Corps commander Brig. Gen. Alfred Pleasonton, who marked the young man for advancement. More serious cavalry fights followed at Middleburg and Upperville between 17 and 21 June. At Upperville, the Federal cavalry inflicted its first significant defeat on the vaunted Confederate cavalry, driving it from the field and back through Ashby's Gap in the Bull Run Mountains.

[15] In February 1863 Burnside was relieved of army command at his own request. His successor was Maj. Gen. Joseph "Fighting Joe" Hooker, who had refit and reorganized the Army of the Potomac that winter and who took a huge and confident army into the field for the spring campaign. Hooker had devised a sound strategy and had begun good execution when he lost his nerve, receiving a dreadful defeat at Chancellorsville on May 2–5, 1863. Despite the defeat, Hooker had managed to keep the army's morale high and keep its combat effectiveness in a high state of readiness, and he did a good job of following the Confederate advance toward the Potomac.

[16] The Michigan Brigade received its orders to march on June 25, 1863, moving out that day.

[17] Located near Leesburg, Virginia, Edwards Ferry marks the spot where Goose Creek empties into the Potomac River. It was a popular and often-used spot for crossing the Potomac. The Army of the Potomac's engineers had constructed major pontoon bridges across the Potomac, and most of the army would cross the river there. The Wolverines crossed on 26 June, leading the army's advance toward its date with destiny in Pennsylvania.

3

The Gettysburg Campaign

*"Never did men do better fighting than did ours that day,
and they won lasting honors, for they defeated the enemy,
at every point."*

WE PASSED THROUGH THE PRETTY TOWN OF FREDERICK, WHICH IS SITUATED
in one of the most beautiful valley's I ever saw, and camped for the night about
one mile out on the Gettysburg Pike;[1] then moving on, we passed through the
now famous town of Gettysburg, where we were hailed with delight by the
union loving people, who brought out bread and apple butter, as we halted for
a short time in their streets.[2] One incident, particularly worthy of note, was a
young lady standing in the door singing the "Star Spangled Banner" as loud as
she could sing. We hailed her with hearty cheers. That night we camped just
beyond the town, and were visited by a throng of people, who brought out
nice cakes and pies for us, which were very acceptable after eating hardtack

---

[1] This is modern-day U.S. Route 15, which connects Frederick and Gettysburg, passing through
the town of Emmitsburg, Maryland, just south of the Mason-Dixon Line.

[2] The Federal cavalry arrived in Gettysburg on 28 June. The townspeople were especially happy
to see Union soldiers, as Confederate infantry and a small detachment of cavalry had visited
the town on 26 June, ransoming and plundering it and terrorizing the inhabitants. Any friendly
soldiers were greeted with open arms by the relieved citizenry. For further details on the first
Confederate visit to Gettysburg, see Linda J. Black, "Gettysburg's Preview of War: Early's
June 16, 1863 Raid," *Gettysburg: Articles of Lasting Historical Interest* 3 (July 1990): 3–8. See
also Wilbur S. Nye, *Here Come the Rebels!* (Baton Rouge, La.: Louisiana State University
Press, 1965), pp. 266–82.

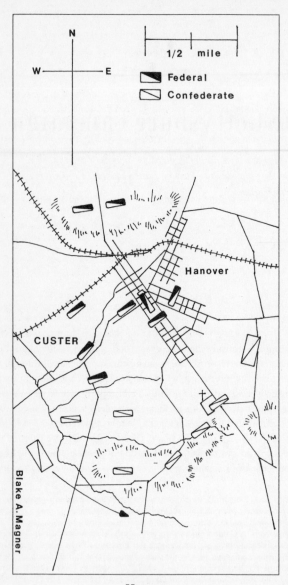

N

W——E

1/2   mile

Federal

Confederate

Hanover

CUSTER

Blake A. Magner

Hanover

so long. The next morning we were on the march early, and were moving off to look up the johnnies, who were prowling around toward Little York and Harrisburg.[3]

We passed through Emmitsburg and on toward Hanover, when we received orders to dismount to fight action front.[4] As this was our first order of the kind, and came so suddenly, we were somewhat flustered, officers and men, but we were quickly in line, leaving every fourth man to care for the horses.[5] The line advanced in good style, met the rebs, and after a short time beat them back, when we mounted and followed on a charge through Hanover.[6] This was our first skirmish, and without loss, except Captain Dutcher, wounded. Some time before this, he had been promoted, Vice Captain Williams resigned, which I should have mentioned before. Dutcher never served with us

[3] "Little York" refers to the city of York, Pennsylvania. After leaving Gettysburg, Maj. Gen. Jubal A. Early's Confederate infantry division marched east, crossed the Susquehanna River, and briefly occupied the town of York. Brig. Gen. Albert G. Jenkins's brigade of Confederate cavalry skirmished with Union defenders in the outskirts of Harrisburg, the state capital of Pennsylvania, on June 29–30, 1863. See Nye, *Here Come the Rebels!*, pp. 266–342.

[4] Avery appears a bit confused as to dates here. The Battle of Hanover occurred on June 30, 1863—not the 29th, as the narrative seems to indicate. On 29 June, Brig. Gen. Judson Kilpatrick assumed command of Stahel's independent division of cavalry, which was then designated the 3d Cavalry Division and formally made a part of the Army of the Potomac's Cavalry Corps. See *O.R.,* vol. 27, part 3, p. 376.

[5] This is a standard tactic for cavalry who were fighting dismounted. Because someone had to watch the horses of the men who were fighting dismounted, every fourth man was detailed to hold his and the horses of three companions. The mounts were kept nearby, so that the men could mount quickly and move out if necessary. The problem is that doing so reduces the available fighting force by one-fourth.

[6] The Battle of Hanover was a classic meeting engagement. Union Brig. Gen. Judson Kilpatrick, commanding the 3d Division, of which the Michigan Brigade was assigned, was moving into Pennsylvania, looking for the large Confederate force known to be operating between Gettysburg and York. Instead, Kilpatrick found three brigades of Confederate cavalry under the personal command of J. E. B. Stuart. As Avery correctly points out, the fighting began as dismounted skirmishing, but a decisive mounted charge, led by newly promoted Brig. Gen. Elon J. Farnsworth, routed the Southern horsemen from the town and nearly succeeded in capturing Stuart himself. Hanover was a significant victory for the Federal cavalry, as Stuart was driven north toward Carlisle. This meant that his route of march was made significantly longer and that neither Stuart nor his three fine brigades would arrive in Gettysburg until July 2, 1863, while the battle was already under way. For more on the Battle of Hanover, see Historical Publication Committee, *Prelude to Gettysburg: Encounter at Hanover* (Hanover, Pa.: Hanover Chamber of Commerce, 1963); Edward G. Longacre, *The Cavalry at Gettysburg: A Tactical Study of Mounted Operations during the Civil War's Pivotal Campaign, 9 June–14 July 1863* (Rutherford, N.J.: Fairleigh-Dickinson University Press, 1986), pp. 161–79. See also *O.R.,* vol. 27, part 1, pp. 986–87 and 991–96. For more on the specific role of the Michigan Brigade, see Longacre, *Custer's Wolverines,* pp. 121–42; James H. Kidd, *Personal Recollections of a Cavalryman in Custer's Michigan Brigade* (Ionia, Mi.: Sentinel Publishing Co., 1908), pp. 113–32; and *New York Times,* 6 August 1863 (setting forth the official reports of the commanding officers of all four regiments of the Michigan Brigade).

after receiving this wound. Here we saw our first dead rebs, and we were highly elated over our first victory.

Here too, our boy General Custer first took command of the Michigan Brigade; it was a good beginning, and was well followed up.[7] This was on June 30, 1863, after which we moved toward Gettysburg again. At this time, a detachment of our company, under Lieutenant Safford,[8] went on a scout to Little York. Meeting with a suspicious person, the lieutenant, with the advice of the sergeants, arrested him, and as he could not, or would not show a pass, we marched him into camp, and he proved to be General Meade's spy.[9] For this, the lieutenant was, without reason, put under arrest, but was soon released again and on duty. We now had a new captain assigned to our company, G. W. Townsend,[10] a good and efficient officer.

July 1st, we began to hear the boom of guns at Gettysburg and were hurried forward to take positions on the right of the infantry, a point we reached none to soon.[11] On the second of July, although the First, Sixth and Seventh

---

[7] Along with Capts. Elon J. Farnsworth and Wesley Merritt, George A. Custer was promoted from brevet captain to brigadier general of volunteers at the behest of Brig. Gen. Alfred Pleasonton, Cavalry Corps commander, on June 28, 1863. The three so-called boy generals were immediately assigned to command brigades in the Army of the Potomac's Cavalry Corps. Farnsworth, a soldier of great promise, would die seven days later at the Battle of Gettysburg. For more on Farnsworth's death, see Eric J. Wittenberg, *Gettysburg's Forgotten Cavalry Actions* (Gettysburg, Pa.: Thomas Publications, 1998). Merritt went on to have one of the longest and most distinguished careers of any American cavalryman, and most Americans are familiar with the untimely and unfortunate end met by Custer and nearly three hundred men of the 7th Cavalry at the Battle of the Little Big Horn, June 26, 1876.

[8] Lt. Charles H. Safford of Detroit. Safford eventually became a divisional assistant adjutant general, serving in that important staff billet with great merit.

[9] Maj. Gen. George Gordon Meade of Philadelphia assumed command of the Army of the Potomac on June 28, 1863, when Hooker was relieved of command at his own request. While the specific individual referenced by Avery cannot be identified, it is known that Meade had sent out numerous small parties in an effort to locate the widely spread elements of the Confederate army, known to be operating in various parts of Pennsylvania. For further information, see Edwin C. Fishel, *The Secret War for the Union: The Untold Story of Military Intelligence in the Civil War* (Boston: Houghton-Mifflin, 1996), pp. 484–537; Eric J. Wittenberg, "Ulric Dahlgren in the Gettysburg Campaign," *Gettysburg: Articles of Lasting Historical Interest* 23 (December 1999).

[10] Lt. George W. Townsend of Greenbush. With the coming of war, the thirty-eight-year-old Townsend entered service as a second lieutenant in Company G of the 5th Michigan. He was promoted to first lieutenant in the fall of 1862, and would be commissioned captain of Company I in November 1863. He was discharged for disability in July 1864.

[11] The Battle of Gettysburg began at sunrise on July 1, 1863, and continued for three long, bloody days. It has been the subject of more books than any other battle of the Civil War. For a comprehensive overview of the campaign and Battle of Gettysburg, see Edwin B. Coddington, *The Gettysburg Campaign: A Study in Command* (New York: Charles Scribner's Sons, 1968).

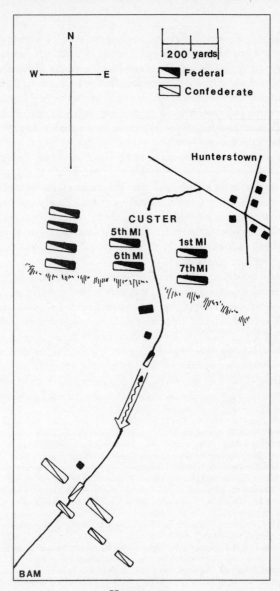

Hunterstown

cavalry were doing splendid fighting, repulsing the enemy at every point, our regiment was held in reserve.[12] We were in line of battle, dismounted in an open field where the shot and shell would come crashing along, tearing up the earth, or demolishing a tree or building. Still we lay in line on the ground, with guns ready for instant use, but no order came for us to move, as it was our duty to support those in front. During our stay on this part of the field, one man was detailed at a time to take all the canteens he could carry and go to a well at some distance for water.

When my turn came, I went to the well, and as I was getting the water, two women came out of the house and wished me to tell our colonel that there was a lieutenant down in their cellar who was abusing them for being afraid of the shells which came flying through the air. I went down to see that it was none of our regiment and told him I thought him in good business hiding away, and then misusing the ladies, but I had no time, nor business there, so returned with my canteens to the thirsty boys and reported the case, but I guess they let the coward stay.

The long, hot day, at length, wore off at night, settled down on the tired army, as the men cooked their coffee, and eat their hard tack. The roar of guns ceased with darkness, and the guards were placed on the line to keep watch in the still hours of the night, beside their fallen comrades, while the soldiers off duty rolled themselves on the ground to sleep with guns in hand, and without shelter. The night passed peacefully, though quickly, to the sleeping men, many of whom were to awake for the last time on earth in the early dawn.[13] The morning of the third was ushered in with the booming of cannon, as the gunners began to get range on the enemy, and soon the steady, regular roll of

---

[12] Avery refers to another meeting engagement between Kilpatrick's division and Stuart's cavalry that occurred near Hunterstown, Pennsylvania, about five miles from Gettysburg. In that short but intense fight, Kilpatrick's advance elements ran into the rear guard of Stuart's column, finally making its way to the battlefield at Gettysburg. In the action at Hunterstown, Custer personally led an unsuccessful charge of the 6th Michigan Cavalry and was nearly killed when his horse was shot and fell on top of him. Only good luck and the courage of Sgt. Norvill F. Churchill of the 1st Michigan Cavalry saved Custer. Churchill rode out and pulled his general to safety. For the only known detailed examination of the Battle of Hunterstown, see Paul Shevchuck, "The Battle of Hunterstown, Pennsylvania, July 2, 1863," *Gettysburg: Articles of Lasting Historical Interest* 1 (July 1989): 93–104.

[13] The Michigan Cavalry Brigade spent the night of 2 July holding an important road intersection about four miles from the center of the town of Gettysburg. The intersection, where the Hanover and Low Dutch Roads met, was behind the main lines of battle of both armies. The Low Dutch Road provided a direct route from the far right flank of the Army of the Potomac to the rear of the center of its position; it had to be held at all costs. It sits about two miles from the high ground known as Culp's Hill.

volleys of musketry, and the increasing roar of artillery, brought every man to his feet, to mechanically buckle on his arms, for the fray.[14]

Nor had we long to await orders, for boots and saddles sounded, and soon all were ready; the last thoughts of home indulged and stern reality before us. Arriving at the point assigned to us, Colonel Alger dismounted the regiment to fight action front, and left. We deployed in heavy line, then advanced toward a fence which ran along the edge of a wheat field, in front of a piece of timber. As we advanced through the wheat field, the rebs poured volleys into our lines. When we were ordered forward, we dashed ahead and with such a fire from our Spencers, that the rebs were quickly dislodged and driven back, where we held them for some time, continuing a heavy firing all the time, effectively checking their advance, which they undertook several times. We were beating back the columns of Lee, who was trying to push around the flank of our army.[15] If he had succeeded, he would probably have beaten us, but the Michigan brigade was there, and no rebel troops could move it out of the way. Thus we held the line until mid-day, when we were ordered to mount, and the regiment fell back to where our horses were.

Here I wish to relate a little adventure of my own. As the company retired, I thought I could catch up, so lingered on the line looking for johnnies. As I was walking along on a rising piece of ground, I turned to follow the company, and just as I turned, a ball passed my head. I turned in time to see the smoke of a gun, and a man standing in a field of oats. I raised my gun as if to shoot a squirrel, and down went Mr. Reb. I saw no more of him, so joined the company.

We mounted our horses just in time to repel a charge of the enemy. Here General Custer rode in front of our troops, and with his flag in one hand,

---

[14] Intense Confederate attacks on the Union left and then right failed during the late afternoon and evening of 2 July. Early on the morning of 3 July, fighting for the crucial high ground known as Culp's Hill resumed. This fighting is probably what Avery refers to here. For details on this fight, see Harry W. Pfanz, *Gettysburg: Culp's Hill and Cemetery Hill* (Chapel Hill, N.C.: University of North Carolina Press, 1993), pp. 284–309.

[15] Actually, the opposing force consisted of four brigades of Confederate cavalry, personally commanded by Stuart. Stuart, on a mission to try to flank the Union position so as to make mischief in the Army of the Potomac's rear, intended to pass down the Low Dutch Road. Instead, he ran into the Federal cavalry near the Rummel Farm on that portion of the battlefield that is today known as East Cavalry Field. For a detailed overview of the fight on East Cavalry Field, see Marshall D. Krolick, "Forgotten Field: the Cavalry Battle East of Gettysburg on July 3, 1863," *Gettysburg: Articles of Lasting Historical Interest* 4 (January 1991): 75–88. For specific information on the role of the Wolverines, see Longacre, *Custer and His Wolverines,* pp. 143–65; Kidd, *Personal Recollections,* pp. 136–60; Samuel Harris, *The Michigan Brigade of Cavalry at the Battle of Gettysburg, July 3, 1863, Under Command of Brig.-Gen Geo. A. Custer* (Cass City, Mi.: Annual Reunion, Co. A, 5th Michigan Cavalry, 1894).

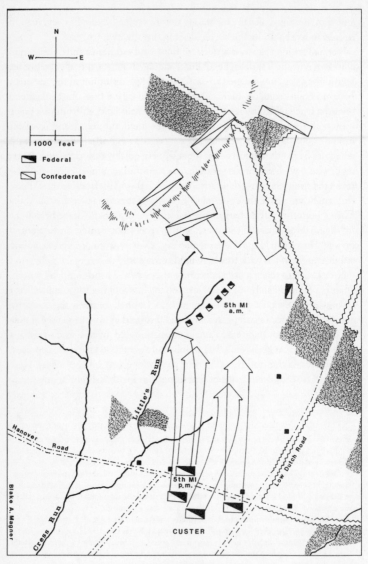

N

W —— E

S

1000 feet

■◣ Federal

◪ Confederate

5th MI
a.m.

Little's Run

Hanover   Road

Blake A. Magner

Cross Run

5th MI
p.m.

CUSTER

Low Dutch Road

Gettysburg

and his sabre in the other, ordered us forward, and with a cheer, the brigade rushed to meet the charging rebs, driving them back in confusion; but they rallied and came again, only to be repulsed a second and third time, after which they were willing to keep still a spell.[16] It was during this desperate fight that Major Trowbridge of the Fifth, had his horse shot under him, and being likely to be taken prisoner, Billy Dunn of Company I, gave him his horse, and was himself taken prisoner. Just before dark, when the regiment was in line of battle, Billy came to us again, having succeeded in escaping from the johnnies, all right. For this brave conduct, he was promoted to lieutenant, and was afterward raised to brevet major.[17] It was while in this line of battle that I came very near getting a call. I noticed a cannon smoke in front, and a little to the left; the ball came past my horse's head, brushed my knee, and struck the man beside me, tearing his leg and passing through his horse, rolling them together on the ground.

Never did men do better fighting than did ours that day, and they won lasting honors, for they defeated the enemy, at every point. Although the loss of our company was comparatively light, yet we lost a great many noble men that day. The regiment lost Major Ferry, shot in the head; and many other officers and men.[18] My company lost John Nolting, killed; Moses Cole and Caleb Bennet, wounded; besides many horses killed. As darkness came that night, all was still in our front, except an occasional shot or shell, as the gunners still tried to get the range in the deepening gloom, which was settling down on the bloody field, where the killed, and wounded laid in heaps, literally piled in swaths.

In different parts of the field, where the two great bodies of infantry and artillery had struggled, the continued heavy roar of over a hundred cannon, and the rattle of musketry was terrible to hear.[19] Then, at intervals, the shouts and cheers of contending masses could be heard, as they plunged at each

---

[16] Custer personally led two charges of his Wolverines during this fight. In the first charge, he led the men of the 7th Michigan forward to meet the enemy, yelling "Come on, you Wolverines," as he spurred ahead. In the closing action of the engagement, Custer led the 1st Michigan forward in a second headlong charge that shattered a massed charge of the Confederate cavalry, which then withdrew. See Longacre, *Custer's Wolverines,* pp. 150–165.

[17] This soldier, interestingly, does not appear on the regimental roster.

[18] Major Noah Ferry, a popular and quietly competent soldier, was killed instantly, as Avery relates. His brother Thomas W. Ferry was a powerful and influential United States senator from Michigan. Ferry was sorely missed.

[19] Avery refers to the grand and heroic Confederate infantry assault that marked the climax of the third day's fight and that is known to history as Pickett's Charge, an assault that was preceded by a lengthy and loud cannonade.

other with the bayonet. Three days of this awful storm of shot and shell, one continued flash, and roar, except as night gave short relief, and the battle of Gettysburg was done, and darkness again closed over the terrible scene.

Again, for the third night, the army bivouacked the bloody field, and as the tired soldiers laid down to rest, they might well have sang, for a consoling lullaby; "The soldiers weary from the fight, tho heeded not the rebels might, for Michigan's on guard tonight; Michigan, my Michigan, the Michigan Brigade had been baptized in blood and fire, and ever after, were entrusted, with the place of honor, under its noble commander."

The rebels had again, and again, pushed forward a heavy force to break our line, so as to strike Meade's rear. And were as often repulsed by our brigade, and Meade was saved.

The Fourth of July dawned bright and hot, and the soldiers were ready for the fray, by the first streak of light in the east.[20] But why this deathly stillness? What mischief are the johnnies brewing this Independence Day? Something is the matter; we are waiting for them to open the ball; we are ready to fiddle, for them to dance, but the word comes that they took a jig in the night and put in a double shuffle for the old Potomac. Therefore we were ordered out on the trail, and after rations were issued to the men, and each had his cartridge box and saddle bags filled with ammunition, we were quickly on the road, led out by the Fifth, following in the wake of the rebs.

Reaching Emmitsburg, we stopped for a spell, and cooked our supper. Our pleasant morning had changed to a stormy afternoon and night, but we pushed on toward the mountain and reached Monterey Gap up which we began to climb just as darkness was settling down on the wet, wet columns, as they wound their way beside the stream and across the bridge of a creek passing along the foot of the towering cliffs.[21] Up, up we went, four abreast, in the pitchy darkness, relieved only by flashes of lightening, followed by rolling thunders. When a bright flash lit up the scene, we could see a deep abyss, so close to the path that a stumble would send one down hundreds of feet. On the other side, we could not see to the top of the overhanging cliffs. Thus, we marched that Fourth of July night up the side of South Mountain.

---

[20] Avery is mistaken. It rained heavily that day, nearly all day. The rains had begun around 7:00 P.M. on the night of the 3d and lasted for several days.

[21] Avery refers to the Monterey Pass through South Mountain, located near the town of Waynesboro, Pennsylvania, approximately twenty-five miles from the battlefield at Gettysburg. The passage through Monterey Pass represented the shortest line of retreat to the Potomac River for the Confederates, so possession of the Pass was critical to any efforts to pursue the retreating Army of Northern Virginia.

Soon the crash and boom of cannon, mingled with the roar of thunder, told us we had work to do. We had to face a battery that we could not see, but the darkness was as favorable to us, as to the enemy.[22] When we reached the top, a level piece of ground was found to extend to the left over which two companies were dismounted, and moved forward, flanking and capturing the battery, without loss, and on the column moved. Quickly we came in contact with a heavy train of wagons with a strong guard, who held their own well for the darkness, but they were soon overpowered, and the Michiganders were again the victors. When morning finally dawned, we found a curious sight, something that appeared like men covered with mud, surrounding a long train of wagons with nearly a brigade of prisoners, and lots of horses.[23] It was a good night's work. The train was burned, such of it as was not needed for use.

Again we found the enemy at Smithtown [Smithsburg], and defeated them after a sharp fight;[24] and again we were on the march to Boonsboro, and went into camp for the night, getting a much needed rest. July 6th, we marched to near Williamsport, where we could see a heavy train, which Kilpatrick took into his head to capture, but finding a strong body of rebs to obstruct the way.[25] He formed his division in order for a forward move, and the shot and

---

[22] Actually, the force consisted of one company of Maryland cavalry, approximately fifty men, with one piece of artillery that had extremely limited ammunition. The combination of the unfamiliar territory, the terrible weather, and the effective tactics of the Confederates convinced the Union soldiers that they faced a much larger force. That small force of fifty dogged horse soldiers held off Kilpatrick's entire division for several hours that night. For a detailed examination of the fight for Monterey Pass, see Eric J. Wittenberg, "'This Was a Night Never to be Forgotten': The Midnight Fight in the Monterey Pass, July 4–5, 1863," *North and South* 2, No. 6 (August 1999): 44–54.

[23] This was the wagon train of the Army of Northern Virginia's 2d Corps, commanded by Lt. Gen. Richard S. Ewell. Kilpatrick claimed to have destroyed the entire wagon train except for eight forges, thirty wagons, and a few ambulances carrying wounded Confederate officers. He also claimed 1,360 prisoners, one battle flag, and a large number of horses and mules captured. His own loss was forty-three. *O.R.,* vol. 27, part 1, p. 994.

[24] On the morning of July 5, after the midnight orgy of destruction in the Monterey Pass, Kilpatrick's division encountered the entire Confederate cavalry force strongly positioned at Smithsburg, Maryland, with Stuart in personal command. After a brief engagement, the Confederates withdrew. *O.R.,* vol. 27, part 1, p. 994.

[25] Avery refers to the seventeen-mile-long wagon train of Confederate wounded, waiting to cross the rising Potomac River at the important ford at Williamsport, Maryland. The position was defended by Brig. Gen. John D. Imboden, who with a scratch force of his Confederate cavalry brigade and the teamsters responsible for the wagon train, held off two Union cavalry divisions and saved the wagon train from capture. It was Imboden's finest day. See John D. Imboden, "The Confederate Retreat from Gettysburg," *Battles and Leaders of the Civil War,* edited by Robert U. Johnson and Clarence C. Buel, vol. 3 of 4, pp. 420–28 (New York: Century Publishing Co., 1884–1904).

shells began to fly thickly, passing over our heads, which made some fun for the boys, to see a particular officer on Custer's staff duck and dodge. We could not help laughing at him.

About this time a fire was opened on our rear, and looking back, we saw heavy double columns of rebel infantry coming down and opening with musketry and artillery, completely cutting off our retreat in that direction. We were ordered fours left, and marched by the left flank through a rough, wooded country, and completely fooled the johnnies, for we turned back around their rear, and as night had come, we moved back to Boonsboro, and went again into camp. Now, although we did not capture the train, we did find that the rebs were not all across the river, yet, for we had marched right into a division of rebel infantry.

On the 7th, we lay quietly in camp at Boonsboro, getting a much needed rest after our long night ride. The boys were so sleepy on this march that it was impossible for them to keep their eyes open. Once, when we halted for a few minutes, Sergeant Weeks got off his horse and sat down and getting asleep, his horse went off and left him to walk. During those long marches and numerous fights, we would eat our hardtack as we rode along. Making coffee, and frying meat when we could. A day in camp was therefore always welcome, and then too, we could write letters home, while resting up for the next move.

I often wonder, why it is that history gives no more details of the battle of Boonsboro, as it was as heavy a cavalry fight, perhaps, as any during the war. The 8th of July commenced very rainy, but broke up after a little, and about ten o'clock firing began on our front, and increased as the different regiments got in position. Our brigade was mostly dismounted, and the horses sent under cover, as best they could be. The heavy lines advanced to meet the enemy, who were in force, and the battle raged until late in the day when the rebs had to give way. The horses were then brought forward, and mounted to pursue the retreating rebels, and we chased them to near Hagerstown, where we halted and went into camp for the night. It was in this fight, as my regiment was held in reserve to await special time to move, that Colonel Alger made the famous remark to his men; "Keep under cover boys till I want you, I will watch them." To save his men, he exposed himself, and during the charge that followed, was severely wounded. In this battle, my company lost in wounded, O. P. Eaton and Geo. Hodgetts, besides losing several horses. It had been a hard fight, and we were glad to get a chance to cook our coffee again, as we had nothing all day to eat.[26]

---

[26] Avery is quite correct in his assessment of the fight at Boonsboro. It had been an extremely heavy engagement, involving nearly the entire cavalry commands of both armies, and had

After this, we had a day or two to rest, and I will take this opportunity to say a few words about the company. Officers, of whom no special mention had yet been made, except of a few, and we had by this time learned of what material each was composed, for we had passed through fires that would melt and separate the metal from the dross. First, we will look at Captain Townsend; Cool, brave, quiet, unassuming, but quick to see, and take advantage of a point in our favor, such was the commander of our company. First Lieutenant Safford; a small man, with sandy beard, and very light complexion, generally quiet, always neat and military in camp, but a very lion in battle. I have seen him in front of his company, where the bullets were flying thickest, waving his sword and leading on his men to victory. Such also was our second in command, Sergeant Lonsbury, soon to be Lieutenant; tall, straight, muscular. The best shot with a revolver in the regiment, and not excelled with the sabre. A perfect Bengal Tiger in battle. Woe, woe, unto the man who stood in his path; fiery and quick, but easily counseled with, even when in passion; he was a man whom I loved as a commander and comrade. Sergeant Weeks; a short, wiry, fiery man, always at the front, and ready to punish slinkers, but a good comrade and jolly companion. The rest of the sergeants and corporals I will not stop to mention just now, but will bring them in as occasion requires, except one (name withheld), whom I wish particularly to mention. Although a disgrace to the company, how he ever remained a sergeant I can not see, for he would run at the first smell of powder. The rest of the company had shown themselves to be first class soldiers.

Although there was skirmishing going on near us for two days, we took no part until July 12th, when we advanced in heavy line on the rebel lines at Hagerstown, where they were strongly posted. Soon the shot and shell flew thick and fast, and the flash and soar of artillery made things jingle, cutting the timber in which a part of our company extended, until they were finally silenced by our batteries, and we made a dash, driving them back toward the city, when we mounted and charged the town, driving them out, and beyond. We now halted a short time, then moved out my company in advance of the Williamsport Pike. When just out of town, we were about to cross a small stream when the rebels rose in heavy force, from behind a stone wall not twenty rods away, and gave us a volley which passed over our heads. Returning the fire, and finding them too strong, we returned and halted for the

---

lasted most of the day, the Confederates doggedly resisting all Federal attempts to reach the main body of the Army of Northern Virginia's infantry. Stuart's performance during the retreat from Gettysburg was magnificent. For a detailed discussion, see Longacre, *The Cavalry at Gettysburg*, pp. 259–62.

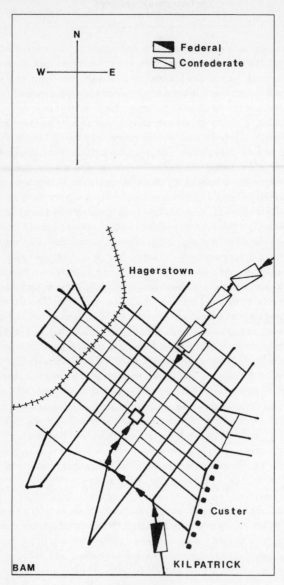

N

W——E

Federal
Confederate

Hagerstown

Custer

BAM   KILPATRICK

Hagerstown
June 12, 1863

night. There was some desultory firing, and finely [finally] darkness again settled down on the scene. In early morning we were again on the Pike, leading to Williamsport, but no johnnies were found, until near the town, where their rear guard were nearly across the river. We charged into town and captured a good many of them and received the parting shots of the enemy as they were huddled on the Virginia shore. But a few shots from Pennington[27] sent them flying.

We next took up our march for Falling Waters, where we again arrived in time to get a parting salute and where we found there had been a terrible battle. The Sixth had charged into the rebel works, and captured a whole brigade; and as only two companies, F and B led the advance and were not supported properly, the rebs seized their guns and shot down most of them. Captain Weber was among the killed.[28] This was the last fight of the great summer campaign of 1863, called the Gettysburg Campaign. Lee had been beaten at every point; lost a great many men, and most of his train, and we of the cavalry believed if he had been pushed, we could have taken his whole army. We now moved down the river below Harpers Ferry, and after resting a short time, from our very hard labor, we followed up the retreating rebels, often pushing them severely.

There seemed to be an impression among the infantry that the cavalry did not amount to much to fight, and it was said that some general, I think it was Hooker, said that he would give so much for a dead cavalry man.[29] Poor man, I think it would have drained his purse very soon after we began in the field.

---

[27] Lt. Alexander Cummings McWhorter Pennington, a West Pointer, who commanded Battery M, 2d U.S. Artillery. This was a unit of horse artillery (all gunners rode horses instead of marching on foot). Pennington's Battery, as it was known, was attached to the Michigan Cavalry Brigade and played an important part in its accomplishments in the Civil War. For detail on this fight, see *O.R.,* vol. 27, part 1, p. 995.

[28] Avery refers to the closing engagement of the Gettysburg Campaign, the engagement at Falling Waters, Maryland. Kilpatrick's division fell upon the rear guard of Lee's army while it was crossing the Potomac River at Falling Waters. A mounted charge by elements of the 6th Michigan Cavalry shattered the thin Confederate defensive line, mortally wounding Confederate Brig. Gen. James J. Pettigrew. Maj. Peter Weber of the 6th Michigan, a most promising young officer, was killed during the charge. Kilpatrick's supporting attacks captured nearly a brigade of enemy infantry and several battle flags, but the bulk of Lee's army had escaped across the river. Had this attack been better coordinated with a similar attack by Brig. Gen. John Buford's 1st Division, the remaining Confederates would have been trapped between the two forces, and a larger haul of prisoners would have resulted. See Kidd, *Personal Reminiscences,* pp. 184–90. See also Garry L. Bush, "The Sixth Michigan Cavalry at Falling Waters: The End of the Gettysburg Campaign," *Gettysburg: Articles of Lasting Historical Interest* 9 (July 1993): 109–15.

[29] Hooker's actual words were, "Whoever saw a dead cavalryman?" Coming events would demonstrate the untruthfulness of these words.

Now I don't see why there should be such a feeling, for every one who knows anything about the war, knows that the cavalry did as heavy fighting, according to numbers, as ever did the infantry, and we certainly felt sorry for them on their long tiresome marches.

Often on the march from Falmouth to Gettysburg, we would jump off our horses and give some poor fellow a ride, to rest his weary, warm feet. But there is one thing that few think of, that is the difference between the two. The infantry have to move in such large bodies, and so slowly, that they have a chance to see but a small portion of country, and they are so long inactive as to cause sickness, and there is nothing left for them in the way of forage, for the cavalry have been ahead of them. This may be in a measure, a cause of their envy.

On the other hand, the cavalry are moving most of the time, in small bodies, sweeping over the country, scouting, or flanking, and always in advance. Thus taking off the cream and leaving the sour milk for the infantry; getting the first choice of pigs, chickens, and honey. I have seen the boys chase turkeys, and clip their heads with a sabre; take bee hives in a blanket and carry them off; go into a smoke house and take their pick of hams and bacon, or into a spring house and drink the milk and get the butter, and of course, little was left for the poor doughboy. Then we had our horses to care for, which gave us exercise when in camp. Our camp, however, was mostly in winter quarters. The balance of our time we were marching and fighting.

4

The Bristoe Station and Mine Run Campaigns

"As the order to draw sabre sounded all over the field from our noble commander, the bright steel blades flashed in the sun like a wave of silver."

ON JULY 14TH, WE CROSSED THE RIVER AGAIN INTO VIRGINIA, EFFECTING the crossing just below Harpers Ferry on pontoons and took up the line of march for Snicker's Gap,[1] where we found the rebs again and drove them out of the gap, and then moved back a short distance and went into camp.[2] On the 19th, we were again on the road leading to Upperville, a wild mountainous route along the east side of the Blue Mountains, but, oh what nice, clear, cold springs, and what scenery; rough, but beautiful. We reached Upperville and went on picket duty for the night, forming our reserve camp, where those off duty could lie down and sleep, or tell stories.

On the morning of the 20th, the cavalry were ordered out on the road leading to the gap, and dismounted. They were deployed to right and left, off the road and in face of the shot and shell (which began to fly thick and fast,

---

[1] Snicker's Gap was a major passage through the Bull Run Mountains and served as a major thoroughfare for east-west traffic through the valleys of western Virginia.

[2] This engagement occurred on July 17, 1863. The official record for the 5th Michigan Cavalry states, "After sharp skirmishing with the enemy, drove them from Snicker's Gap, and occupied the same, capturing several prisoners." *O.R.,* vol. 27, part 1, p. 999.

as we advanced). We soon found a way to cross the stream and drove the rebs back, so that the mounted men could cross, and with foot and horse, the line moved forward over the rough and broken ground. After a very severe fight, we gained possession of the gap, driving the enemy beyond the mountains.[3] We held the gap until the 23rd, to keep the rebs from coming across and striking the rear of our infantry, which was moving toward the Rapidan.

On the 23rd, we marched to Smithsburg, where we went into camp. On the 24th, the Fifth and Sixth moved out on a road leading along the side of a mountain and through a dense wood. On our right was a high mountain, and on our left was a descending slope, for a long distance. When we were well into the wood, we were dismounted and deployed on the left of the road and at right angles, or rather, our line was parallel with the road, and moved at right angles with it down the hill, where we found the enemy in force.

We were in a field of brush and timber in which grew plenty of huckleberries, nice and ripe, and as we advanced, we would pick berries and then fire at the rebs, spite of the shells, which came pretty thick, we were not going past our berries without eating a share. Thus we went down toward the rebel line, not knowing how strong they were and supposing we had to fight them alone, as we did not know that we had a battery with us. Just as we were about half way down, boom went a gun in our rear, and swich-a-swich-a, went a shell over our heads, falling near the rebel battery, and followed quickly by another which burst just above the rebel line, and caused us to cheer, again, and again. For we knew then that Custer was near with good support.

After beating the rebs back, on this line, and finding them too strong to push farther, we returned and mounted our horses, still in the road in the wood. We were then ordered to counter march, bringing the Sixth in front, and to move back the same way that we came in. But just then a volley was fired in our front at close range, and we found that the rebel infantry had closed up the way.[4]

We were in a pickle, sure, as Longstreet's whole division[5] was there, and we were only two regiments with a battery. And Custer had gone back for the rest of the brigade, just before we were closed in, leaving us without a com-

---

[3] The reference to this action is even more cursory, stating, "Occupied Ashby's Gap after slight skirmishing." Ashby's Gap is through the Bull Run Mountains and provides the fastest direct link between Upperville and Winchester. See *O.R.*, vol. 27, part 1, p. 999.

[4] The reference to this engagement is, "Had the advance to Newby's Cross Roads; were at the extreme front during the engagement there, and acted as rear guard when our forces engaged were ordered to fall back." Ibid.

[5] Avery refers to the infantry corps of Lt. Gen. James Longstreet, which was the 1st Corps of the Army of Northern Virginia, the command that had borne the brunt of the fighting on the second and third days of the Battle of Gettysburg.

mander above Colonel Gray of the Sixth. Soon he came riding back, and to my question if he was hurt, replied yes, he had been thrown from his horse, and about forty horses had run over him.[6] This left the command to Major Dake[7] of the Fifth. With but a moment to decide what course to take, he immediately ordered two sections of the battery to the front and then opened with cannister, at short range, sweeping away the first line of rebs. At the same time a part of the regiment was dismounted to support the battery and hold the rebs in check. The mounted men were then ordered left flank, and moved abruptly into the woods, which led us out through an opening between their lines and the foot of the mountain. The battery followed with the dismounted men covering the rear, leaving the disappointed rebs with but a few prisoners, where they confidently expected thousands. They had bagged their game, but had left a hole in the bag, and we were safe again, and soon found Custer, with the balance of the brigade coming to our support; but he thought us lost, and when he saw us, he lifted his hat as each company sent up a cheer.

The route we had traveled was rough, stoney, and thick with brush; but Michigan men knew how to travel over rough ground. One man had been wounded and taken prisoner, but played off so that they let him alone. They told him no men but Michiganders could have got out of the trap laid for us. They were too confident and did not extend their line far enough to the right. Great praise is due Major Dake, for the way he took us out of the trouble. His blue eyes fairly snapped as he took in the situation. We joined the rest of the brigade and returned to camp near Amisville.

The next day the cavalry made a reconnaissance in force, but finding the rebs had left our immediate front. We returned and went on picket and scouting duty for a few days, and then moved to Warrenton Junction, where we stopped some time to rest up and draw much needed clothing.[8]

Our camp at that place was in a low, nasty location, near a small river where we supposed we could get plenty of good water, but found it con-

---

[6] Col. Gray resigned his command in April 1864, as a result of disability. It is not known whether this specific incident contributed to his decision to resign.

[7] Twenty-eight-year-old Maj. Crawley P. Dake of Armada, who was the ranking officer in the 5th Michigan during Col. Alger's absence, Alger having been wounded during the retreat from Gettysburg. Dake resigned his commission in August 1864. The reasons are not known.

[8] On August 1, 1863, another major engagement took place on the familiar ground around Brandy Station. In that fight, John Buford's 1st Division tangled with the entire Confederate cavalry force in a day-long fight intended to feel out the Rebel position. The 3d Division did not participate in that engagement. See William D. Henderson, *The Road to Bristoe Station: Campaigning with Lee and Meade, August 1–October 20, 1863* (Lynchburg, Va.: H. E. Howard Co., 1987), pp. 18–25.

tained dead mules and horses in such numbers as to make a soup. Too thick to drink, and too highly flavored to be agreeable to the taste. Therefore, we dug holes in the ground to get water, which was the best we could do, but it was poor stuff. Add to this the hot August sun and the filthiness of the ground, and it was too much for me to stand. The ground was full of lice, for here the rebel army had camped until vermin were fairly bred into the soil. We could not sit down without their crawling over us. And we had to boil our shirts often to keep them clear of the pests. At this place, I saw the first and last whiskey issued as a sanitary measure. But, although getting sick, I did not take mine, for I thought it hurtful rather than beneficial, and I think so still.

A good many of the regiment were taken sick with dysentery, Frank and myself among the rest.[9] It was at this place that my sickness began which caused the disability on which I now receive the magnificent sum of eight dollars per month. After a few days, the regiment was again to move, and while they were doing splendid fighting, I will follow the course of those who were sent to the hospital. We were shipped into an ambulance, and carried to the field hospital, at the Junction, where large tents had been erected to accommodate all sick and wounded. This was our first experience. The following morning, such as could stand, were ordered into line, and the surgeon in charge passed along, looking at each man. As he came to a man, he looked him over and if really sick, he was ordered into a tent, and if not; "What are you here for?" and away he was sent on duty. I think this was the sharpest surgeon in the army, and he could swear, to beat even Kilpatrick, who was famous on that score.

I have seen him get out in the morning, just his hand up to his eyes to shade them, look around, and if all was not right, begin to fairly scream for somebody to send that man to headquarters. In the hospital when a man gets so he can walk around, he is detailed to help take care of those who cannot. As I got better, the surgeon appointed me as wardmaster; that is, I had charge of two or three tents, and occupied an "A" tent for myself in the rear of the others. One night I heard an outcry from one of my tents, and going there as soon as possible, found a man insane from his sickness. One Dr. and myself took hold of him and he snapped his teeth hold of my sleeve, biting a piece clean out of my blouse. Finally got him to lay down and all was quiet for some time. The next we heard of him, he was out in the field praying; we again got him

---

[9] Dysentery is a parasitic affliction of the bowels often caused by bad or contaminated water supplies. It is a thoroughly unpleasant illness, leading to frequent and painful diarrhea.

into the tent and asleep, but it was the last of the poor fellow; he died the same night.

One day as the surgeon and I were talking, some wounded men came into camp. One a tall, straight, young fellow, had his arm taken off at the shoulder joint, and was walking with a firm step. The Dr. said "my God, is he not a tough one." Our hospital was so far in the rear of the army that we were in constant fear of the rebs breaking in upon us, and we kept a pretty strong guard out on watch. Soon after this, I was in my tent one rainy, cold day, prepared to take a little comfort. I had just got settled when the Dr. sent for me saying "I want you to go to Culpeper with me." So we packed up and got on the cars, but did not move until the next morning.

Previous to this, I had been sent to Washington with sick and wounded. This was a severe task, as the poor boys had to lie on the bottom of boxcars, with nothing but such blankets as they might have. They were jolted along over the rough railroad until they reached the city where they had comfortable beds and good care. The next day I returned to Warrenton, taking a steamboat to Alexandria, and from there by rail to camp to continue in charge until September 18th, when we packed up for Culpeper. We arrived in Culpeper on the 19th and went into a church for a hospital. The next day I was sent to Washington again, with sick and wounded. I stayed all night in the city, where they wished to detail me, but I would not stay, so left on the train for the front again. I had ten men with me but when I reached the train but one was left. All the rest had stayed in Washington, but I had their passes.

Arriving in Culpeper, I reported for duty and found that our doctor had been superceded, which made him swear terribly. He said he would make it hot for them, and I guess he did, for he was reinstated again. I was taken down again and sent to bed, going into an old tavern. This time, I was quite sick, so that I could not sit up. Frank was also there and we laid side and side on the floor, in a room where there were several more sick. By the way, Frank had been able to be about, and went with me on the first trip to Washington; then was down again, when the hospital was removed for Culpeper, which separated us for a spell. As soon as we got a little better, we used to go to the bakery and buy warm biscuits, and then go to the Sutler's and get butter at one dollar per pound, which we thought must be made from spotted cows, as there was a white spot and then a black one. But we were getting hungry and it tasted good, and in fact, we could eat anything. For I have seen hardtack that would almost jump away when you would go pick it up, and bacon that was alive with skippers. We would rattle them out and eat what they left. If you were a soldier, you would eat what you could get.

When I got better, I wished to join the company at the front, having been off duty so long. So an ambulance was ordered out, and myself and another man were stowed within its interior, and thus we left Culpeper to again pass through it in a few days in a different manner. Bidding good bye to Frank and other comrades, we were soon out of sight of Culpeper, and night found us at the camp of the Fifth, near James City. A part of the company were on picket at Robinson River, at which point the rebs made an attack early the next morning very suddenly. Taking prisoner several of my company, among them D. Callaway, who was cooking some fresh meat and had got on his horse. He might have got away, but instead, cast a look at his meat, and the temptation was too strong for his hungry stomach. He dismounted to get his fry pan and was nabbed by the johnnies, and the poor fellow died in a southern prison mess. What a terrible death for a man that was always hungry, to die of starvation. William White and Sergeant Weeks were more fortunate; they did not have time to mount their horses, so struck out on a run with the rebs after them. Coming to a fence, they jumped over just as the foremost rebs asked White to surrender. Instead of doing so, however, he picked up a rail and knocked Mr. Reb on the head, and they got away all safe.

The company lost at this time in prisoners; D. E. Callaway, Wm. Drury, Wm. Goodman, George Pullman, Geo. Thompson, Geo. C. Granger . . . all of whom I think died south.[10]

Early in the morning of October 10th, boots and saddles sounded and we packed up, mounted our horses and formed in line to repel an attack of the rebels who were pushing our line of pickets. We fell back a few miles, skirmishing all the time until night, when we laid down in line and held our horses by the halter, taking turns in cooking coffee and sweet potatoes which we found here. This had been a tiresome day for me just out of the hospital, but I was to have it still worse.[11]

For in the morning, we were again in the saddle and moving back to Culpeper, where the rebs pitched on in earnest, for we were covering the rear

---

[10] Avery has his dates confused. These men were captured at James City, Virginia, on October 11, 1863—not on the 9th, as he reports. Callaway's war record is incomplete. Drury died in captivity on February 27, 1864. Goodman died in the notorious Andersonville Prison on July 24, 1864. Pullman died at Andersonville on April 12, 1864. Thompson survived. He was released from captivity on November 20, 1864, and briefly returned to duty on May 19, 1865. He was mustered out of service a month later with the rest of the regiment. Granger was paroled from Andersonville on May 7, 1864, and returned to duty, serving out his term of service.

[11] Custer reported that, on the morning of October 10, he received orders to march to James City. Arriving about 3 P.M., Pennington's battery engaged, driving a battery of Confederate artillery from the woods overlooking the town. Custer ordered Alger to charge the battery

of Meade's army, and they wanted to harass him. And consequently we had to beat them off and keep them back. From Culpeper to Brandy Station it was lively work. A battery with its support of cavalry would go at full speed and get a position on a hill and open with its six guns, while another battery with its support would go flying by to the next elevation. Thus the dance was kept up until we reached Brandy Station. When we discovered rebs on our right, rebs on our front, and rebs in our rear, well as on our left, we were in fact literally surrounded, by heavy bodies of the enemy. Now, this was a box, but Pleasonton was there, Kilpatrick was there, and better still, Custer was there with the brigade, which could beat the Southern Confederacy in detail, only let them bring them on.[12]

This was the grandest scene I ever witnessed. We were on a level plain, over every foot of which we could see, but on our front, right, and rear, the ground was higher, and on this higher ground the rebs had their artillery. Along our right ran the railroad embankment, which partially covered our columns from that side. Near this was the brigade band, all in order. The brigade was formed in two columns by regiments, the First and Fifth in advance. Custer rode in front, drew his sabre, made a few remarks, which were loudly cheered (in the face of the large body of rebs who held the road in front), then ordered forward, trot, and then charge! As the order to draw sabre sounded all over the field from our noble commander, the bright steel blades flashed in the sun like a wave of silver. The band played "Yankee Doodle" in stirring notes, clear and bold, and on we dashed at full speed. Custer's bright curls, far in advance, we swept on and through the surging rebel ranks. Sweeping them away and driving them into the woods on the right, from which they tried to hold their own, but Kilpatrick came up to the guns and ordered cannister fired into the

---

with the 5th Michigan Cavalry, and Maj. John Clarke's battalion made the attack. Custer wrote, "The charge, although daring in the extreme, failed for want of sufficient support. It was successful so far, however, as to compel the enemy to shift the position of his battery to a more retired point. Night setting in prevented us from improving the advantages we had gained." *O.R.*, vol. 29, part 1, pp. 389–90.

[12] With Maj. Gen. Alfred Pleasonton, commander of the Army of the Potomac's Cavalry Corps, in personal command of the field, and with Kilpatrick also in attendance, another major engagement (the fourth of the war) ensued near Brandy Station. That afternoon, Custer, crying, "Boys of Michigan, there are some people between us and home. I'm going home! Who else goes?," led a charge of the 1st and 5th Michigan and 1st Vermont Cavalry regiments, with his brigade band blaring "Yankee Doodle" in the background. After three or four (the accounts were unclear) separate charges, the Wolverines managed to cut their way free and withdrew to safety. See Longacre, *Custer's Wolverines,* pp. 185–89; *O.R.,* vol. 29, part 1, pp. 389–90. Historian Longacre wrote, "The fight of October 11 had brought the Michigan Brigade to the brink of disaster, but its people had survived to flirt with danger another day." Ibid., p. 188.

woods.[13] The crash and roar was terrific, and the rebs charged, time and again, from the wood to try and break our lines. One party more bold then the rest broke through, and as I saw their flag, I desired to capture it; but could not rally enough to risk it, but one Corporal Rockwell[14] undertook it and his rashness cost him his life. He rode into the midst of them to take their flag single-handed and they literally cut him to pieces. Thus we fought until near night, when Beaufort[15] [John Buford] came on the scene and ended the conflict by striking the rebs on the flank. We then moved across the river and went into camp, where we were glad to get needed rest, but just as we got down to sleep, boots and saddles sounded again, and away we went. Marching most of the night to Grove Church, where we finely camped for the rest of the night.

Let us review this scene . . . Custer orders "draw sabres, forward, trot, and charge!" The shells fly, the band plays Yankee Doodle, the men cheer, their sabres gleam as they rush along, and soon the road is opened and the victory is ours! Was it not magnificent? A couple of hours of this boom and crash and cut and slash and we are done for the day. Now let us count the casualties; Corporal Rockwell killed, but his horse saved by Geo. E. Munn, who rode in and led him off unmolested. This was all, I believe, except I lost a new hat, so had to go bareheaded until I picked one up.

On October 13th, we moved to Bealeton Station and drew rations and then moved to Bull Run where we took our position on the right. On the 14th encountered Stuart's cavalry and handled them roughly.[16] We remained near Bull Run until the 19th. Meade had been falling back from above the Rapidan River, and Lee had been trying to out march him and get on the old Bull Run field ahead. But we kept his cavalry back on the flanks so he did not gain the race. It was truly a race, and one of importance, for had Lee arrived at Bull Run first, he would have had a large advantage. As our cavalry came in on each flank, the rebs were close to our heels, and caused some sharp

---

[13] Canister was an early antipersonnel weapon. Steel balls were packed into something that looked rather like a modern can; when the can exploded, the balls sprayed into the ranks of the enemy, acting like larger buckshot. It was a weapon that was effective only at short range, but its results were usually devastating.

[14] Cpl. William Rockwell of Avery's Company I.

[15] This refers to the 1st Division of Brig. Gen. John Buford, which came to the sounds of the fighting late in the afternoon.

[16] Custer does not note this engagement in his report. He simply wrote, "From the 11th to the 15th instant, my command was employed in picketing and in guarding the flank and rear of the army." *O.R.,* vol. 29, part 1, p. 391.

fighting, but they could not get ahead of the Michigan Brigade. We had to work hard, and we did, and therefore gained the day.[17]

One day as we were on one of these marches, I had noticed a body of cavalry in advance that seemed to be standing quietly. Waiting for our column to move along, and as our company came up with theirs, who should I see among their numbers but my old comrade, Frank. He had so far recovered as to be able to get a mount and return to the front, and I was glad to see him.

On October 19th, we began a forward move chasing the rebs again, and when we arrived at Buckland Mills, found them in force. We dismounted and advanced our lines to the creek called Broad Run. A bridge crossed here, and beyond the run was quite a town in which the rebs were strongly posted, as well as on the hills beyond.[18] As we approached this stream, we were greeted with a shower of lead from the troops in town and plenty of shells from the hills, but we took all the available cover and held fast, giving them the contents of our Spencers as fast as we could work them. Just at this time, Sergeant Hart of my company was struck on the arm with a piece of shell, making a bad wound, and he was sent to the rear and finally discharged on account of the injury. And I did not see him again until the close of the war.

Shortly after this, we were ordered forward. And springing into line as well as we could, we dashed across the bridge and into the town, driving the rebs out and taking possession. This was about noon, and we were ordered to prepare our dinners, and we did so with a will, for we were hungry, and a fight before dinner was a good appetizer. Someone of my company went at once to investigate the commissary stores of the town, and returned with a nice hive of honey, which went well as a dessert. But as our dinner hour was short, we will not linger over it here. As soon as we had eaten, we again mounted and were off in columns of fours, with our brave Alger at our head, and the Fifth in advance of all. We had proceeded but two or three miles when the rebs showed signs of life and began to wake up on our left flank, as we moved down the road. Therefore, the colonel halted the regiment and dismounting one battalion, sent them out as skirmishers and held the rest of us in reserve.

---

[17] On the 18th, Kilpatrick's entire division was ordered to move on the Warrenton Turnpike toward Groveton, on the old Bull Run battlefield. Custer reported that "We soon encountered the enemy and drove him as far as Gainesville, where the entire command bivouacked for the night." *O.R.,* vol. 29, part 1, p. 391.

[18] This is the town of Buckland, Virginia.

Soon the firing began hot and near as they pushed our boys back; then the shell began to fly around and over us thick and fast, showing a heavy body of the enemy pressing our left and rallies in our rear. We could see our colonel was very anxious, as though looking for support, and we were anxious too, for we knew we had got into a nest of hornets, and were in a tight place. Soon an orderly came from our rear, his horse on a dead run and covered with foam; he rushed past us to where Alger sat on his horse watching the conflict in the wood, and gave him the following order, "Custer says take your regiment out as quick as you can."

Alger raised in his stirrups and gave the order, clear, cool and distinct, "Fours, left about wheel, by the left flank, forward, march!" Riding again to the head of the column, he led us back a ways, then turned to the left over a stone wall, leaving the road in possession of the rebs, and then across a field to the creek where he plunged his horse in and we followed. The water was deep but the noble horses swam safely over and up the steep bank we went. Climbing slowly while the shot and shell whistled and screeched and burst all around us, but the rebs came no further, for, as we reached the top, we found the infantry in force ready to receive them. In this scrape, the First Battalion, which had been dismounted, was nearly all taken prisoners.[19]

That night, we again camped on the old Bull Run field, and the next day Colonel Kellogg,[20] of Michigan, addressed us, and then we went on picket duty for seven days. About this time we were so short of food that we had to get dry corn in the ear and roast it, to last us until we could get supplies.

On November 7th, we broke camp again to follow the johnnies who were again on the move. We went down near Falmouth and camped at night at Grove Church where we could hear heavy firing along the Rapidan. The next

---

[19] In fact, the Battle of Buckland Mills was one of the worst and most embarrassing defeats suffered by the Union cavalry in the entire Civil War. The Union plan for the day was based on faulty intelligence; Pleasonton believed that the enemy cavalry was miles away and that the enemy mounted force in his front was weak. In reality, he faced the entire Confederate cavalry corps. After the initial success described by Avery, the Confederates turned the tables and drove the Federal cavalry from the field in a wild rout. When Kilpatrick's division was broken and driven from the field, Custer lost his command vehicle filled with his personal effects and official correspondence. The panicked Yankee troopers fled, with the Confederates in hot pursuit. After taking many prisoners, the gray-clad horse soldiers finally called off the chase. They derisively referred to the humiliation suffered by Kilpatrick that day as the "Buckland Races." See Henderson, *The Road to Bristoe Station,* pp. 200–205. The Michigan Brigade suffered more than two hundred casualties between October 9 and 19. O.R., vol. 29, part 1, p. 392.

[20] Avery refers to Rep. Francis W. Kellogg, a Michigan congressman who played a major role in raising the 5th, 6th, and 7th Michigan Cavalry. Kellogg's son was an officer in the 6th Michigan.

day we crossed the Rapidan, and marched to within eight miles of Culpeper, and on the next, charged a signal station on a mountain, running our horses several miles.[21] As we were returning from this charge, we crossed a dry stream which angled across the road, and as my horse went to raise the bank, which was slippery, he being tired and rather weak for want of food, fell and caught my leg between his shoulder and my sabre, and the stoney bottom holding me down until the boys helped him up. It is a wonder that I got off without a broken leg. And as it was, I was rather badly hurt, and it lamed me for several days. We were next on picket duty again for a few days, marching down to near Fredericksburg and then back. Then to Raccoon Ford and afterward into camp.

I should now give an account of the moves of the regiment during my stay in the hospital. They first moved to Kelly's Ford, where they were engaged with the enemy in a heavy battle.[22] I could hear the thunder of guns all that and the next day where I was at Culpeper.[23] From there they moved to Raccoon Ford.[24] My company losing on the way, Benjamin Bliss, killed at White's Ford, September 21st,[25] and Jack Shop, September 26th.[26] From each place

---

[21] On November 7, 1863, the entire Army of the Potomac was to move forward from the vicinity of Warrenton to Rappahannock Station, a distance of about sixteen miles. Kilpatrick's 3d Division was to cover the left flank of the Army's advance. See Martin F. Graham and George F. Skoch, *Mine Run: A Campaign of Lost Opportunities, October 21–May 1, 1864* (Lynchburg, Va.: H. E. Howard Co., 1987), pp. 8–10. This advance was the opening of the Mine Run Campaign, which was aborted when the Federal high command realized that Robert E. Lee had set a trap for the Army of the Potomac, and Meade wisely withdrew rather than falling into the trap. The withdrawal ended the year's campaigns for 1863.

[22] This refers to an engagement that occurred on September 13, 1863. Kilpatrick's division had still another engagement near Brandy Station, defeating the Confederate cavalry. See Henderson, *The Road to Bristoe Station,* pp. 33–41.

[23] On September 14, the fighting resumed early. Again, the Confederate cavalry was driven back in the direction of Orange Courthouse. Ibid., pp. 42–44.

[24] Raccoon Ford is a major crossing of the Rapidan River. It is due south of Culpeper and would serve as the crossing point for both sides many times throughout the war.

[25] On Monday, September 21, 1863, Kilpatrick's division left Stevensburg and met Buford's 1st Division north of the Robertson River. The combined force advanced on James City and entered Madison Courthouse around sundown, driving out a small Confederate outpost of twenty men. They then camped there for the night. Henderson, *The Road to Bristoe Station,* p. 53.

[26] The Battle of Jack's Shop, fought on the 22d, was one of the largest all-cavalry fights of the war. Buford's division pitched into the Confederate cavalry near modern-day Rochelle and routed it. Kilpatrick's division came up and joined the fighting, and a vigorous pursuit occurred, called off only when the Federals reached their objective, Liberty Mills on the Rapidan River. At one point, Jeb Stuart, watching the fighting, called out, "Boys, it's a fight to captivity, death or victory!" Through skillful handling, Stuart extracted his badly defeated command in reasonably good order. Ibid., p. 60.

many wounded were sent back. They then went on picket at James City, where I joined them October 9th.

We will now return to Stevensburg, where we had established a camp from which we did picket duty on the Rapidan, after driving the rebs across the river. On November 26, 1863, we made a move which was, I think, very foolish; at least it looked so to me, as I could see no object in it.[27] We were marched in the cold rain to the river at Morton's Ford, beyond which the country raised in abrupt hills from the river. Of these hills, the first or nearest to the stream were not as high as those further back. They were covered with rifle pits and earth works, behind which the rebs were strongly posted with infantry, and artillery. On our side, the country descended from a long distance back from the river until it reached a wide strip of low plain next to the stream, and reached this flat land which was covered with a growth of tall grass, and in parts with cornfields.

We were formed in line and advanced in the face of the rebel works, from which came showers of lead and iron. It would have been totally impossible to have carried their works, even with a heavy army, and this could be seen, at a glance, but somebody wanted to get the men killed off; or else someone was drunk; at least so it looked to us. Our company did not lose any, however, although many narrow escapes were told of afterward. After remaining under this fire long enough to satisfy someone's curiosity, we were withdrawn and returned to camp.

---

[27] The move described is the general advance of the Army of the Potomac on the strong Confederate position at Mine Run.

5

Winter Encampment and the Reorganization of the Cavalry Corps

"Thus we passed from 1863 to 1864 . . . on picket duty."

AFTER THIS, OUR DUTY WAS SCOUTING AND PICKET ALONG THE RAPIDAN, and some cold nights during the winter were passed pleasantly in various ways. I had charge of a post at Jacob's Mill for several days, and we used to go to the mill and get corn meal and make hot cakes. I used to post my guard and then lay down by the fire and sleep two hours; then get up and post the next and continue this all night.[1]

At Germania Ford,[2] where I was next on guard, there was an old building close to the water where we stood guard. As this was a point where deserters came into our lines, it was a very important post. For it took a larger reserve to assist in case they were pursued. When they came in and gave themselves up, we always protected them. Being in charge of this line of pickets, many was the night both dark and light, that I rode along the river, beyond which

---

[1] The Army of the Potomac established its winter camp in the area between Brandy Station and Stevensburg, and the Cavalry Corps spent the winter picketing a twenty-five-mile front along the Rapidan and Rappahannock Rivers. It was difficult and trying duty that took a heavy toll on the horses of the Cavalry Corps.

[2] Germanna Ford on the Rapidan River.

we could see the rebs camp fires, and many a time I listened to the tunes played by their bands. I even heard them play "Hail Columbia," and "My Native Land" but never "Yankee Doodle."

At Jacob's Mills, they would come down to the water and call out "hello yank." We would say "hello johnny, what you want?" "Got any coffee?" "yes, you want some tobacco?" "yes," "all right, throw it over." Then a stone would be tied to a sack of coffee or a plug of tobacco and thrown across. Thus, the johnnies would get their coffee and the Yankees their tobacco. When the news of some victory would reach us, we would tie a stone to a newspaper and throw it over for them to consider.[3]

Occasionally, as our patrol was passing in sight of the rebs, or a wagon would come in view, they would send a shell screeching along and the mule drives would whip up and get under cover as soon as possible, or the cavalry men would pick up a little faster to get out of range. We had one man who was fool-hardy enough to cross over and play cards with the rebs. One day he traded horses with them. Thus it was reported all quiet along the Rapidan for the winter of '63 and '4, except an occasional raid.

Thus we passed from 1863 to 1864, still on picket duty, until February 6, 1864. When we broke camp early and marched to the river and crossed. The rebs retired and we took possession of their works.[4]

I was put on picket away out to the front, in a piece of timber so thick that it would be hard work to get through. And it was so dark that I could not see my hand before my face. There I sat for four long hours, far from any one, in the drizzling rain. Suddenly I heard the sound of horses splashing through the mud and sang out "halt, who comes there?" The answer came back "relief." Quickly I said "advance, relief" and with my revolver in readiness, I awaited

---

[3] So much fraternization and trading took place that the high command of both armies grew unhappy. An informal arrangement developed that the pickets would not fire on each other, except in the event of a foray. The two armies managed to pass a quiet and not altogether unpleasant winter that way.

[4] This was the beginning of the infamous Kilpatrick-Dahlgren Raid, intended to fall upon Richmond and free the large contingent of Federal prisoners of war held at either Libby Prison or Belle Isle. The raid, while well planned, was not well executed and must be considered a disaster. Local militia ambushed one branch of the raiding force, commanded by Col. Ulric Dahlgren, and Dahlgren was killed. The locals claimed they found papers on Dahlgren's body indicating a scheme to kidnap or execute Confederate President Jefferson Davis, and the enraged locals mutilated his body. The raid was an unmitigated disaster. See Longacre, *Custer's Wolverines,* pp. 201–2. Not long after, Kilpatrick was relieved of command of the 3d Division and sent west to command the cavalry of Maj. Gen. William T. Sherman, who said of Little Kil, "Kilpatrick is a hell of a damned fool, but he is just the sort of fool I want to command my cavalry."

the coming of the officer. Soon Sergeant Weeks came up to me, gave the countersign and I fell in, and we made our way toward the camp through the inky darkness. After going a few miles we began to see the campfires of our troops as they flickered in the distance. Soon after we arrived in camp, unsaddled our horses and cooked our coffee, and laid down to sleep. The night soon passed and daylight came with its cold, gray mist, after a winter's rain. What a place we found ourselves in. Close to the right of us was a deep hole or shaft. What was it, a well? No, for there was another just at our rear, and another and yet another. It was actually dangerous to move, even by daylight, and what must it have been in the night?

We soon found that we were in an old gold mine. Where many pits had been dug years before for gold. It is singular that none of us fell into those pits, for it hardly seemed possible to avoid them. We cooked our breakfast and after a while saddled up and mounted our horses and moved out for the river. Again crossing[, we took up] the line of march for camp, where all was quiet again as before. Nothing but camp and picket duty. A little incident occurred this time that fixed me for some time. I was on picket with a man named Homer Wasson, of Company I.[5] We were to tent together for the time, and I was to be cook. After making a good rail fire, I put the coffee pot on with our coffee in it, and was cooking meat and such other food as we had.

Wasson was a great fellow to be dancing and jumping around, although he danced like a cow. He came to near the fire and his big foot got tangled in the rails and upset the fire. Away went the coffee, and away he went, I following after. He ran and I ran; I could not catch him, for his legs were long, being a six footer, therefore I tried to give him a kick in the rear, but as I was too far back to reach him, my foot came down so hard that it knocked my knee out of joint and dropped me flat on the ground from which I could not raise. Turning around, he picked me up and carried me to the tent, where I laid until morning suffering terrible pain. In the morning I was lifted on my horse and sent to camp. This was tedious, as every step my horse took wrenched my knee. But I arrived safely, and several of the boys helped me dismount and carried me to my tent, where I called the surgeon, and he bound up the knee and said I was to use cold water. I had a very bad knee for about six weeks.

In referring to my diary, I find that on January 25, 1864, I was promoted to commissary sergeant. A place I had filled since the fight at Buckland

---

[5] Twenty-one-year-old Pvt. Homer Wasson of Otsego. Wasson served his entire term of service honorably.

Mills, therefore the duty was not new to me. Being off duty now, I appointed F. Miller to act for me. When I so far recovered as to get about on crutches, I went to the tent where a Mr. Brown took photographs. And as the regiment was on muster, I had to go in front of them to get to the tent. There was a ditch running across the ground for me to get over, and as I went to swing myself over, my crutch caught and let me down into the ditch, in fair view of the whole regiment, but I made the best of it I could and hobbled on out of sight.

About this time, Kilpatrick undertook his famous raid to Richmond. A detachment was taken from the company, and I was sent to the hospital at Brandy Station. The second day after my arrival at the hospital I sat on my bed, which was at the end of the tent; the flap of the tent being tied back, thus opening as a door. Some one says "hello Avery," I looked up and saw a face looking out from another tent a few feet away. I at once recognized one of my company, Giles A. Piper, who had been wounded, and had taken the small pox from which he was just recovering.[6] Red enough too, was his face.

At this place some of the convalescents used to get the metal off from the shells that were laying around, to make rings. One day three or four of them were at work at a shell when it exploded, though strange to say, it did no harm, but this made them more careful in the future. When I got able to do duty and return to camp, I found the company back from the raid to Richmond, except those taken prisoners, and wounded, whose names I will here give. They were Sergeant Weeks and White; privates E. J. Burlingame, James Dyre, Abiul Emmons, John Hill, Godlep Miller, Chas. Moses, Geo. Shupart, prisoners; and Orlando Masson wounded. Masson was hit in the eye, losing it. This took away our first sergeant and first duty sergeant, leaving me to act as first sergeant—a duty which I performed for the next year, in addition to my duty as commissary, with the assistance of Frank.

Sometimes during this long stop in camp, the officers would get together and have a regular tear or spree, where poor whiskey sometimes played a prominent part. One night there was a gathering of this kind near the tent occupied by myself, Frank and Harvey Mann. It was a pretty loud time they were having, and had got to be rather tiresome to the boys who wanted to rest. I had been wishing it would stop when it appeared my wish was granted, for

---

[6] Twenty-year-old Giles A. Piper was from Avery's home town of Allegan. He would be captured at Trevilian Station on June 11, 1864, and was released in December 1864. He returned to the regiment in the spring of 1865 and served out the balance of his term of service.

someone threw a box of cartridges down the chimney into the fire. At once they began to explode, causing the officers to scatter out doors without stopping to learn the cause, and broke up their fun for that night at least. The next day they tried to find out who did it but no one knew.

One day the regiment was ordered out and formed in a hollow square, facing inwards, when the Provost Marshal brought in a prisoner; a man, I think, from Company D, who had stolen some clothing from some of his companions. He was seated in a chair, and had one side of his head shaved smooth as his face. Another time during the night, the sutler's tent was raided, and his goods taken. But I will not let the Fifth, or any of the brigade be accused of this, for it was their sutler, and as other troops were camped near, we laid it to them. In these various ways, the long, long months passed quickly away, and the spring came, which was to usher in one long bloody campaign in the vicinity of Richmond and the Shenandoah Valley.

On April 17th, General Kilpatrick took leave of the Third Division and went to the Department of the Tennessee. Our brigade was transferred to the First Cavalry Division and was afterwards the First Brigade, First Cavalry Division, Cavalry Corps, with General Merritt division commander, Custer still remained brigade commander.[7] We moved our camp near Culpeper and made a new camp which gave us plenty of work to do to clean up, and as the warm days came on, the boys began to scrunch and then to boil their shirts, for the Grey Backs[8] had again made their appearance, and we discovered them along the seams of our clothing and had to get them disposed, or they would have made it extremely disagreeable for us.

Later on, when the hot days came, reviews and inspections were of almost daily occurrence, which we knew meant preparations for the coming campaign. Then our clothing was looked to and every man was rigged out in a new suit, as far as needed. Our arms were next looked over, and the number

---

[7] In March 1864, Maj. Gen. Alfred Pleasonton was relieved of command of the Cavalry Corps, and a new commander, Maj. Gen. Philip H. Sheridan, was brought east to take command. The Cavalry Corps was immediately reorganized, and new division commanders were appointed. John Buford had died of typhoid fever in December 1863, and thirty-year-old Brig. Gen. Wesley Merritt, the senior brigade commander, temporarily assumed divisional command. In the interim, Brig. Gen. James H. Wilson, a favorite of the newly appointed Federal high commander, Lt. Gen. Ulysses S. Grant, was brought east and given command of Kilpatrick's division. Because Custer outranked Wilson, his brigade was transferred to the 1st Division and a brigade of the 1st Division assigned to the 3d Division. Not long after, Brig. Gen. Alfred T. A. Torbert of Delaware was assigned to command the 1st Division despite his having no prior experience in commanding cavalry.

[8] This was a commonly used slang name for body lice.

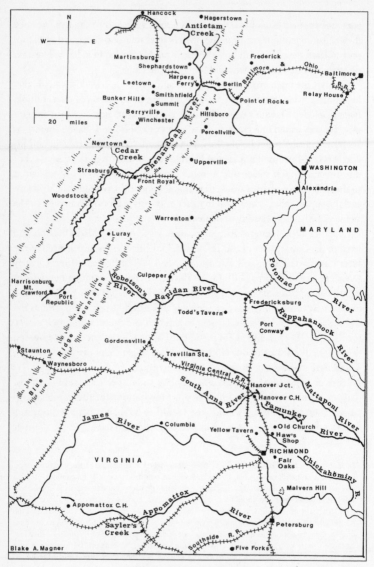

Virginia-Maryland Theater

and caliber of each carefully noted. Then came a day when ammunition was issued, forty rounds to every man, which he stored away in his saddle bags and cartridge box. Next in order was rations, with which each man was supplied for five days.

Now let me give the explanation, etc. before we were in proper order for heavy marching. First a man's saddle is examined and found all right, to which is buckled bed blanket, shelter tent and poncho. Then comes coffeepot, fry pan, tin cup, and over coat, which as it comes hot weather is turned over to the Quartermaster. Then the soldier buckles on his sabre, revolver, and cartridge box, straps his carbine over his shoulder and hangs it on his right side. Then his haversack and canteen completes the outfit. Thus, he had his house, bed and cooking utensils, and is himself a moving arsenal. This is the way each man appeared, mounted and in line on the morning of May 4th, 1864, when we took up our route toward the river.[9]

---

[9] On May 4, 1864, the Army of the Potomac crossed the Rapidan River and began advancing toward the Wilderness, near the Chancellorsville battlefield of the year before. This move announced the beginning of the spring campaign season, a campaign that lasted for six long, bloody weeks. This is known as Grant's "Overland Campaign."

-6-

Campaigning with Sheridan

"We were a cheerful, contented set, ready to march and fight, and go hungry without complaining. We were fighting for our country."

IT WAS A WARM DAY AND THE TROOPS WERE GLAD TO REST A SHORT TIME AT noon and cook their coffee. As we were waiting orders to mount, the surgeon from brigade headquarters came along where several regimental officers were talking; taking a bottle from his pocket, he passed it around to each and they took a drink. As it was passed to Colonel Alger, he had the courage to say no, and did not touch it. This I saw and therefore know and I believe, Alger never used strong drink while in the service. That night we encamped at Stoney Mountain; a towering pile which seemed to be composed entirely of stone. The surrounding country was rough and broken.

On the 5th, we marched to Ely's Ford, on the Rapidan,[1] where we crossed and took the road leading south. Soon we heard the thunder of cannon away to our right, which was the first beginning of the Battle of the Wilderness. We however, went into camp just at night without taking part in this day's struggle.

Chaplain Gunderman[2] took this opportunity to hold a meeting, and going back under a tree, he soon had a large audience. He had been a lieutenant of

---

[1] The bulk of the Army of the Potomac splashed across the Rapidan River at Ely's Ford.

[2] According to the regimental roster, the chaplain of the 5th Michigan Cavalry was Oliver Taylor. There are four troopers named Gunderman listed. It appears that Avery refers to Capt. John Gunderman, age forty-six, who was a member of Company G of the 5th Michigan Cavalry.

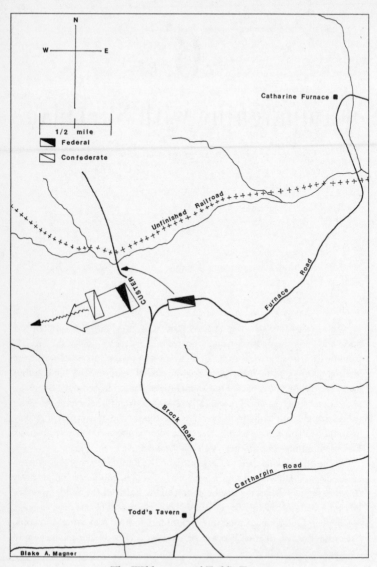

The Wilderness and Todd's Tavern

Company G, and was a very common, every day man, just the sort to take well with the boys, and not afraid of duty of any kind. I have seen him mount a horse and lead one or two more, as occasion required, to water. He always drew a large crowd, as he was a good speaker, and when any of the boys were sick, he would visit them and cheer them up with pleasant talk. And would not put on a long face and converse in dry, uninteresting subjects. In fact, he was a man, as well as an officer.

The morning of the 6th, we were in line and marched to the left of our infantry, where we went into action in a field where there was a good many scattering scrub pines.[3] We had to run our horses to get into line of battle in this field, and the shot and shell flew thick and fast.[4] It was here that I happened to look back, just in time to see (name withheld) going back to the rear as fast as his horse could carry him, and he was out of reach of us, or I should have been tempted to have brought my Spencer to bear upon him, the cowardly dog.

As we were brought into line, we were halted for some particular move, which was not yet ripe. We remained for a time in that position taking the shells as they came. Just in rear of our company lay a wounded reb pleading for water. Some of the boys were rather inclined not to notice him, but I dismounted, went to him, raised his head and gave him a good drink from my canteen. Again I mounted my horse and was ready to charge, or dismount to fight, which we did after a while.

After dismounting we moved forward to a piece of wood, through which we charged on foot, driving the rebs back on their main lines. In this wood we found one reb who had the back of his skull taken off, but was still alive,

---

[3] In fact, this area was known as the Wilderness. It was largely dense secondary growth, with heavy underbrush that made mounted operations nearly impossible.

[4] The Wolverines received the order to march at 2:00 A.M. on May 6. They were to take a position along the southern flank of the Army of the Potomac. They reached their objective near the junction of the Brock and Catherine Furnace Roads and briefly bivouacked there. Around 8:00 A.M., the Federal cavalry received orders to attack with a division of cavalry all along Longstreet's flank. This order was based on the false assumption that Confederate infantry held the area, when it was instead held by Brig. Gen. Thomas L. Rosser's cavalry brigade. A brisk cavalry fight occurred, with the 5th Michigan rescuing the 6th Michigan from a tight situation. Rosser's men were driven back, and a heavy engagement, including counterbattery dueling, ensued. A member of Rosser's brigade recalled May 6 as the "bloodiest day of the war." See William N. McDonald, *A History of the Laurel Brigade* (Baltimore: Sun Job Printing Office, 1907), p. 237. See also *O.R.*, vol. 36, part 1, pp. 816, 827. The latter is Alger's report of the activities of the 5th Michigan Cavalry. For the finest work available on the Battle of the Wilderness, see Gordon C. Rhea, *The Battle of the Wilderness, May 5–6, 1864* (Baton Rouge, La.: Louisiana State University Press, 1994), pp. 343–49.

although helpless, and as the bursting shell had set the leaves on fire he was liable to be burned. We took him to a piece of moss and laid him carefully down where he could die, and not be burned.[5] There we left him and rushed on to keep pace with our company.

It was a terrible place. The brush was thick and brambles ran over the ground tearing our clothing, while the dry leaves caught fire filling the woods with smoke. We pressed on until near night, when a halt was ordered, and we returned to our horses and went back into camp for the night, and this is a good chance to review our experiences of the day. I had just got a new pair of pants with a wide sergeant stripe down the legs, and these stripes were completely scratched off. The rest of my clothing was also badly torn. The others fared better. Although the balls flew thick around us, we lost no men from the company, except the very few who ran, by this I mean the one who, when there was no danger, was a host of himself, but just at that time shrunk up to a very few, not enough to support himself, so he had to fall back to a safe place.

On the 7th, we were again on the line of battle, and as usual, pushed the enemy back to their [earth]works, where, after a long, hot day of hard fighting, night found us posted in heavy lines behind piles of rails and logs, awaiting an expected advance of the rebs. As we were thus watching, we could hear their bugle sound all the calls. They seemed to be so near that our guns were cocked and ready to give them a warm reception. They moved in some other direction and did not put in an appearance in our front. It was nearly dark when suddenly a cheer was sent up and carried to the extreme left. I think no one knew the cause, but I do believe the rebs thought we were reinforced. We were ordered to mount and were led out to the road and off toward Fredericksburg, near which place we went into camp for the night.[6] During those two days the infantry had been heavily engaged; the roar of musketry was terrific, and considering the nature of the ground, the enemy's artillery had played havoc with our ranks, as many of our men were killed, but the loss on the rebel side was equally as great.

Those two days of the Battle of the Wilderness was to be followed by still harder fought fields in the near vicinity, for this was to be Grant's grand push

---

[5] Unfortunately, many of the wounded of both sides were burned to death by fires in the underbrush ignited by sparks from powder or artillery shells.

[6] In fact, Maj. Gen. Philip H. Sheridan, commander of the Army of the Potomac's Cavalry Corps, had received orders to take the entire Cavalry Corps on a raid toward Richmond. They departed early on the morning of May 8.

by the left flank with success, although with heavy loss.[7] That night we got little rest for the rumble and rattle of wagons and artillery as they passed along the stoney street, disturbed our slumber, and besides this, the band struck up about twelve o'clock, which added to the din, but the morning of May 9th, my birthday, found us ready for the march, when the whole Cavalry Corps joined to strike the rear of Lee's army around his right flank.

The columns moved out early, led by the Michigan Brigade, the first in advance. I think this was the first time the Corps ever moved together, on one road. And when on an elevation, it was a splendid sight to look as far as the eye could reach each way, and see the same blue line of soldiers, relieved only by the white tops of the wagons, and the more somber covers of the ambulances. They extended twelve miles or more in one solid column, four abreast. The artillery, of which there was one battery of six guns with each brigade, looked the same as cavalry, for we could not see their guns, they being so low. We moved leisurely along, having considerable fun with the colored population, who would look and stare at us and wonder if there was any more left where we came from. Sometimes we saw an ancient looking individual, whom we would ask how far it was to Richmond? He would answer "A right smart ways, I reckon. Say soldiers, how many millions is there of you?"[8]

Thus we marched, talked and laughed as we passed far beyond the flank of the enemy. Sometimes I was on the flank, as we kept our flankers on each side; then again in the column.

As we neared a point on the Virginia Central Railroad, our scouts reported a train of wagons in sight, and Custer ordered Major Brewer, of the First, to capture them.[9] He at once led out, closely followed by the Fifth, supported by

---

[7] Avery is correct. Despite having suffered a tactical defeat in the Wilderness, Grant pushed his army around the Confederate flank at a place called Todd's Tavern, looking to reach the important crossroads town at Spotsylvania Courthouse before the Confederates, thereby getting between Lee's army and Richmond. Only a determined stand by Confederate cavalry under Maj. Gen. Fitzhugh Lee and poor execution by the Union subordinate command prevented Grant from reaching his objective. See Gordon C. Rhea, *The Battles for Spotsylvania Court House and the Road to Yellow Tavern, May 7–12, 1864* (Baton Rouge, La.: Louisiana State University Press, 1996), pp. 21–54.

[8] Because it was very hot and dry, the column moved at a leisurely pace so as to conserve horseflesh. For the best account of the Richmond Raid, see Louis H. Carpenter, "Sheridan's Expedition around Richmond, May 9–25, 1864," *Journal of the United States Cavalry Association* 1 (1888): 300–324.

[9] Maj. Melvin Brewer, commanding officer of the 1st Michigan Cavalry. Avery refers to Beaver Dam Station, a stop on the Virginia Central Railroad, the most important east-west railroad link to Richmond.

the Sixth and Seventh. We dashed ahead for two or three miles, and came up with the rebs, capturing their train guards, and a little farther on, a heavy guard who had in charge some four hundred of our men, prisoners. Among the prisoners we found one colonel and two lieutenant colonels, besides many majors, captains, etc. They had been captured during the first days of the Wilderness, and were on their way to Richmond. They had nearly reached the train, which was in waiting with steam up, ready for them. But our descent on them was so sudden, that before they were aware of what was going on, we had their train also.[10] And not only this train, but one loaded with provisions for Lee.

Besides this, there was a large stack of bacon, corn meal, and molasses, and several stand of arms, from which the boys we had liberated, armed themselves, and marched and fought with us to the James River, where they took a boat for Washington. We took what supplies we could carry and set fire to the rest, cars and all. The bacon made a big fire which lit up the night far and near. We destroyed that place, about nine day's ration for Lee's army [and] thousands of dollars worth of railroad property. Late in the evening, we laid down to rest as best we could, holding our horses by the halter.

The day following our success at Beaver Dam Station, we were at work tearing up the railroad track of which we destroyed several miles. On the 11th, at a place called Yellow Tavern, we found a large body of rebs under General Stuart, strongly posted across our path where they proposed to dispute our way, but although within seven miles of Richmond, their strong hold, we did not propose to stop, or let them hinder us much. Therefore our lines were formed with the Fifth and Sixth dismounted and moved forward; the First and Seventh and First Vermont to move mounted.[11]

The line was pushed forward and the fight began to be hot, and still continued to increase as the different regiments got into position. Our company was on the left of the line and reached into a piece of woods, where we were pushing the rebs back from tree to tree. The noise and excitement was such that I did not hear an order to fall back, and kept pushing on after a party of

---

[10] These officers have not been identified. Lt. Carpenter, of the 6th U.S. Cavalry, recalled that these men "were overjoyed at their unlooked for good fortune and expressed their gratitude in unmeasured terms." Mounts had to be found for these men, who accompanied the column. See Carpenter, "Sheridan's Raid," p. 305.

[11] The 1st Vermont Cavalry had been assigned to the Michigan Brigade in late 1863. A well-respected unit, the Vermonters were called "the 8th Michigan" by the Wolverines. In the spring of 1864, when new recruits swelled the ranks of the Michigan Brigade, the 1st Vermont was assigned to serve with the 3d Division.

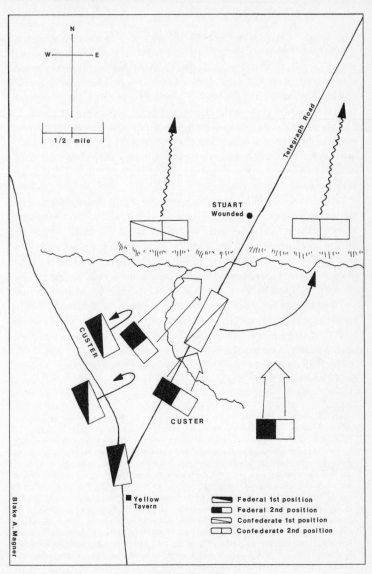

Yellow Tavern

rebs, firing my Spencer as fast as I could with the johnnies only a few rods ahead of me. Just then I glanced back and could see none of our men at all. I was alone, fighting a large party of rebs. Thinking they might see their advantage and take me to Richmond, before I wished to go, I turned back quickly and left them masters of the field. It appears the line had been withdrawn from this front to support the center, and being the farthest in advance, I had not noticed the move, so got left. I soon found the rest of the company engaged in an open field in about the center of the line, where the brave Stafford and the heroic Lonsbury were leading on the no less brave and heroic company, where the storm of leaden hail was dealing death and destruction in their path.

Lewis Herner was killed, then Henry Werner wounded, and the balls came zip, zip, close to our ears, making a man duck his head without seeming to know it. About this time, Custer, with the First and Seventh, charged the lines of rebel battery, capturing it, and we mounted and charged the lines of rebel cavalry, routing and driving them back, giving them a severe whipping. During this battle a ball struck Henry Werner in the mouth, passing out near the neck and breaking the jawbone. Fox and myself helped him to the rear and then went in again. I never saw him again until in 1880, when we met he cried like a child, saying "If it had not been for you and Laph [Lafayette Fox], I no be here now." To this day he cannot open his mouth enough to put the point of a ten penny nail between his teeth.[12]

The Fifth is entitled to the honor of displacing one rebel officer, General Stuart, who was killed by a man named Huff, of Company E.[13]

---

[12] Avery has briefly described the first day of the great Battle of Yellow Tavern, one of the largest all-cavalry battles of the Civil War. After the better part of a day was spent in dismounted fighting, the Wolverines received orders to make a mounted charge on the Confederate position, anchored on some high ground fronted by a stand of woods. With the 5th and 6th Michigan supporting them, the 1st Michigan charged over five fence lines and a narrow bridge. Their charge captured two pieces of Confederate artillery, forcing the enemy cavalry to fall back behind a ravine. Custer then committed the 7th Michigan, which was repulsed. In response, the 5th and 6th Michigan advanced dismounted. The combined attack carried the day. In the process, Jeb Stuart was mortally wounded by one of the Michigan men, although the precise identity of the soldier who fired the shot has never been ascertained. Alger claimed that Pvt. John A. Huff of the 5th Michigan had fired it. Asa B. Isham of the 7th Michigan claimed that Maj. Henry Granger of his regiment fired the shot. Stuart was taken to Richmond, where he died the next day. See *O.R.,* vol. 36, part 1, pp. 815–20 and 827–29 (Alger's report). See also Longacre, *Custer's Wolverines,* pp. 210–15.

[13] There is some dispute and controversy over whether Huff actually fired the shot that fatally wounded Stuart. Robert E. L. Krick, a gifted young historian, makes a compelling argument

Just at night, when we formed a camp, George Earle, whom we had not seen during the action, came in with his arm in a sling. "Hello Earle, who hurt you?" was asked. "My horse fell with me and hurt my arm," he replied. So he carried his arm in a sling for several days, until our farrier, Andrews, who had a suspicion that he was playing off, watched him, and saw that he could use his arm as well as ever, when he thought no one saw him. This raised the ire of Lieutenant Lonsbury who told me to put Earle on duty the first detail made.

The same night we went into camp at Bottom's Bridge,[14] where the rebs shelled us as we were going in, and there was a detail for picket from our company. I went to Earle and told him he was to go on duty that night. He tried to get off, saying "I can't, my arm is lame." I told him that would make no difference, he must go, and he went. After that I remember nothing about him and care nothing about him. I have done with him entirely.

The next day we moved to the Chickahominy River, which runs through a dense swamp, crossed by a railroad and wagon road side and side, with a very heavy ditch along the south side of the road. The wagon bridge [Meadow Bridge][15] made impassable for cavalry, and the rebs had a splendid position on the other side of the swamp for their artillery on a rise of ground, perhaps half a mile from the river. The road being straight and wide, they had a splendid range for their guns, covering the bridges.

We had to repair the wagon bridge, and therefore the Fifth and Sixth were dismounted and marched across the railroad bridge, forming a heavy line on the left of the road, as we advanced to engage the enemy from the swamp, while the bridge was being repaired. The artillery in the meantime opening from the other side in our rear. Thus we held them while their shells flew along the road. It is said that while the men were at work on the bridge, Custer was sitting on a piece of timber when a shell struck it knocking it from under him.

As soon as the troops could move across, a heavy line of dismounted cavalry with their Spencer's and revolvers, moved over with irresistible force,

---

that the fatal shot was not fired by Huff, but rather by an unidentified member of the Michigan Brigade. He argues that Huff was nowhere near Stuart at the time that he was wounded. As Huff was later killed in action, the primary source crediting him with firing the fatal shot was Alger's report, cited above. See Robert E. L. Krick, "Stuart's Last Ride: A Confederate View of Sheridan's Raid," in *The Spotsylvania Campaign,* edited by Gary W. Gallagher (Chapel Hill, N.C.: University of North Carolina Press, 1998), pp. 127–69.

[14] Bottom's Bridge was an important crossing over the Chickahominy River near Richmond.

[15] This is the Meadow Bridge over the Chickahominy. The Confederate cavalry division of Maj. Gen. Fitzhugh Lee stoutly defended it.

sweeping over the rebel breastworks, and beyond them we went leaving our path strewn with dead, many of whom lay behind the works, shot in the head, showing how well had been our aim. After driving them a mile or two, we returned to mount and follow as far as prudence would allow.[16]

During our fight in front, the Third Division had been pounding away at the gates of Richmond, but as there appeared to be a very heavy column advancing to attack them, it was thought best to withdraw.[17] Therefore, following on the road we had opened, they were all in due time on the other side of the Chickahominy, at Meadow Bridge, near which we soon after went into camp for the night, with everything quiet and serene, and not a reb to be seen. The tired army fixed their blankets and went to sleep. Again you might have heard the now familiar song: "Michigan's on guard tonight, Michigan my Michigan."

On May 13th, the Fifth was in the extreme rear, the very worst place in marching, when there is an enemy on the look out to harass the rear guard, but we moved quietly along all day without being molested. We were then passing through the country where McClellan fooled away such time and thousands of lives in his foolish campaign of 1862.

We passed through Fair Oaks, White Oak Swamp, Chickahominy, Gaines Mill, and Seven Pines.[18] As we marched along, we could see the tall pines, with their boughs literally trimmed, and many a one with its top cut entirely off with shot of shell. The trees were marked with balls from the ground up, as far as we could see. One can imagine that in such a storm, many men must die. We marched into a level field, at a point called Bottom's Bridge, to go into camp. As we were unsaddling, the rebs threw some shells at us from the other side of the river, but a few pills from one of our batteries made them hunt their holes, and they did not trouble us any more for several days. The

---

[16] Col. Peter Stagg's 1st Michigan Cavalry, supported by the 7th Michigan, made the decisive mounted charge, driving the Confederates from their strong position and opening the bridge. The 7th Michigan then made a concerted charge that broke the enemy line. Custer praised the 5th Michigan's participation, writing, "The assistance of the Fifth and Sixth Michigan Cavalry, by engaging the attention of the enemy in front, was also most important." See *O.R.*, vol. 36, part 1, p. 818.

[17] Wilson's 3d Division engaged enemy artillery along the Mechanicsville Pike, near the Seven Days' Battlefields in the outskirts of Richmond. A strong detachment of the defensive garrison assigned to Richmond came out to face Wilson, prompting him to draw back. See *O.R.*, vol. 36, part 1, pp. 791–92.

[18] Maj. Gen. George B. McClellan, then commanding the Army of the Potomac, had fought a protracted and bloody campaign over these fields during the 1862 Peninsula Campaign. For a detailed treatment, see Stephen W. Sears, *To the Gates of Richmond: The Peninsula Campaign* (New York: Ticknor & Fields, 1992).

next morning we were out early in route for the James River, passing over more noted battlegrounds. And commenting on the chances McClellan had to have ended the war, if he had only pushed things at the proper time.

As we neared the James River, we passed through a wooded country and then into a large tract of cleared land, which rises gradually until it gets quite an elevation above the river. This was Malvern Hill.[19] As our advance reached the top of this high ground, we heard the boom of heavy guns, followed by others not so heavy, near our line of march. Soon we saw the cause of this, we had gunboats on the river and they had mistaken our dusty columns for the rebs. And had brought their big guns to bear on us. One huge shell resembling a joint of eight inch pipe came tumbling along and stopped just beside our regiment. This was decidedly dangerous, but one of the boys recklessly jumped off his horse and tipped it up on end. Looking off to the right we saw a signal flag waving in the air, which the officers on board the gunboats had also discovered, telling them that we were not rebs.

We went into camp on Malvern Hill. The following morning we went down to the river at Harrison's Landing, where we got supplies and returned to camp. At that place, the soldiers we had taken from the rebs at Beaver Dam left us, taking steamer for Washington. We were once more in communication with the world, and you bet we improved the time in writing letters home. We also went into the James River to bathe, which was a luxury after our long dusty march in the burning southern sun.

On the 16th of May, we listened to the boom of Butler's guns away to the south of James River.[20] The next day we broke camp and marched all night down the river until near the Pamunkey River, where we went into camp for the night. The next day we remained in camp foraging for our horses, we found some guns which we brought to camp and destroyed so that the rebs could not bushwhack our pickets with them.

On May 20th, our brigade marched to Hanover Court House, where we tore up the railroad track, destroying the rails, and also burned a bridge. The usual mode of destroying rails was to pile the ties up, set them on fire and then

---

[19] An extremely strong defensive position and outstanding artillery platform, Malvern Hill was the site of the final engagement of the Seven Days' Battles, fought on July 1, 1862.

[20] Avery refers to Maj. Gen. Benjamin F. Butler, commander of the Federal Army of the James, then attacking the Confederate positions at Bermuda Hundred on the Peninsula. Butler was to attack Richmond from the east, while the Army of the Potomac advanced from the northwest. Butler was incompetent, and his attack failed, removing his large force from the fighting and ruining Grant's grand strategy. See Edward G. Longacre, *Army of Amateurs: General Benjamin F. Butler and the Army of the James, 1863–1865* (Mechanicsburg, Pa.: Stackpole Books, 1997), pp. 90–96.

take the rails and put them on the fire. When sufficiently hot, about three men would take hold of each end and twist them around a telegraph pole. This was a big job, but many men made quick work, and a long distance of track was soon spoiled. We moved back about ten miles and went into camp. The next day we again moved out beyond Hanover Junction, where we found the rebs in force. We tried them on, and after a short fight, found them too much for us, so we withdrew. As we were drawing off, our regiment, my company came in the rear as rear guard. The advance seemed so long moving out that it got to be pretty hot for us before we fairly got started.[21]

The johnnies pressed us so hard that it looked as though the brigade would have to turn and beat them back, but we kept them off until the column had got fairly out on the road and moving off briskly. Our mode of action was for Captain Safford to form his line, he having charge of one half of the company and myself the other, and he would keep them in check until I had my men in position; then he would fall back and form a line again in advance of mine; then we kept those fellows back for a long distance, until we crossed a stream, when they gave up and left us alone.[22] The last time that they made an attempt to push us, I was the farthest in the rear and a ball struck my saddle, but as it did no damage, I rode on with my men and was safe at last.

That night we went into a beautiful field of clover, unsaddled and went into camp. The following day we procured corn for our horses and then took up the line of march for the Pamunkey River, which we reached at White House just before night; we drew rations and then moved across a few miles and camped for the night.[23]

We crossed the river on an old railroad bridge, which had been partly burned. There had been plank laid down to cross on, but the bridge was at least twenty feet above the water and with no railing, besides being rather shaky, I carried a box of hardtack on my horse in front of me so that I could not see the track. I had divided up the supplies for several to carry, but I took the only box of hardtack, and would rather be where bullets fly then try it

---

[21] According to Custer's report, the 1st and 5th Michigan had been sent on a reconnaissance to test the strength of a garrison of Confederate infantry known to be holding the bridge over the South Anna River. Custer wrote, "They had not proceeded beyond 2 miles, when the enemy was discerned in strong force in front, while a heavy column of his was reported to be moving on our left flank. Not desiring to bring on an engagement at this point, and having accomplished the main object of the expedition, the command was withdrawn." *O.R.*, vol. 36, part 1, pp. 819–20.

[22] This tactic is known as retreating by echelons.

[23] At this time, White House Landing on the Pamunkey River was the primary Union supply depot.

again. The old bridge swayed and shook until one pack mule lost his balance and toppled over into the water below; it is strange that so large an army with wagons, artillery, etc., could cross without more loss. We got safely over however, and went into camp a mile or two away. I issued the rations to each man, and we cooked our coffee and pork and went to sleep. The next morning we were again on the road early, and before night were within hearing of Grant's guns as he persistently pounded away at Lee.[24] The next day we marched all day in the heat and dust, shooting horses as they played out along the road, until a dead horse or mule could be seen every few rods along the way, making the boys hold their noses as they passed that way days after. They would sing out; "pass it around, don't be a hog and take the whole."

Again we heard the heavy boom of guns, and as we got nearer, we found that our brave army was much nearer Richmond than when we left them fifteen days before.

On Wednesday, May 25th, we joined the Army of the Potomac again, and as we moved along in the rear of the contending lines, we could see the horrors of war in every shape. We were marching along when we met a column of infantry; they soon recognized the long curls of Custer and sent up three hearty cheers for the young chief, who had saved them from Richmond. They were again on the way to the front.

That day as we went into camp, we were where we could get the first mail from home since leaving on the raid, May 9th, and I got six good long letters from home, which I at once proceeded to read, feeling much encouraged by the good news they contained about home and friends and especially about my wife. The following day we took up the march for the front again to work as usual on the flank, where we would engage and hold the enemy until relieved by the infantry, when we would strike for a new point. We arrived at night at the Pamunkey River and went into camp. Early the next morning we were in the saddle and on the way again. We had to dismount to cross the river on pontoon bridges, for we could not ride our horses across, on account of the motion of the boats. Getting safely over we massed on the other bank, advanced, and formed a rebel line of battle, which we soon disposed of and drove them several miles. At night we went into camp as usual.

Perhaps it would be well to be a little more explicit about this going into camp for the benefit of those not used to military terms. Going into camp literally covers the whole part of the time when not on a march. That is, after marching or being on the march, we stop to rest, sometimes during the day

---

[24] The Army of the Potomac was trying to force a crossing of the North Anna River, not far away.

as well as at night, when the order is to unsaddle and go into camp, which means prepare ourselves for rest and to cook our meals. We arrange ourselves in a perfect line, dismount and unsaddle, staking our horses with a pin carried for the purpose, to which we tie the halter. After snapping two together by means of a short strip with a snap on one end and buckled to the bridle of the other horse. This is a strap used in dismounting to fight, which I will describe further on, but to return to the camp; now that we are in line and staked, we take off the saddles, bringing them in front of each horse and laying them down on the ground; then we unbuckle our belt, taking off sabre, revolver and carbine, and laying them beside the saddle; now we are in camp.

The first thing to do is to procure forage for our horses; for this one man goes for two horses, leaving the other to cook the coffee, after making a fire, if fuel is handy, if not, he goes to work to find some, for if he delays, some one else has it all. Thus the feed and wood are first procured, the beasts fed, and the fire started. Then the tents are staked up, if the weather is foul, if not, we put up no tents. Our tents consist of a piece of cotton cloth about one and one half yards square, one piece to each man. These we button together, as they are furnished with button and holes. We then put up a couple of stakes about six feet apart with a pole on top, putting the cloth over it and staking the lower corners spread out to the ground, this makes the roof. We then take our ponchos and button them on each end and our tent is done. Our blankets are then spread on the ground inside and we have a house in which to keep out the storm, but if we lay straight, our feet stick out at one end. We next put our arms inside, and after eating our supper, crawl in and lay down to sleep.

If the weather is fair, we spread the ponchos on the ground, then our blanket on them and still another, under which we get, and we are in bed with the starry skies for a cover. If the night is pleasant this will do first rate, but many a night I have seen rain or snow storm come up and catch the sleepers unaware. I have gone to bed in this way, tired and worn, so that I would not awake even if it rained, until morning, when I would find myself laying in a pool of water held by the rubber blanket underneath, or the still colder cover of snow, which had come on in the stillness of the night. But what of this? We were soldiers, and must expect a taste of all the good as well as poor comforts and hardships. While our friends at home were snugly housed, and in nice warm, soft beds. What do we care, did we not say we will go and risk our lives and health for our country and for them? Did we not fulfill our promise, and did some of our friends fulfill theirs? We shall see further on.

We found no fault; we were a cheerful, contented set, ready to march and fight, and go hungry without complaining. We were fighting for our country.

On the morning of the 28th, we moved out toward a place called Hawes Shop, where we struck the enemy's lines. They were posted in a heavy wood on each side of the road and behind breastworks, we had found their outer lines and charged them mounted, and had driven them to the wood, when we dismounted, and forming in heavy double lines, moved forward in columns of battalions. The ground we had to traverse was open, with the exception of some small shrub pines. As we advanced in this field the musket balls began to greet us, and increased in volume until a perfect hell of fire and smoke broke from the rebel works. Even the air we breathed seemed thick with lead and sulfur. It did not seem possible for balls to fly thicker. The boughs were dropping constantly from the pines. The leaden messengers splished and spat and chucked as they passed or struck the mark, burying themselves in a human target, when fell all sides, some to rise no more, some to get up and stagger off to the rear, while others started for the rear with arms dangling helplessly, and then were overtaken and brought down again, perhaps forever. I never saw men fall so fast, and still the storm increased, and the surging lines wavered, but bracing up, we made a tremendous charge, driving the enemy from their works and dealing death and destruction as we jumped over their breastworks and pursued the congruelling rebs. The victory is ours, but at what a cost. About fifty men from the regiment lost in a few minutes. Company I is fortunate, considering the storm of leaden hail, only losing one man killed, and three wounded. Fox had a gun shattered in his hands, but picking up another from the ground he pushed on. You could see heroism all around; every man made himself a hero in this terrible cyclone.[25]

After the battle, I had occasion to assist in helping care for the wounded, and looked over the field. The ground was covered with guns, revolvers, and other arms; the dead lay thickly around, and in the rear, close to the field, the wounded were gathered together, and the surgeons with their assistants, were busy over them, here probing a gunshot wound in the leg, and if necessary, off it comes; there dropping off an arm; yonder, under that tree is a man

[25] The veterans of both sides recalled the Battle of Hawes Shop, fought May 28, 1864, as the heaviest or most severe cavalry fight of the war. It was a meeting engagement, where the two opposing cavalry forces came together, and the combat soon became general. The 5th Michigan carried much of the brunt of this fight, making both mounted and dismounted charges. As Avery quite correctly points out, the regiment took heavy casualties in this action. See *O.R.*, vol. 36, part 1, p. 821, for Custer's account. Eighteen of the Wolverines were killed in action that day.

Hawes Shop

Blake A. Magner

whose deep drawn breath, accompanied with a suppressed groan as the surgeon examines a puncture in the breast, tells you of death soon to follow; others with slight wounds are awaiting to be treated. As fast as the surgeon is through with one he passed to another; soon all are cared for, then placed in the ambulances and sent to the hospital. The dead are examined for the purpose of finding something by which to identify them, and then are given a soldier's grave. The cold earth is their winding sheet, the sod their coffin lid.

After this severe battle, in which the brigade lost more men than in any other during the campaign, we went into camp until May 30th. About three o'clock on May 30th, we moved out toward Old Church, at which place we found the rebs beating back the Fifth New York regular cavalry.[26] We were ordered to dismount, action front, jumping off our horses we formed a line by the side of the column, then marching by the right flank, we moved out to a field in which was a rise of ground. As we passed Custer and his staff, he said, "I have a good place boys, under the brow of that hill, and when they come over give them hell." This was the only time I ever heard Custer use hard language. But we deployed on the right of the road and when the Fifth New York came back through our lines, we started on the run, and meeting the johnnies, completely routed them, firing our Spencer's and yelling as only Michigan men can yell, Wolverines sure.

We drove them three miles as fast as our legs and lungs would allow, and on the way many prisoners were taken. Fox was after one fellow whom he ordered to surrender; the reb not stopping soon enough to satisfy the fiery red-headed Fox, he up with his gun and brought him down. Our regiment went in with such a rush, that we entirely outstripped the seven who were mounted on the left of the road, therefore leaving both our flanks uncovered; but we were all right, no rebs wanted to interfere with us.

This engagement was with a heavy body of mounted infantry sent out, as a reb prisoner told us, "to whip the Michigan Brigade," but the first time they had a chance, said Michigan Brigade scared them out of their hides, or at least their wits.[27] The last we saw of them, they mounted their horses and started for Dixie, double quick. They had learned that the Michigan men were not like honey bees, in one sense, sting once and stop, but more like the hornet, keep on stinging, and sting fast and quick.

---

[26] Avery refers to the 5th New York Cavalry of the 3d Division. This was a volunteer regiment, not a regular army unit.

[27] Avery refers to the South Carolina cavalry brigade of Brig. Gen. Matthew C. Butler, armed with Enfield muzzle-loading rifles and not cavalry carbines. Butler's brigade became one of the finest cavalry commands on either side during the Civil War.

May 31st, we were flanking the enemy at Cold Harbor, fighting a very superior force, holding the ground all day, and resting on our arms, in position, all night. In this fight it became my duty to be with the horses, therefore did not witness the battle on the lines, but saw some destruction among the horses with shell. Next morning the rebs made a vigorous attack on our lines, but we were too much for them again; we held our position until relieved by the Sixth Corps, when we moved to Paisley's Mills, and went into camp. June 2nd, moved to Bottom's Bridge and encamped. 3rd, still at Bottom's Bridge; our guns try the rebel lines, but without effect. 4th, move to Old Church where we again encamp. June 5th, go on picket at Anna Church; rebs attack our lines, but are repulsed.

June 6th, again return to Old Church, where we take a bath in the Pamunkey River, [a] great treat which the whole regiment enjoyed. This river is noted as being in the country of Powhatan, chief of the tribe of Indians that captured John Smith. Who has not heard of John Smith who was taken prisoner by these savages, his companions all killed and he only escaping by his cunning and tact in showing his pocket compass and writing, which the Indians looked upon as superman. All such things strike the superstitious nature of the savage, and most of them would suffer death rather than harm such a person; but this particular tribe seemed to think it best to be rid of such influences, and would have killed Smith finally had it not been for the chief's daughter, Pocahontas, who interfered to save his life. Pocahontas married Rolf, from whom sprang some of the present families of this part of Virginia, noted as the "F.F.V.'s [First Families of Virginia]."[28]

All over this part and along the James River, is where the terrible sufferings of the colonies which first settled in this region took place. Every foot of their land is historic; not only from the Indians career here, but also by the War of the Revolution; and now again we make a new history, of the same by the War of the Rebellion.

During the day it was learned that we were to make another grand raid, this time to Gordonsville, which is probably about one hundred miles north and west of Richmond.[29]

---

[28] Avery facetiously refers to the so-called First Families of Virginia, typically wealthy, powerful plantation owners, the ranks of whom included Robert E. Lee himself.

[29] Gordonsville is a strategically crucial point. At the junction of the Orange & Alexandria and Virginia Central Railroads, it was the major transit point for rolling stock headed for Richmond from the fertile Shenandoah Valley. Contrary to what Avery wrote, however, Gordonsville is only sixty miles northwest of Richmond, not one hundred. The destruction of the Virginia Central Railroad was one of the principal goals of the raid mentioned by Avery.

James Henry Avery, shown in his Grand Army of the Republic uniform not long after the Civil War. *Michigan State Archives*

Avery in old age. *Karla Jean Husby*

Maj. Gen. Philip H. Sheridan, commander of the Army of the Potomac's Cavalry Corps during 1864–1865. *Library of Congress*

Maj. Gen. Alfred Pleasonton, the second commander of the Army of the Potomac's Cavalry Corps. Pleasonton promoted Custer to command of the Michigan Cavalry Brigade. *Library of Congress*

Maj. Gen. Julius Stahel, commander of the Third Cavalry Division until Maj. Gen. Judson H. Kilpatrick was appointed. *National Archives*

Maj. Gen. Judson H. Kilpatrick, also known as "Kill-Cavalry," commanded the Third Cavalry Division during the time that the Michigan Brigade served with it. *Library of Congress*

Maj. Gen. Alfred T. A. Torbert, commander of the First Cavalry Division for most of 1864 and 1865. *Library of Congress*

Maj. Gen. Wesley Merritt succeeded Torbert as commander of the First Cavalry Division. *Library of Congress*

Maj. Gen. Thomas C. Devin, final commander of the First Cavalry Division. *Library of Congress*

Brig. Gen. George A. Custer. *Library of Congress*

Col. Sir Percy Wyndham, the foppish British lord who briefly commanded a brigade that included the 5th Michigan Cavalry. *Library of Congress*

Brig. Gen. Joseph T. Copeland, the officer who organized the 5th Michigan Cavalry. Copeland was the first commander of the Michigan Cavalry Brigade. *Library of Congress*

Bvt. Brig. Gen. James H. Kidd of the 6th Michigan Cavalry, who briefly succeeded Custer in command of the Michigan Brigade. *Bentley Historical Library, University of Michigan, Ann Arbor, Michigan*

Bvt. Brig. Gen. Peter Stagg of the 1st Michigan Cavalry, the final commander of the Michigan Brigade. *Library of Congress*

Col. Russell A. Alger, who commanded the 5th Michigan Cavalry, 1863–1864. *United States Army Military History Institute, Carlisle, Pennsylvania*

Bvt. Brig. Gen. Luther S. Trowbridge of the 5th Michigan Cavalry.
Library of Congress

Lt. Alexander C. M. Pennington,
commander of Battery M, 2nd
U.S. Artillery, which served with
the Michigan Brigade. *Library of
Congress*

Maj. Gen. Benjamin F. Kelley. *Library of Congress*

"A Skirmish Line Advancing," by Alfred Waud. *Library of Congress*

"The Charge of the 5th Michigan Cavalry at Third Winchester," by Alfred Waud. *Library of Congress*

"Custer's Charge" by Edwin Forbes. *Library of Congress*

Maj. Gen. James E. B. Stuart, legendary Confederate cavalry commander. *Library of Congress*

Lt. Gen. Wade Hampton, commander of the Army of Northern Virginia's Cavalry Corps, 1864–1865. *Library of Congress*

Maj. Gen. Thomas L. Rosser, Custer's friend and commander of the Confederate cavalry in the Shenandoah Valley, 1864–1865. *Library of Congress*

Maj. Gen. Lunsford Lomax, Confederate cavalry division commander. *Library of Congress*

Col. John S. Mosby, the notorious "Gray Ghost" and Confederate guerilla chieftain.
Library of Congress

Mosby and some of his Rangers.
Library of Congress

Lt. Gen. Jubal A. Early,
whom Sheridan vanquished
in the Shenandoah Valley.
Library of Congress

7

The June 1864 Trevilian Raid and an Ordeal to Remember

"We knew not where we were going; we cared not, only that we were after rebels. We took them, we took their horses, and all was confusion and still we rode."

WE ALWAYS HAD TWO OR THREE MEN WHO LIKED TO REMAIN WITH THE wagon train rather than with the company, and such was the case with some of the Dyre boys.[1] It seems that one of them had got rather tired of the train and thought he would come to the company for a while, as all appeared to be quiet. He reached camp just at night, bringing with him a very nice horse he had picked up somewhere. As soon as he found out there was to be a move he wished to trade horses, so I having one that was nearly played out on the long hard marches, told him I would trade. All right, he took my old horse and went back to the train, and I had a good smart one to start out with in the morning; and he was a splendid beast, not large, but quick and wiry, with speed like an eagle; and could jump a fence or a ditch like a deer.

Such was the kind of a beast I mounted on the morning of June 7, 1864, on

---

[1] There were four brothers from Allegan named Dyer—James, Robert, Russell, and Seth—who served in Avery's Company I. James Dyer had been captured near Richmond on March 1, 1864, during the Kilpatrick-Dahlgren Raid, and died in captivity at Andersonville on September 29, 1864, so he could not have been one of the brothers specifically referred to by Avery here.

the memorable trip to Trevilian Station, which proved to be the most severe and trying campaign of the war thus far.[2] As near as possible I shall give the full details of this raid, and the subsequent trials of myself and my companions in misfortune, for a soldier should take everything as it comes in good part and all for the best and in fact, this is the light in which I used to take everything. As I take up my diary, which I carried at the time of which I write and made an entry of each day's incidents, marches and place of encampment as I learned of it on the spot.

I find we broke camp in the morning of June 7th and crossed the Pamunkey River on our course to the north. I did not notice the order of marching every day, so do not know which brigade took the advance this day.

It may be of interest to detail the regular order of marching on a long journey, as many do not understand a regular military move. We will take a division, for example, taking three brigades to constitute a division. The Michigan Brigade was composed of four regiments. Now the first day, the first brigade takes the advance, and the first regiment in order is in advance of the brigade; the first battalion takes the advance of the regiment, and the first company (or Company A) takes the advance of the battalion. The next day this company takes the rear of its battalion, the battalion the rear of the regiment, and the regiment the rear of the brigade. Thus each brigade, regiment, battalion and company alternate each day. Then a guard is thrown out in extreme advance, and one back in the extreme rear; one man is also sent to the right and left of each company as flankers, thus forming a complete guard around the entire column.

We will now look to the officers of each command, just behind the advance guard, and some little in advance of the column, you will find the general commanding division, the brigade commander of the leading brigade with their respective staff officers and the head quarter [headquarters] flags of each. Thus you will see at once the division and brigade which leads. Now comes the colonel of the leading regiment with the regimental staff, next comes the company officers, at the head of each is the captain, the first lieutenant and orderly sergeant, the second lieutenant and commissary sergeant with one corporal march in the rear. This now is a perfectly formed column, which when an order is given, works to time like a clock. On the right and left are

---

[2] Trevilian Station, named for a local wealthy landowner named Charles Goodall Trevilian, was a stop on the Virginia Central Railroad. The little town of Trevilians is located in Louisa County, Virginia, about five miles west of Louisa Courthouse and about six miles southeast of Gordonsville.

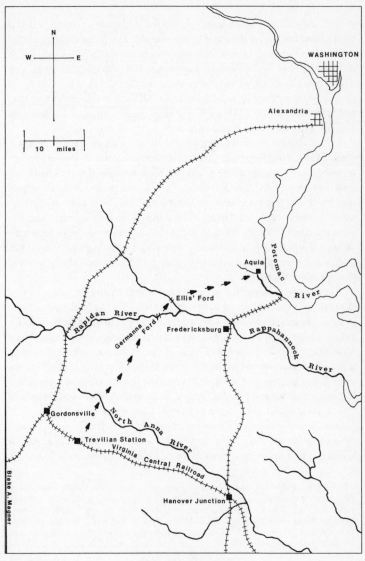

Avery's Trevilian Trek

perfect skirmish lines as we march, supported by the main column, which is formed into line, either mounted or dismounted in an instant, and ready for work. Now here you have a column in heavy marching order as it keeps its form day after day. It is quickly formed into line of battle, does its fighting and as quickly, moves off in column again. As the men thus pass along the dusty roads, they must do something to pass off the time, therefore they talk, laugh, whistle, and are a jolly set. But at times the order is given to "March in silence" when the enemy is suspected near.

As I said before, we broke camp on the 7th and took up our line of march toward Gordonsville, passing over some very nice country as well as some terrible poor.[3] Such as had been used for tobacco plantation, but had since grown up with a thick growth of scrub pines. We marched cheerily along until night, and went into camp near the Mataponia River.[4] Next day was spent the same—march, march, yes, "tramp, tramp, tramp, the boys are marching, like a grand majestic sea," we marched to the Polecat Station on the Gordonsville railroad [Virginia Central Railroad].[5] Spending a quiet night in camp at this place we were again ready to move out early in the morning. The next day was the same thing over again.

The 10th was a change for me, as I was out with a party for forage all day. We rode over the country on each side of the road, picking up such articles in forage as we could. Corn, oats, or other grain. One barn I went into appeared as though the corn husks were three foot deep on the floor. When upon examination, we found a nice pile of corn in the ear underneath. Filling some sacks, we returned to the column. On these foraging expeditions we often found bummers, or camp followers, who made it their business to follow along and rob and plunder helpless and defenseless families, and at one time, I threatened to shoot a party of two or three if they did not let up.

One day I was sent with a detachment to search a house for arms. When I entered, followed by my soldiers, the lady of the house wished to know our business. I told her we were there to search for arms, "ahms, ahms," she said,

---

[3] The objective of this raid was for Sheridan to take two divisions of the Cavalry Corps, the 1st and 2d Divisions, march along the route of the Virginia Central Railroad to Gordonsville, destroy the critical rail junction there, then march to Charlottesville, where the cavalry would join the Union army of Maj. Gen. David Hunter, then advance up the Shenandoah Valley. Once the two forces combined, Sheridan was to escort Hunter's army back to the main body of the Army of the Potomac, thereby significantly reinforcing it. See *O.R.,* vol. 36, part 1, pp. 784–86.

[4] Actually, the Mattapony River, a tributary of the James River.

[5] Polecat Station is actually a stop on the Virginia Central Railroad. There is no Gordonsville Railroad.

"we have no ahms in the house." But we were ordered to search, and not take the word of anyone, therefore, directing my men to be lively, we made a thorough search. The house was well fitted up for comfort, although in rather ancient style; in fact it was a regular southern planter's habitation. In a large upper room I found not only comfort, but splendor, and hanging on the wall was a life size portrait of General George Washington. I made the remark to the lady that it was a wonder that that picture did not take life and curse them for trying to break up the Union. Feeling at the same time that the picture itself was almost a certain guard against vandalism, I wondered, if the house had been searched by some roughs, if they could have proceeded after seeing that noble picture. Finding no arms, I withdrew my men and left all things unmolested.

Duty is duty, but I have known of men, under the guise of duty, to pillage buildings of everything, even beds and carpets. I once heard of some men, rather rascals, taking feather beds and cutting them open for the fun of scattering the feathers to the wind. Now what is the need of this lawlessness? No good soldier will do such a thing, nor will he molest women or old men. But it is a shameful fact that there were men, calling themselves soldiers, who would not stop at robbery, but even insult defenseless ladies. I say such men were not soldiers, but the worst kind of sneaking dogs, who would never meet an honorable death in battle, but always in a coward's place. But, we have a very important move on hand, and if I don't proceed, I fear my name will get pricked for being tardy.

Early in the morning of June 11, 1864, boots and saddles sounded, and we were soon in line and counted off in fours.[6] We marched in a westerly direction for some little ways, and then formed a line of battle in an opening facing south.[7] After remaining a short time in this line, we again broke off by fours and moved to the front, striking a road leading west,[8] which we followed for some distance until we heard firing in our front when the column

---

[6] On the night of 10 June, Sheridan's column camped in the area around Clayton's Store, several miles north of Louisa Courthouse, near Carpenter's Ford on the North Anna River. Custer was to take his Michigan Brigade along a wood road, arrive near Trevilian Station, and there join the rest of the Federal column, which would advance on Trevilian Station via a different route. See *O.R.,* vol. 36, part 1, pp. 820–25, for Custer's report on the Battle of Trevilian Station.

[7] Early that morning, the Confederate cavalry brigade of Brig. Gen. Williams C. Wickham, of Maj. Gen. Fitzhugh Lee's Division, made a sortie from Louisa Courthouse and briefly engaged Custer's pickets along the Louisa Road. After a brief skirmish, Wickham's men broke off and withdrew to Louisa, and Custer began his march. See *O.R.,* vol. 36, part 1, p. 823.

[8] This is the main stagecoach road between Louisa and Gordonsville, which is modern-day U.S. Route 33. It parallels the course of the Virginia Central Railroad.

was put on a trot, which was kept up for some time, with the order to keep well closed up. Next came gallop, and then charge with revolver in hand. We soon picked up a reb with some horses, then a wagon, then more horses and more wagons with a good many rebel soldiers. A heavy column of lead horses had been left by dismounted cavalry out on the skirmish line, and we had struck their rear.[9] We hauled in the horses, and men, and wagons, lively, leaving a man to take care of them as we went along. Thus we rode fast, faster, and yet more fast, as the rebel bullets began to fly, and we rushed on to face them.

Lieutenant Lonsbury and myself rode side by side in this head long race. We knew not where we were going; we cared not, only that we were after rebels. We took them, we took their horses, and all was confusion and still we rode. Edwards,[10] who rode a mule, fell out and we urged him on, but he replied he knew what gait this horse took to be safe. He was taken prisoner. It got hotter and thicker; we passed Custer; we rushed through the rebel line of battle; on, on, led by Alger. Our column was reduced in length; many had been left with the captured horses, and to take care of the wagons; others took back the prisoners.

Still on and on we pressed until we were past the rebel lines. They closed up the gap, and we were cut off from the brigade, forty men close to Alger, we would not be out done by our Colonel and were almost by his side, surrounded by rebels everywhere, we had some prisoners still and kept them under our revolvers. We were Michigan men, full of grit, with the feeling that the honor of our state was in our keeping so we hang on until the last. Where was our support? We had none. We were alone, within the rebel lines where brigade could not help us and we had to help ourselves. Finally we reached a piece of timber where the Colonel called a halt, and we grouped together to talk matters over. The rebels were all around us; we could see their heavy columns pass, hither and yon, as we watched them.

I covered the prisoners with my revolver, for they must not be allowed to say a word. We were soldiers, and did not intend to be prisoners. Captain

---

[9] Custer had found a seam in the Confederate position. Maj. Gen. Wade Hampton's Confederate cavalry division was engaged with the rest of the 1st Division along the Fredericksburg Road, to the north of Trevilian Station. In the fields surrounding the train station, Hampton had established his divisional wagon park and holding area for the horses of the men then fighting dismounted, and Custer's line of march had brought him into a seam between Hampton's and Lee's divisions, and in the rear of both.

[10] William Edwards of Detroit, a member of Avery's Company I. Edwards was captured that morning and survived his captivity, receiving his discharge in Detroit in June 1865.

Judson,[11] a staff officer was with us, and he and Lonsbury consulted with the Colonel [Alger] during the lull that ensued. Frank dismounted to investigate a rebel saddlebag, which was decidedly cool, considering the place. Thus we stood in that bit of wood surrounded by rebs, a gun was fired close by, and instantly Alger led out and on we rushed, over fences and ditches; over hills and vales; through the tangled bush wood, my revolver still covering six prisoners. Soon we struck the enemy again. Someone said counter march, and we broke in two. On pressed the Colonel, and all but twenty five with him crossed the lines. I was with those left. We tried to cross, but the rebel line was doubled and we could not get through. It seemed all up with us, for we were alone and surrounded by rebs.[12]

I left my prisoners with others and carefully reconnoitered the rebel lines; they were too strong for our numbers. We dismounted and crept through the bush to other parts of the line, but with no better success. We were in a bad pickle. There was but a handful of us, surrounded by thousands of rebs. It was strange they did not look up and secure us, they must have thought we passed their lines. But there we were, and we had to depend on ourselves for safety. We had men who did not give up for trifles. There were seven sergeants, two or three corporals, and about fifteen men. Every company in the regiment was represented with us. We concluded to try and pass around the rebel flank, and moved off lively for quite a distance.

Passing through a small opening, we were fired on by a picket, but were not followed, and still kept on until we came to a large field in which we saw a division of cavalry, which we thought was ours, and were just about to rush out when we discovered that they were rebs.[13] We kept under cover and they did not see us. We then gathered in the woods to consult. Some were for following up our army, but I said no, for by doing so we could go directly to

---

[11] Thirty-five-year-old Capt. Robert F. Judson of Kalamazoo, who served as the Michigan Cavalry Brigade's acting assistant inspector general, riding with Alger that morning.

[12] In fact, Alger was nearly captured when he and his little force blundered into a strong enemy position. They bluffed their way out of the tight spot and spent the rest of the day riding around the Confederate flank until they finally found their way back to friendly lines that night after riding nearly twenty miles. A large portion of the 5th Michigan was captured during the heavy fighting that ensued, much to Alger's chagrin. For Alger's report on the Battle of Trevilian Station, see *O.R.,* vol. 36, part 1, pp. 829–32.

[13] This is most likely Maj. Gen. Fitzhugh Lee's division, which advanced out the Gordonsville Road from Louisa Courthouse and engaged Custer's embattled Wolverines near the train station around noon. Thus Custer's force was entirely surrounded, and he had to fight for several hours a desperate and lonely action to save his command until a massed attack by the rest of the 1st Division finally cut its way through to him.

Richmond, as prisoners, for we could not keep clear of the rebs. So I proposed to move as straight as possible, and thus by going from the rebel army with a chance of safety.

This difference in opinion caused a temporary split in our ranks, and the majority were for following the army. I said go, but I go alone the other way, for I don't propose to be a prisoner. One boy, a little fellow from Kalamazoo, belonging to Company L, said, as the tears came in his eyes, "which ever way the sergeant goes, I go too." He called me sergeant, I thus had one on my side, and then Dan Collier, one of my own company, signified his intention of following me. Things stood in this way without shape, when a Negro came along through the woods. We halted him and learned that he was going to try to get into our lines. He said he could pilot us across the rebel lines that night, and could take us twelve miles on our course toward the Potomac. This settled the matter and pleased me, for he said we could not rejoin our command, because Fitzhugh Lee's division of cavalry was between us and them.

We mapped out our course, and as night came on, left our horses tied to trees and started out on foot, hiding our sabres under logs, as they were a useless appendage, buckled on to tangle our feet, but every carbine and revolver was taken good care of, and put in prime condition. We moved silently along, through the tangled bush, often stopping to listen, and all the time on the look out for danger. About ten o'clock our guide whispered to us to lay down, and we laid low for perhaps an hour when he said all right. We then moved on again for a long ways. When again we stopped, he then told us we had crossed the rebel lines, near Trevilian Station.[14]

We moved on until we thought we were at a safe distance, and when daylight began to appear in the east, we sought the thickest brush we could find, and crept into [it to] pass the day. During the day our guide looked around outside and posted himself about the enemy, and just before night, returned and reported. He said the rebs had been scouring the country all day for some yanks who were somewhere around. But the Negroes had misled them, and sent them off on a different route. At dark, we again started and marched until

---

[14] During the late afternoon phase of the fighting on 11 June, a determined Union attack drove the Confederate cavalry away from Trevilian Station. Sheridan's men camped in the fields near Trevilian that night. Lee's men camped in Louisa, and Hampton's division camped in an area known as Green Spring Valley, partway between Trevilians and Gordonsville, along the Gordonsville Road. There is no satisfactory modern treatment of the Battle of Trevilian Station. For the best overview to date, see Walbrook D. Swank, *The Battle of Trevilian Station: The Civil War's Greatest and Bloodiest All Cavalry Battle* (Shippensburg, Pa.: Burd Street Press, 1994).

near midnight, when we stopped to rest. That night one of our prisoners complained of being sick, and I shared my blanket with him, both sleeping under one cover, while one of our men stood guard over us. Thus we passed the second night.[15]

In the morning, we held a consultation, in which our prisoners were allowed to take part, as it concerned them. We proposed to let them go, as our rations were low and we would have to provide for them, as well as ourselves. They said they would go with us without trouble, or they would return if we said so, but on the honor of southern soldiers, would not betray us. Trusting them, we parted; they feeling quite affected, shaking hands, and wishing us good luck, they set out on their way to friends, and we took up our line of march moving by daylight.

One little incident I want to mention; As we were on our horses and trying to find our command, I noticed a horseman off to the left, who seemed to be watching us in an undecided manner. I rode toward him and he also advanced toward me. As I got near enough to see, I discovered that he was a reb, and not knowing how many more there were, I turned and rode back to my column and he, discovering my identity, also turned and rode the other way. I think the fact of our having prisoners with us led them to believe that we were their own men, as they often dressed in blue. Surely, I did not wish to investigate further, under the circumstances, but to proceed.

After marching until mid-day, we took up our camp in the bush again to rest until dark. Our rations were now exhausted, and our guide went to the house of some friends of his, also Negroes, and from their scant store they gave us some warm hoe cake. When he came to camp with it, he also brought along a friend, who wished to go with us. This was good, for it increased our strength, as he brought a gun with him. This made us twenty-seven, and all determined men, who could have made a big fight. Again we moved out of our concealment at dark, taking the stars for our guide. As we now had to cross our opening, we moved very low, almost on our hands and knees. On the other side, next a piece of wood, ran a high fence.

Just as we got under the shade of the fence, our advance guard made a motion to lie down. Instantly all were flat on the ground, and still as mice.

---

[15] On 12 June, the fighting resumed to the west of Trevilian Station. There, the Confederates, safely ensconced behind a strong defensive position, repulsed seven separate attacks launched by the Federal cavalry, which eventually withdrew in defeat. That night, Sheridan began withdrawing back across the North Anna River at Carpenter's Ford, and the return march began. The body of Sheridan's command would not reach safety until 25 June and would not rejoin the Army of the Potomac until 2 July.

Pretty soon a horse was heard coming, we listened anxiously. Nearer and nearer it came, breaking the dry brush in the wood. It stopped and somebody spoke and another answered. A low conversation ensued and then the horse moved on again, and the sound grew fainter and then all was still. A rebel picket had been relieved, almost within our touch. It seemed as though we must be discovered, but we made a careful survey of the place. Moving like shadows, and crawling like snakes, flat on our faces. Then we got on our hands and knees, and then bending low, we ran for the wood, and in the darkness we managed to pass undiscovered. No one spoke and all was still, with no sound to be heard but the gentle sighing of the wind as it rippled the leaves of the forest; under which we still crept on and on. Our guide had doubled on his track, and got bewildered.

I had been used to the forest, and taking the lead, ordered them to follow me, and struck a course straight through the wood, but it was near morning by the time we got through, and we had to crawl under the bushes and lay still. Out of some meal we made porridge, which was pretty thin, but we could do no better, so we laid down to sleep, hungry, tired, and foot sore, but we were not discouraged, and were determined not to be taken prisoners if we could help ourselves. We were ready to run or fight as necessity might determine. Each man had his Spencer and revolver with him, ready for use.

We traveled all the fourth day and reached a region we had been over before near the Rapidan. We struck the rebel works south of the river, and had a fair view of them.[16] They extended five or six miles back from the river, we passed through them and took the road to Germania Ford, reaching the Ford about mid-day, all was clear as we forded the river and reached the country, where we had been on picket duty day after day. Everything was now familiar and we knew just where to go. We moved on a little to the north and went into camp for the night in a piece of woods where we had camped before. We rested well, but were getting weak from hunger.

In the morning, we again moved out on our journey, taking the road to Ellis's Ford, on the Rappahannock, at which place we arrived near noon. Here we found an old boat, which we pressed into the service of Uncle Sam as a transport, crossed the river in safety, and found a family who gave us some meal and a little milk. We went into a piece of wood further on, cooked some gruel, and after a rest, concluded to go on in the night. We were not yet out of danger, for the country was swarming with rebels, but we put in good time, for every hour put us so much nearer our lines.

---

[16] This area is probably somewhere around the Wilderness battlefield, or perhaps the Chancellorsville battlefield, just a few miles farther east.

On we went over hill and vale, through wood and field, and becoming bolder, took a wagon road leading to the Potomac. On our route we passed a house at which we got some beans and salt fish, which we carried along. About three o'clock in the morning, of the 18th of June, seven days after our fight at Trevilian, tired, hungry, sick and sore, we laid down to rest until daylight, when we kindled fires to cook our beans, at the same time putting up a flag and a shelter tent for a signal.

Before our beans were done, our signal had been sighted by a gunboat from afar, which at once steamed toward us. As they neared us, their guns were brought to bear on us, and when near enough to land, a plank was thrown out after the captain had found out we were not rebs, and we were told to come on board, where to the wondering officers our story was told. At once the captain told us not to eat our beans, which we carried on board with us, and ordered his steward to bring us canned beef, cautioning us to be careful not to eat too much, as he would have a good dinner for us in a little while. Our adventures had to be told over to all the officers; our Spencers were examined, they had never seen such guns, and everything they could see on shore was made a target of, cattle, sheep, pigs or geese, as we steamed away up the Potomac, and we lounged away the time in what shade we could get on deck.

Soon dinner was ready and we were served with a bountiful supply of bean soup, which would have done credit to the best of our cooks at home. Thus we glided along over the bosom of the grand old Potomac, as we talked and laughed loudly, for now we did not care for Johnnies; we were out of their reach and I could say, "boys, this is better than going to Richmond, escorted by Lee's cavalry."

Just at dark, we passed the guard ship at Alexandria, and after the officer of our boat had reported to the admiral, we steamed into port. The captain accompanied us to the provost marshal, and reported our care to him, where upon he orders wagons to take us to what was known as convalescent camp, about six miles up the river opposite Washington. There we arrived, after seven days of hardship and privation. Some of the boys were really sick and others nearly so, and all tired and dirty. We were immediately surrounded by an anxious crowd of soldiers, asking questions. Next day a detailed account of our travels was published in a paper that was printed in camp, and called "The Soldiers Journal," and I still have the item and also Sheridan's report of our loss. I at once sat down and wrote to Lonsbury; telling him of our escape, and the regiment was all ordered in line and the letter read to them. I am told there was exceeding great joy at our good luck in keeping out of rebel hands, for they supposed we were prisoners.

As soon as we arrived at Alexandria, we procured a situation for the Negro who aided us to escape, in the quartermaster's department. A good place at good pay.

Having briefly sketched the escape of our party from the perils that environed us, let us go back and see how the rest of the regiment came out.

The party with Alger, after crossing the reb lines, soon joined the brigade, where some more of the Fifth gathered in, being lucky enough to be on the right side of the lines so as not to be obliged to cross. The buglers were ordered to scour the woods and sound the brigade call, and in this way many were guided to them and the command, but we had been to far off to hear these calls. We were therefore given up as lost, and reported us missing in action, and the brigade took up the line of march back again for the Army of the Potomac. Where they were when my letter was received. Their subsequent work for the next three months I cannot follow, as I was away from them for that time, and when next I saw them, they were in the Shenandoah Valley.[17]

To return to my own experience, after a few days in convalescent camp, to get recruited up, our party was sent to remount camp, just below Washington on the hills. It was customary for them to send a guard with each party sent through the city, but the officer in charge of the camp said he did not think such men as we needed a guard, and therefore, he would merely send an orderly along with dispatches for the provost marshal and the officer in charge of the remount camp, and would not insult us by placing a guard over us. At this time we met Mr. Brown, the photographer, who gave us five dollars to buy some little articles with, we were very thankful.

We crossed the Potomac at Long Bridge, and took our way into the city, where we reported to the provost and were furnished with proper authority to proceed to camp. Crossing a low, nasty stream [Anacostia River] that empties into the Potomac at the Navy yard in the south side of the city. We were soon climbing the hills south of Washington, on which we find remount camp, which was called Camp Stoneman.[18] Here I found Sergeant Baldwin, Geo. Shupart, and O. P. Eaton of Company I, with whom I took up my quar-

---

[17] In fact, the Cavalry Corps got a few weeks of rest and relaxation in July and then was sent west into the Shenandoah Valley with the express task of hunting down and destroying the Confederate army of Lt. Gen. Jubal A. Early, sent west in the hope of drawing off Federal forces from the siege lines around Petersburg.

[18] Named for Maj. Gen. George Stoneman, the first commander of the Army of the Potomac's Cavalry Corps and first commander of the Cavalry Bureau, this was a major remount camp. Its purpose was to train replacement cavalry horses for the rigors of service. It was one of several major remount camps established throughout the North.

ters. I made up my mind to take a good rest as there was no prospect of getting a mount for some time. During several days of our stay at this camp, we had nothing to do except to cook and eat.

We went down town one day and drew pay, so that we had some money with which to buy some little extras, and I also sent some home. We were furnished reading matter by the Christian Commission, and therefore had plenty to read.

8

A Temporary and Very Reluctant Infantryman

"We had established quite a reputation with the infantry for pluck."

ON JUNE 27TH, WE DREW ARMS AND EQUIPMENT FOR CAVALRY, AND ON THE 3rd we were mustered for pay. The weather was extremely hot excepting the mornings. On July 4th, we turned over our cavalry arms and took muskets, as we learned that the rebs had crossed into Maryland and we were to go out with the infantry.[1] We were organized into a separate command of dismounted cavalry, thirteen hundred strong, armed with guns that we were not accustomed to,[2] and officered by men we did not know. We were in fact, an awkward squad and therefore needed to be drilled, we knew nothing of infantry tactics or the manual of arms. We drilled a little on the 4th, but it takes

---

[1] Early's Army of the Valley crossed the Potomac River into Maryland on July 4, moving on the Federal armory at Harpers Ferry. For a detailed study of Early's raid on Washington, D.C., see Joseph Judge, *Season of Fire: The Confederate Strike on Washington* (Lexington, Va.: Rockbridge Publishing, 1994).

[2] Avery and the other cavalrymen were used to carrying rapid-firing, breech-loading carbines that were semiautomatic in nature. Fighting as infantry, they were now armed with unfamiliar muzzle-loading Springfield muskets. Instead of being able to fire seven shots per minute and being able to load while lying down, the dismounted cavalrymen had to learn to fire a shot or two per minute with a weapon that could not be loaded while they were lying down.

longer to teach the infantry drill to a man who is used to the cavalry drill, than to teach a new recruit.

Early on the morning of July 5th we packed up, shouldered our muskets and moved out of camp down to the city, where we took cars on the B&O Railroad for Harpers Ferry. The boys were full of fun and were shooting at everything they saw as the train passed slowly along. Just above Washington, one of them cut the telegraph wire with a bullet; another scamp, in firing at some geese, hit a woman who was walking along. The cars were crowded inside, between and on top; as they were boxcars with wide bumpers, several could stand between. One fellow in trying to climb up, accidentally fired off his musket. An officer asked his name and he replied, George Washington; the officer asked "what business have you with such a name, do you think George Washington would be fool enough to cut such a caper with his gun?" The poor fellow looked as though he would like to sink out of sight.

We crept slowly along all night, and in the morning arrived at Sandy Hook, where we disembarked, and for a short time took up our quarters along the rocky road for breakfast. When breakfast was over we set out on our first attempt to march on foot.

The Virginia side of the river was held by rebel sharpshooters, who covered the road leading up to the [Edwards] Ferry. We took the road leading up Pleasant Valley from Point of Rocks. Going up the valley a mile or two, we struck a route leading by a long detour up the eastern slope of the mountain to the top of Maryland Heights,[3] which we reached about noon in the burning July sun. It was a high point, towering above the Ferry several hundred feet, on top of which were earthworks containing several heavy guns, one of which used a hundred pound shell, and brought the country for four miles around within range of its terrible power. During the night you could see the fuse of the monster as it passed over into the tower, and the explosion was like a big gun in reply. I saw several buildings burned by those shells.

We were marched down on the flats and into rifle pits, where we remained for two nights, expecting an attack from up the river. During the first day that we were in this position, Sergeant Sigel[4] came in with his command and also

---

[3] Towering high over the confluence of the Potomac and Shenandoah Rivers at Harpers Ferry, Maryland Heights was an impregnable defensive position featuring 100-pound naval guns. While the town of Harpers Ferry could not be held, Maryland Heights could not be taken but by siege.

[4] This sarcastic remark probably refers to the command of Maj. Gen. Franz Sigel, which had been thrashed by a scratch Confederate force, including cadets from the Virginia Military Institute. Sigel fell back into the defenses of Harpers Ferry and was then relieved of command. His record as a combat commander was not especially good.

Colonel Mulligan.[5] We had no engagement however, except slight skirmishes in front. On the third day we moved out and down the river to Pleasant Valley again. The route along the Potomac was very wild, as it cuts its way directly through the Blue Ridge, and the river canal and railroad are side by side.

We moved down to Point of Rocks,[6] where we again halted for a short stop, and then proceeded to Pleasant Valley[7] where we went into camp, drilled for a few days and then moved to Sandy Hook, where General Hunter[8] arrived and took command.

On July 15th, we crossed the river by fording and moved on to Hillsboro, where we went into camp for the night. Hillsboro was a small town, nestled in the mountains, several miles from the Potomac. By this time I had begun to understand the infantry drill, as far as marching was concerned, for every night I was so tired that I could hardly put one foot ahead of the other, and was ready to get down to rest as soon as a halt was called, even if I did not get any supper. At Hillsboro we had plenty of stones for pillows, for they were so thick that we had to roll them aside to get a place to lay down. Finally, however, we got to sleep, and in the morning arose refreshed and ready to move again. About 8 o'clock we expected an attack and formed a line of battle on the mountain side, and remained in line until 3 o'clock when we moved out, marched to Purcellville and went again into camp. The rebs continued to harass our advance, and our pickets, but we did not find them in force.

On July 17th, we remained in camp all day, and listened to a sermon preached by the chaplain of the 18th Connecticut Infantry. On the 18th, we crossed the mountains at Snicker's Gap, fording the Shenandoah River at Island Ford. We there met the enemy in strong position a short distance from the river, and as we crossed we went into line of battle on the bank; after some sharp firing, we took position close under the low bluff, which made a breastwork for us, but over which they could see our heads and shoulders, which made a good mark for their sharp shooters, and their bullets came very thick, sending death into

---

[5] Col. James A. Mulligan, who commanded the Federal garrison at New Creek. A lawyer and newspaper editor by training, Mulligan would be mortally wounded on 23 July. For his bravery, he was brevetted to brigadier general of volunteers effective July 23, 1864. Roger D. Hunt and Jack R. Brown, *Brevet Brigadier Generals in Blue* (Gaithersburg, Md.: Olde Soldier Books, 1990), p. 437.

[6] An important landmark, Point of Rocks is a crossing over the Potomac River near Leesburg, Virginia. It was a frequent target for Mosby's guerrillas over the course of the war.

[7] Pleasant Valley was another major Federal remount camp located near Harpers Ferry.

[8] Maj. Gen. David Hunter, known as "Black Dave" for his unforgiving policy of total war, including warring against civilians, was the theater commander for the Shenandoah Valley. His army had been defeated by Early at Lynchburg and had fallen back. Hunter then went to Harpers Ferry and took command of the remount camp at Pleasant Valley.

our ranks, thick and fast. The dismounted cavalry and infantry were mixed up promiscuously.[9]

A tall, fine looking Virginian, who carried his regimental colors, stood beside me. I heard a ball strike, and as I turned to him he fell, shot in the head and instantly killed. Lorin Chapman of the cavalry picked up the flag and set it against a tree, when instantly a ball struck the tree, cutting the tassel cord. My old musket bothered me terribly in this fight; it would not go off as I had forgot to bite the cartridge, so I drew the ball and set my ramrod beside a tree just as we were ordered back. To remedy this evil, I picked up a gun that was in order, as my gun was of no use without a rod.[10] I made a good change. We were now ordered back, and as we were rather closely pressed on the river, it made some confusion. As the soldiers ran into the water, many were shot and the stream was red with blood. When we reached the bank and had proceeded a short distance up, we were gladdened by the sight of a heavy body of our troops, which a few minutes before had moved into position and ready to meet the rebs. We were not to be troubled any more that night however, for the enemy did not follow us across the river, and we therefore went into camp again on the east side of the Shenandoah.

The following day we lay in camp all day, and although we could hear heavy fighting at the front, we took no part. On July 20th, we again crossed the river, getting a double portion of wet, as it rained very hard, and wet us above water as well as below. The river was so deep that we had to hold our guns and ammunition up to keep them out of the water. But they got somewhat wet. We went into camp again within hearing of heavy firing in the direction of Winchester.

On July 21st, we were in camp all day, but on the 22nd marched to Winchester, passed through the town and went into camp just south of it, where we established a picket line. The next day the rebs attacked our lines and were beaten back. During those days, when off duty, we picked black berries, read and wrote, as having no horses to care for, we had lots of time in which to get homesick if we would.

---

[9] A Union force commanded by Brig. Gen. George Crook, part of the Department of West Virginia, moved out from the defenses of Martinsburg, West Virginia, on 18 July. Crook attacked Early's forces at Snicker's Ferry on the Shenandoah River, undoubtedly the engagement described by Avery. This became a large engagement, as the 6th Corps, detached from the Army of the Potomac and sent to clear Early's army from the valley, engaged the Confederates. See *O.R.*, vol. 37, part 1, p. 287, and part 2, p. 392.

[10] The Springfield rifles required a ramrod to push the ammunition and cartridge down the barrel of the gun. Without a ramrod, a weapon could not be reloaded effectively.

We had a very good position on the south side of a high elevation, where we built up piles of rails for breastworks, behind which we could watch and hold the rebs, and we considered our position very strong. We had established quite a reputation with the infantry for pluck, if not for correct movement, and we had got so as to be able to load and shoot our old muskets. The loading took some time, for it was new to us to bite the end off a cartridge, but once loaded, the Johnnies needed to look out, for we could point them straight, and shoot a long ways.

We had a good deal of fun as we lay behind our works, waiting for the Gray Coats to put in an appearance, but the day passed off at length without a battle. The country to the west of the town of Winchester is quite hilly, making a natural defense from the front; at the south it is somewhat hilly, but not so high, while on the east, a nice level plain extends for miles, only broken by now and then a knoll or ravine along some little stream. This plain extends to the Shenandoah and is crossed by the Opequon and some other smaller streams. The Shenandoah runs along the eastern border near the Blue Ridge.

I now, and did at the time, insure General Crook for his miscalculation, or inability to comprehend the situation. Our small army of about seven thousand men was posted mostly in the hills at the right of Winchester, and in front facing south; and apparently reaching but a very short distance to the left, or else very weak at that point. Some will say, the commanding officer knows best, but, I say sometimes a private can see as well as a General. The General must not be found fault with, and all the honor of success is given him, while the rank and file do his work, whether good, bad, or indifferent. Our army was small compared to the one brought against us consisting of from twenty five to thirty thousand rebs.[11] To extend our lines far enough to cover the front made a very weak show, and to try to hold our position under such circumstances showed very bad management.

In the morning of July 24th, the rebs advanced on our lines, and the battle became heavy. Colonel Mulligan was killed, and his command pushed back upon the second line, which in turn gave away before the weight of the rebel columns. The fight raged along the right and front, and still heavier on our left, and the rebs doubled up our left flank. Soon our lines began to move back slowly, then a little faster, and then they became broken and disorgan-

---

[11] This engagement is known as the Second Battle of Kernstown. Actually, Early had only about twelve thousand men. His effective management of this force made it seem much larger than it actually was.

ized. The rebs pushed us vigorously and we got demoralized and confused and retreated back past Winchester, Crook was defeated.[12] The men had no confidence in him. Many soldiers were lost on his account.

Had he knowing the enemy's strength, withdrawn to a better position, or nearer the ferry where they could not have flanked us, we might have kept them back; but he did not and a perfect Bull Run took place. All skedaddled as fast as their legs would carry them; infantry, artillery, and wagons were in a confused mass. Averell's cavalry[13] made a show of covering our rear, but such a show. If they had given us their horses we could, that is, the dismounted cavalry could have checked them somewhat and kept them back, but instead of this, the cavalry even ran over and into the rear of the infantry. This was not good behavior for cavalry, who were placed in that place to keep the enemy back, but it was everyone for himself, and we all tried to make it good.

Sergeant Baldwin and I were together in this skedaddle, we did our best to save ourselves and succeeded. I threw away my gun into the river, dropped my blanket and everything to lighten myself, but I still hung to my haversack, which was nearly empty; as I passed a broken wagon in which were lots of hard tack, an officer said, "fill your haversack." I therefore took all I could put in, and on I went. Run, run, all was run, until we reached Bunker Hill, about twelve miles north. It being then night, I threw myself under a bush beside the road, and without cover, went to sleep. Awaking in the night, I found it raining, but did not stir until morning. When I got up, wet and lame from the previous day's work, I had traveled twelve miles, mostly on a double quick, after fighting all the forepart of the day.

As soon as daylight came, we were on the road again, moving north as fast as our sore feet and lame legs would carry us, through rain and mud until we reached Martinsburg, on the Potomac River, where we awaited orders. Soon

---

[12] Crook claimed, "On the 24th, . . . I was attacked by a large force of the enemy near Winchester. I repulsed their force twice, and was driving them when they partially turned my left and threw it into some confusion. At the same time a heavy column was moving around my right, and I gave the order to fall back. My left soon reformed, and the whole line moved back in good order; the enemy pressing both my flanks and center hard all the time." He continued, "I regret to say that the greater portion of my dismounted cavalry, along with some infantry, the whole numbering some 3,000 or 4,000, broke to rear the first fire, and all efforts to stop them proved of no avail. They mostly got into Martinsburg, circulating all manner of reports. A few of them were captured endeavoring to escape my guards. I lost over one-third of my cavalry in this way." *O.R.,* vol. 37, part 1, p. 286.

[13] Brig. Gen. William Woods Averell commanded the cavalry attached to the Department of West Virginia. These were not the best-mounted soldiers assigned to the eastern theater of the Civil War, and their performance was mixed.

the dismounted cavalry were ordered on board the cars to go to Washington. But before the train could start, the rebs occupied the railroad, and attacked the town. We were now taken backward over the B&O railroad to Cumberland, where we unloaded and lay down to rest again.

In the morning we fixed up a camp in the only place we could find, which proved to be a pest hole, or a place where small pox were buried, and a shanty was standing in which a man had died of on Friday, and we went in on the next Monday night. This looked bad, but only two men took the disease, though the shanty was used for a sutler's store. We stayed in this camp six weeks, doing nothing but eating and sleeping, except some small incidents which I will mention as they come along. We had a pretty good time generally.

Having no tents, we called upon the quartermaster and received tents, with which we soon fixed up a nice camp and slicked up the ground, making all in good order. Fox, whom I failed to mention as with me, he and I put our tent together. I don't remember just where Baldwin and [Dan] Collier were located, but they were somewhere near us. We were between two mountains, where the water would run down in torrents when a heavy rain came, as was after the case. We were also near the town which lies on the north side of the bend of the Potomac. The B&O railroad ran near our camp, and two flat cars were fixed up for scouting duty. One was rigged as a fort; with a turret made of rails from the track, set up end ways, which made a defense from which the balls would glance off. A piece of artillery was mounted inside, which could be turned around to be fired from a porthole on each side and the rear end.

The other was a boxcar, covered with heavy sheet iron, with loopholes for muskets. These moveable fortifications would run out on the railroad to reconnoiter every day. It seemed to me they could be easily captured by tearing up the track at a distance on either side.

We soon got our camp in perfect running order and drew our regular rations of soft bread, coffee, sugar, and meat. As we got plenty of coffee, I had more than I could use, as I did not like strong coffee, and I used to take what I had left and sell it and buy baking powder. I also often exchanged my soft bread for milk, as we had a man from Company C who would go out and milk some cows and bring the milk to me. Letting it sour and getting some flour, I made some very nice pancakes of which Fox and I were very fond, and they were good too, if soldiers did make them. At other times, I would go to a vineyard on the side of the mountain and get grapes which were large, and made a good sauce. Thus we lived nicely in this camp.

One day, an alarm was caused by what we supposed to be the report of a cannon, but it afterward proved to be a store in town blown up by some reb. We were not out of reach of the rebs, and therefore, were on the outlook for adventures, but if they had come, we would have had to fight with fists and clubs, as we had no arms at all, everything having been lost in our skedaddle from Winchester.

It may be of interest to tell how General Kelley[14] earned his extra star. The rebs were raiding Maryland, had burned Chambersburg,[15] and were threatening other points. Kelley had command at Cumberland, and one day the scouts reported the approach of rebs, where upon we were all ordered into the fort just south of town, on a high knoll, without guns. We marched up this hill into the fort, where there was nothing but a small three pound piece called a Jackass Battery.[16] This was all we had for defense.

In the meantime, the rebs had approached with a flag of truce, and demanded the surrender of the town and all the troops in forty minutes. Kelley held a parley, during which the main army of the rebs crossed the river, and finally Kelley refused to surrender. For this brave battle Kelley was promoted. Two hundred good soldiers could have taken the whole thing. I don't know which should have been promoted, Kelley for his parley, or the boys for their brave defense in settling down without arms and quietly awaiting the end of the conference, when we are quietly moved back to camp and took up our old quarters.

On August 7th, I went up on the mountainside, where for the novelty of the thing, I sat down and wrote some letters home. It was a place to be remembered; away up above the city of Cumberland.

On the 8th of August, there was another scare in town, as rebs were reported again in our front, threatening our place, but the day passed off without bloodshed, and night settled down peacefully, overshadowing all things

---

[14] Brig. Gen. Benjamin F. Kelley, at age fifty-seven, was one of the older soldiers commanding troops in the field. Most of his service during the Civil War was spent in West Virginia, guarding the line of the Baltimore & Ohio Railroad from the numerous enemy attempts to cut the railroad. In February 1865, some of Mosby's men captured Kelley and Crook in Cumberland, Maryland. Kelley was released by special exchange, and then he resigned from the army. On August 5, 1864, Kelley received a brevet to major general of volunteers for the reasons set out by Avery.

[15] Confederate cavalry commanded by Brig. Gen. John McCausland had burned the town of Chambersburg, Pennsylvania, on July 30, 1864, as punishment for Hunter's many acts of depredation in the Shenandoah Valley that spring.

[16] Avery refers to small mountain howitzers, typically firing three-pound shells, that were normally pulled by mules or donkeys.

good and bad. Each day everything was told off, as usual, and all our duty was to cook, eat, and sleep, or read and write. Sometimes we took a turn at washing our clothing, to keep off the gray backs, and for the good of our health.

On the 10th, there came up a sudden storm of rain and wind; the rain came in torrents, soon forming a swift stream down through our camp like a small river. While the wind was so strong as to blow down a building in which were some sick soldiers, killing one and severely injuring several others. The storm was of short duration, and soon all was calm and bright again, and as hot as any August sun could be, making the poor fellows pant under their thick woolen clothing.

One day a soldier came into camp, and at once the boys set up a whistling, as though calling a dog. Everywhere that he went he was greeted with this salutation. It was all on account of his wearing a paper collar, but collars afterward became popular, and really made the soldier look slicker.

Our camp was organized into several divisions, with a commissary to each division. The division which I drew rations for numbered forty-four men.

We were getting tired of this inactive life and often applied to the officer in command to send us to the front; but a certain amount of red tape had to be used, and we had to wait our time.

One day we heard that the Michigan Brigade was in the [Shenandoah] Valley, and the news made us still more eager to get out of our irksome quarters.[17] We had stayed too long in one place, and wished to be with the brigade again, which was doing excellent work. I received several letters from home and from Frank; one of Frank's told me of a party of our regiment being captured by rebs and murdered in every way. Some were shot, some had their throats cut, others hung and tortured in every style, equal to savages. This happened at or near Berryville, and Custer at once sent out a detachment and burned several buildings near the place. It seemed to be a point to retaliate, and make them stop such work.[18]

We finally prevailed on the commander, or else his roll of taffy had run out; and on September 2nd, we were ordered on board a freight train for Hancock. We were piled and jammed in and on box and stock cars, and went

---

[17] In fact, Grant had sent Maj. Gen. Philip H. Sheridan west, with the Army of the Potomac's Cavalry Corps in tow, with orders to take command of the Middle Military District and destroy Early's army. With the 6th, 8th, and 19th Corps and two divisions of cavalry, Sheridan had a powerful army. Little Phil and the cavalry arrived in the vicinity of Winchester on August 10, 1864.

[18] At Berryville, Virginia, on August 19, 1864, some of Mosby's guerrillas captured and murdered thirteen members of the 5th Michigan, supposedly in retribution for their burning of houses.

rolling away from Cumberland. The track was rough and our motion slow, so that we did not reach Hancock until late in the day. The next day we drew rations and marched fifteen miles to Clear Springs, and the next day to Hagerstown.

On the 5th, we marched to and through the Antietam battlefield, where we saw the debris left by that terrible battle.[19] As usual, where there is timber, the trees were cut and torn, splintered and broken, from the ground up. A brick church standing on the field seemed to have been an especial target, for it was completely riddled with cannon balls.[20] Near this church was where Burnside's columns made their terrible road through the rebel ranks, and where the noble 17th Michigan put in its first marks for its state; never did veteran soldiers do better than did this splendid regiment of raw men. On this field Hooker, Sumner, Franklin, Ricketts,[21] and others dealt the rebels hard and heavy blows. The 17th in this battle, led by the brave Colonel Washington, charged up South Mountain, driving the enemy from behind stone walls. It was one of the severest battles for the time it occupied during the war.[22]

After passing the historic ground, we halted at Antietam Creek, and went into camp at the stone bridge. We found there an old log house in which a part of our column took up quarters, and as it was a rainy night, we thought ourselves lucky to find so good a shelter. In the morning, we again took up the march and reached Harpers Ferry in the afternoon, and I went to Pleasant Valley where I found Sam Shaffer [Shaver][23] with the headquarters wagon, and the mail for the company. I received 18 letters, which had accumulated

---

[19] The Battle of Antietam, fought near Sharpsburg, Maryland, on September 17, 1862, was the single bloodiest day of the Civil War. For a detailed description of this brutal and bloody fight, see Stephen W. Sears, *Landscape Turned Red: The Battle of Antietam* (New York: Ticknor & Fields, 1983).

[20] This is the famous Dunker Church, a focal point of the fighting during the morning phase of the battle.

[21] Maj. Gens. Joseph Hooker, Edwin V. Sumner, and William B. Franklin, all corps commanders at the time of the battle, and Brig. Gen. James Ricketts, who commanded a division in Franklin's 6th Corps.

[22] Avery has confused his battles here. The 17th Michigan Infantry, commanded by Col. William H. Withington, was a brand new regiment in September 1862, having only been mustered into service two weeks earlier. At the Battle of South Mountain, fought September 14, 1862, the men of the 17th Michigan, seeing combat for the first time, performed admirably, driving Confederate infantry from a series of stone walls in Turner's Gap, near the spot where Maj. Gen. Jesse Reno, commander of the 9th Army Corps, to which the 17th Michigan was assigned, was killed.

[23] Samuel Shaver of Saugatuck served in Avery's Company I.

since I left the regiment at Trevilian, and read them as soon as I could. On the 7th, we again took the cars and started for Washington. We were on the road all night and I slept on top of a box car all the time the train was not in motion, but when it was running, the track was so rough that I had to hang on tight or roll off.

Once during a short stop, some of the boys got off and picked some large grapes that grew wild near the track. On the morning of the 8th, we arrived in Washington, and went back into our old Camp Stoneman. We had accomplished nothing, except to learn the country, and more of the ways of war and red tape.

On September 12th, we got our horses; all new and vicious ones. Mine was a nice looking one, but as I went behind him to make him stand around in order to feed him, he kicked with both feet, one going on each side of my head like lightening. I was so surprised that I did not move, but fortunately, he did not kick again. It is a wonder that his feet did not strike me in the face. I saw one horse rear and fall back on his rider, killing him almost instantly. We soon, however, took the temper out of them, for on the 15th we broke camp and moved out through Washington and Georgetown, and on.

The 19th we crossed the river at Harpers Ferry, and marched all night as train guard.[24] The next day we passed through Winchester and Newtown, and went into camp south of the latter place. On the 21st, we joined our brigade and moved to Port Conway, where we went on picket. The boys were very glad to see us again, after our long absence from our company. I again had the pleasure of shaking Frank by the hand, as well as Lonsbury and the others whom I had not seen since the Trevilian fight. The boys were alive and well except Harvey Mann, who had been killed at Shepardstown, where they had quite a hard fight.

It would be well at this point to review the work of the regiment during my absence. After trying without success to recall us at Trevilian, it moved with the brigade back to the army of the Potomac, where it took part in the second battle of Cold Harbor. July 21st, the cavalry was then transferred to the Shenandoah Valley where the brigade was in action at Winchester, August 11th; Front Royal, August 16th; Leetown, August 25th; Shepardstown, August

---

[24] That day, a major battle raged, the Third Battle of Winchester, in which a magnificent five-brigade charge of Federal cavalry, led by Custer and the 5th Michigan, broke Early's defensive lines and drove his army through the town in a wild rout. It was a major victory for Sheridan's newly formed Army of the Shenandoah.

25th; Smithfield, August 29th; Berryville, September 3rd; Summit, September 4th; Opequon on September 19th; Winchester, September 19th.[25]

Batchelor[26] gave me a description of the battle of Winchester, which was one of the most splendid and successful of the war, equally in brilliance and excelling in result even Brandy Station. During the hottest part of this battle, when all was smoke and confusion, with shells and balls flying thick and fast, Lieutenant Lonsbury saw a chance to capture a battery, which was lightly supported. Rallying a few brave fellows, he boldly charged upon the rebel guns, and had he been properly supported, would have secured them, but the rebs rallied in heavy force, and finally beat our brave boys back, inch by inch, and hand to hand, and saved their guns. I guarantee this made the gallant Lonsbury foam. I can even now imagine his tall, straight figure, writhe under the repulse. There must have been terrible odds, for if he had not been opposed by more than ten against one, I would have vouched for his success.[27] Nearly every day the company and regiment were in a fight. And the scouting and reconnoitering duty was immense; all the time on the move with scarcely time to catch more than a few minutes rest.

---

[25] This was some of the most intense cavalry fighting of the Civil War and one of the phases of the war that made George A. Custer's reputation as a fighter. For a detailed description of these actions, see Jeffry D. Wert, *From Winchester to Cedar Creek: The Shenandoah Campaign of 1864* (Carlisle, Pa.: South Mountain Press, 1987).

[26] Pvt. Harvey D. Batchelor of Gun Plains, who served in Avery's Company I.

[27] Custer specifically mentioned this incident in his report of Third Winchester, writing, "Lieutenant Lonsbury, Fifth Michigan Cavalry, with great daring, advanced with a handful of men to within a few paces of the battery, and was only prevented from capturing it by an infantry support, hitherto concealed and outnumbering him." *O.R.,* vol. 43, part 1, p. 457.

━9━

Fighting with Little Phil

*"Like figures of iron bolted to our saddles, we pressed for-
ward with pale cheeks, eyes flashing fire, teeth set firm, and
revolvers clasped in our right hands."*

IT WAS THE 20TH OF SEPTEMBER, THE DAY FOLLOWING THE BATTLE OF
Winchester, that I joined my company, right in the midst of a very active campaign. We made a move up above Front Royal, capturing a few of Mosby's
men at Front Royal. They were recognized as a part of the band that had
recently captured a lieutenant and some men of our advance guard and murdered them. Being caught and recognized by the lieutenant before he died,
they were sentenced without court or jury, and two of them were given over to
our regiment. Being brought in front of us, the colonel, [Hastings],[1] said; "If
any of the Fifth had a spite against Mosby's men to ride out." This was wrong.
We all had a spite against them, but did not feel like murdering them in cold
blood. The only proper way would have been to detail a firing party, under
orders. Only two men rode out; one was a man who had just had a brother

---

[1] Maj. Smith Hastings, who was promoted to lieutenant colonel of the 5th Michigan Cavalry in
November 1864, was in temporary command of the regiment, Alger having resigned his commission on September 20, 1864. In August 1864, Alger had apparently gone AWOL from the
regiment and had resigned to avoid being court-martialed. The taint of this incident haunted
Alger for the rest of his life, supplying his critics with plenty of ammunition when Alger was
nominated to be secretary of war under President William McKinley. See Longacre, *Custer's
Wolverines*, pp. 252–53.

killed by them at Berryville;[2] the other was the bugler of the regiment,[3] who had nothing but his own spleen to vent.

The boys, one about sixteen, the other about eighteen years old, were to be shot. They begged of the chaplain a chance to run for their lives, but no such boon was allowed them. They were placed a short distance away, and the two men began firing at them. The first shot killed the younger, but the other received two or three balls before he fell. I pronounced this barbarous, and some of the boys muttered at me, but I did not care, why should we be obliged to see those boys shot down like dogs, right at their doors in this savage style? Two others were led along to a piece of wood and hung to a tree. This was a terrible warning to bushwackers, and this kind of work was carried on until Mosby was glad to quit.[4]

That same day we went into camp on a creek near Front Royal, and had everything ready for a good rest. Several of us had taken off our shirts and were in the creek washing them when Boots and Saddles blew, and we had to put on our wet shirts and march all night up the valley.

On the 24th, we found the rebs at the village of Luray, posted behind piles of rails, strung across the valley. Our brigade was formed in line on the left of the road, our regiment on the extreme left, with our company on the left of the regiment. The battery got in position and threw in some shells, effectually removing some of the rails, and then ceased firing to give us a chance. We charged with a terrible yell, our sabres flashing in the sun, and in a few moments the rebel lines were broken and scattered in all directions. Many

---

[2] This appears to be George Warner of Company C of the 5th Michigan Cavalry, whose brother Oliver M. Warner was killed by Mosby's guerrillas at Berryville on 19 August.

[3] This may refer to J. Allen Bigelow, who had been the 5th Michigan's chief bugler for more than a year. However, Bigelow was a first lieutenant at the time of this episode, so it is not possible to confirm the identity of the soldier Avery mentions here.

[4] Not long after, Mosby's men killed a popular Union officer, and several of his men were hanged in Front Royal in retaliation. Mosby, in turn, executed several members of the Michigan Brigade, and then a truce ensued in which both sides agreed to cease executing each other's prisoners. It was one of the ugliest incidents in the Civil War. While Mosby blamed George Custer for ordering the executions in Front Royal, the order originated with Torbert. Mosby also lied when he said that he only retaliated against the Wolverines. In truth, infantry and artillerists also participated in Mosby's infamous "death march," and of the seven men actually selected for execution, only two of them were Wolverines. For details, see Roberta A. Fagan, "Custer at Front Royal: 'A Horror of War'?," in *Custer and His Times: Book Three,* ed. Gregory J. W. Urwin and Roberta A. Fagan (Conway, Ark.: University of Arkansas Press, 1987), pp. 17–81. See also James A. Ramage, "Mosby in the Valley," *North & South* 3, No. 1 (November 1999): 10–22.

were taken prisoner or killed, and others got away, and our victory was complete.[5]

On October 1st, we moved into the [Rockfish] Gap near Port Republic and back. On the 2nd, we moved to Brown's Gap and crossed in the night. Our way being blocked with trees and rocks, and everything to impede our progress, so that it took us the entire night to get through. After a short stop, we returned to Harrisonburg and went on picket duty. The next day I was assigned six men for duty near the Shenandoah at a farmhouse where a Mr. Miller lived. He had a great many apples which we made into cider, as there was a hand mill at the farm. We also got flour, chickens and meat there, and fared very well.

There soon came a day, however, for us to get out, as the rebs got on our flank, and gave us a close rub. In that affair, I noticed how cool Colonel Hastings was in close quarters. Keeping his regiment in good order, he kept in the rear where the rebs were pushing us closely. Cool and quiet, he was just the officer to inspire confidence in his men. Although pressed hard, we were taken out in good shape and went back to Harrisonburg.

On October 8th, the Fifth was rear guard as we were moving down the Valley, and the rebs kept picking away at us all day. When we got to Woodstock, they were so close as to be within pistol shot. We were in the town at the same time that they were and some one set a building on fire, which burned several others. We were so closely pressed as to require the attention of the brigade, and several columns were formed on each side of the road, which soon gave them a severe drubbing.[6] In this little muss, Lonsbury had his horse shot under him. I was near him and saw the horse as the ball struck. When night came, we went into camp. And right here I want to say that we went into camp just the same, whether there were rebs in the way or not; for if they were in our bed, we would pull them out and get in ourselves. In other words, if in our way, we would drive them off and then pitch our tents.

---

[5] Wesley Merritt, now commanding the 1st Division, reported, "The march was then resumed, when Wickham's cavalry was met near Luray and routed by the [Michigan] and Reserve Brigades, with the loss of nearly 100 prisoners and one battle-flag belonging to the Sixth Virginia Cavalry." O.R., vol. 43, part 1, p. 441.

[6] On the 8th, the 5th Michigan engaged in severe skirmishing the entire day. When the pesky enemy cavalry was finally driven off, the pursuit by the Michigan Brigade came upon heavy enemy reinforcements near Woodstock, and Col. James H. Kidd, the new commander of the Michigan Brigade, wisely called off the pursuit. With the 5th Michigan as the column's rear guard, Kidd withdrew. O.R., vol. 43, part 1, p. 460.

As I have said before, the worst place to fight is in the rear guard, for you have got to have your back to the enemy some of the time, and then they pitch in. I would rather face the enemy than back them.

Early on the morning of the 9th, we were in the saddle and ready to pay the Johnnies for the trouble they had given us the day before. We moved out on the road we had traveled for some distance, and then taking another route, went through timber and across fields, over hills and up mountains, until we were on an elevated position overlooking the valley on the right. We were there given the honor of supporting a battery. Our whole regiment was in line on either side of the battery, where we had a splendid view of the movement of the Third Division of cavalry, under command of Custer; who, by the way, had been promoted to Major General, and given the command of this Division, Colonel Alger commanding our brigade.[7]

There was a heavy line of rebs in front of Custer, under the command of General Rosser,[8] and they proposed to dispute our way. General Averell had the low ground to the left and we occupied the center. The rebel line in our front was rather weak, which gave our battery an opportunity to play entirely on the rebel battery in front of Custer. We were in such a position that we could see all the moves nicely. While our guns were playing away lively at the rebs, Custer formed his division in heavy double columns, and with sabres and revolvers, swept on like a whirlwind, swooping down on the astonished Johnnies, who could not withstand the onset; and he completely wrapped his columns around them.

As Custer's lines neared the rebs, our guns ceased firing and every man raised in his stirrups, the better to see the result of the charge. For a second, all were breathless, and then, with a mighty cheer we rushed on to keep pace with the right as they followed after the defeated rebs. The lines in our front were swept out of the way, and Averell was doing well on our left. On, on, we went, at the top of our speed, until ten miles were traversed and everything cleared for that distance from rebs. The fruits of the victory were twelve pieces of artillery, and lots of wagons and horses, with many prisoners. This

---

[7] Alger had resigned his commission. Col. James H. Kidd of the 6th Michigan was Custer's handpicked successor and commanded the Michigan Brigade briefly during the Shenandoah Valley Campaign. Custer, while given divisional command, had not been promoted. He received a brevet to major general of volunteers, but that did not occur until the spring of 1865.

[8] Maj. Gen. Thomas L. Rosser, commander of the Confederate cavalry assigned to the Shenandoah Valley.

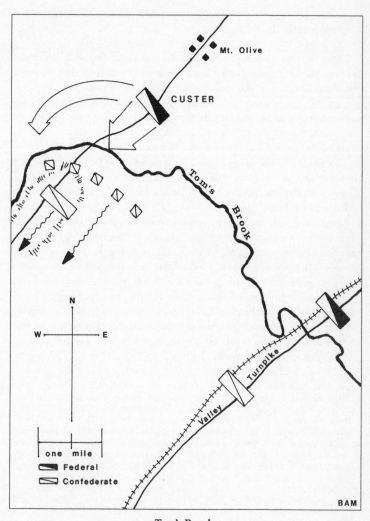

Tom's Brook

ended the day at Woodstock. We had paid them off with heavy interest for their temerity the day before.[9]

On October 10th, we went into camp near Fishersville to rest up again.

I have referred to Custer's being with the Third Division. I think the transfer occurred during my absence from the brigade, and soon after his grand success at Winchester. The brigade was very glad of his promotion, but sorry to part with him as a commander, although Alger did well. Always when we met Custer on a march, he would lift his hat to each company, and was greeted with hearty cheers by the passing soldiers. All loved him, yes, they idolized the curly headed general, who had led them in many a hard fought battle.

The Third Division of cavalry had been commanded by General Wilson, and when he was sent to the west, leaving the division without a commander, Custer was given the command.[10] It afterward appeared that he could handle a division as well as a brigade.

On October 13th, the rebs appeared again in front of our lines and opened with shells. Our brigade moved into position on the right, and they soon stopped. During this campaign, I was in charge of the company, and had to make all the reports, and do all the business, including making the monthly and tri-monthly returns, muster and pay rolls, etc. Lonsbury was with Company M, and we had but one duty sergeant with the company, Sergeant Batchelor, who helped me. Frank acted as commissary, drawing and issuing the rations. At one time during the summer, the company could muster but thirteen men for duty, but at this time, its strength was increased considerably.

Our lines extended along the north side of Cedar Creek.[11] The infantry

<hr/>

[9] In fact, this fight, the Battle of Tom's Brook, was probably the worst defeat suffered by the Confederate cavalry in the Civil War. In the battle, which was known derisively as the "Woodstock Races," the Federal horse soldiers chased the routed enemy for nearly twenty-six miles before calling off the pursuit. In a short but intense battle, the Southern cavalry was flanked and driven from the field in panic. Merritt proudly claimed, as his prizes for the day, forty-two wagons, three ambulances, five pieces of artillery with limbers, four caissons, five forges, twenty-nine mules, thirty-nine horses, twenty-five sets of harnesses, fifty-two prisoners of war, and a wagon filled with new Enfield rifles. *O.R.,* vol. 43, part 1, p. 448. Col. Kidd praised the performance of the 5th Michigan, writing, "I cannot speak in terms of too great praise of the gallantry of Major Hastings and the officers and men of his command, who three times repulsed desperate charges made by a greatly superior force of the enemy." *O.R.,* vol. 43, part 1, p. 460.

[10] Wilson was given the task of organizing a mobile army designed to take on and defeat the force commanded by Lt. Gen. Nathan Bedford Forrest, the so-called Wizard of the Saddle. Custer was given division command on October 1.

[11] Sheridan, after defeating Early again at Fisher's Hill on October 10, had gone into camp on the banks of Cedar Creek. He then proceeded to Winchester for meetings with Grant, leaving command of his army in the hands of Maj. Gen. Horatio G. Wright, commander of the 6th Corps.

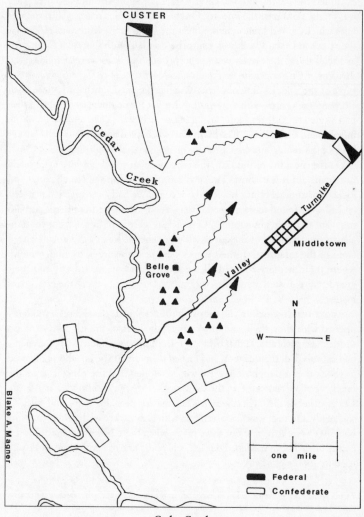

Cedar Creek

occupied the center, and the cavalry the right and left flanks. Our brigade was on the right near the infantry. On the 17th, the rebs made a sortie on our lines which caused some commotion at the front. Some historians claim that the attack at Cedar Creek was a surprise on the Eighth Corps, if on any, for as I shall show, the cavalry was not surprised. Our lines were as follows: the division of Custer on the extreme right; Merritt next to Custer, and on the right of the pike leading out from Winchester; the Eighth and Nineteenth Corps in the center, with Powell's cavalry[12] at Front Royal on the left, as we had a small brigade on a long line, it left a weak point between the left of the infantry and Front Royal. The Sixth Corps occupied a position a little farther back of the center, and were brought up as soon as the fight began.

On the morning of the 17th, the rebs made an attack and we were ready for them, but it was short. The next morning we were again all ready and looked for another attack but it did not come. We had an inspection that day, and all were found to be in good order. We were looking for a battle and did not want to be caught napping. Our pickets were kept at the front continually to give warning of the approach of an enemy. I can't say how it was in front of the infantry, but their works were near the creek on high ground, where their artillery covered all the south banks of the stream, and their guards were posted along the creek at the very point where the attack was made.

About four o'clock in the morning of October 19th, the rebs suddenly opened with shot, shell, and musketry on the lines of the Eighth Corps. So sudden was their attack, that before our troops knew what was up, the enemy had captured all their cannon and turned them on our boys, who vainly tried to check the onslaught. The rush was so sudden that the pickets along the creek were overpowered in the darkness before they could give the alarm. Under cover of the night, the rebels had massed near the creek, and when all was ready, the rush was made, striking with heavy force and sending our line back. We were driven about three miles, when the rebs halted and threw up earthworks. They threatened our left, where the line of cavalry was weak, and tried to double our flank.[13]

---

[12] Col. William H. Powell's 2d Division of the Army of the Shenandoah, which was formerly Averell's command. Sheridan had summarily relieved Averell of command after the Third Battle of Winchester.

[13] Early's plan of attack was well thought out and well executed. However, when he paused to re-form his lines, his attack lost its momentum. Many later criticized Early for pausing, arguing that the pause had cost him the Battle of Cedar Creek. For the best treatment of the Battle of

About ten o'clock, our brigade was ordered to move to the left to check the rebs at that point. Passing along in the rear of the infantry, we were in reach of the shot and shells as they came tumbling along after striking the ground. One was noticed bounding toward our column as we were marching along the road. It would strike the ground then bound about four feet high, then strike the ground again, until it passed through our column between our company and Company L, next in our rear, doing no damage.

A little further on, I saw a shot cut the flag staff above the head of the color bearer. As we passed on we formed a line of cavalry with drawn sabres, keeping the stragglers from going to the rear. This was new to us as we had never seen a guard placed over the rear of our lines, for when we went back, we all went together. We moved into position on the left of the infantry in heavy columns, and held the rebs in check until about four o'clock. Once we were ordered to charge, and our battalion rode close up to the rebel guns and were then ordered back again, amid a tremendous shower of grape, canister and balls, which fell like hail around us, and rattled in the cornstalks through which we had charged. [We were] only one battalion in the whole line. We could do nothing, it was a bad mistake, but I don't know who was to blame for it.

The battalion retired past its original line, across a ravine and up a hill, on which it halted, faced about in good order, moved forward again and took its old position on the line. When on the hill, the shells screeched and screamed, and burst all around, tearing up the earth and whatever they struck in a terrible manner. One shell struck a post just in front of me and burst, shivering it as a stroke of lightening would have done, and sending the pieces all around. Soon after we were again in our former position.

George Hicks,[14] a good steady, reliable and brave soldier of Company I, was shot in the head and instantly killed. We had on[e] young man, a recruit, whose name was Force,[15] he was very slow, and the boys used to laugh at him, on account of the strangeness of his manner and slowness. But here he sat on his horse and delivered his fire as cool and steady as the best of them, showing that he had force in this direction at least.

Cedar Creek, see Theodore C. Mahr, *The Battle of Cedar Creek: Showdown in the Shenandoah Valley, October 1–30, 1864* (Lynchburg, Va.: H. E. Howard Co., 1992).

[14] Cpl. George H. Hicks of Trowbridge, who had been captured at Trevilian Station, paroled, and returned to the regiment only at the end of July.

[15] Pvt. Benjamin Force, who had just joined the regiment on August 9, 1864, at the tender age of sixteen. He joined the regiment just in time for the Battle of Fisher's Hill on 10 October, and served the rest of the war.

Our old dad, M. Andrews,[16] would take a deliberate aim, fire, and then laugh. Frank was as cool as though shooting squirrels. Sam Atkins,[17] or fatty, as we called him, seemed to have great sport with his Spencer and the rebs, Goncher's[18] eyes would twinkle in his sharp set face, and Batchelor would fire with a cool determination, not to be beat. In fact, I did not see a sign of fear. All were ready for any move. Fox had a horse shot under him, yet he was on the line and at work. I can't describe my looks, as I could not see myself, but having no carbine, I kept two revolvers hot. A sergeant of Company E dismounted to adjust his saddle girt, and had just put his foot in the stirrup to mount again, when a shell struck his horse and burst between them, rolling both over in a pile.

About 4 o'clock, we heard that Sheridan had arrived, and fresh courage was given us.[19] The war of cannon and volley of musketry increased. An aide dashed up to our general, a short conversation ensued and then we were ordered forward. Every man felt that the decisive moment had come, and grasped his reins tightly.

Like figures of iron bolted to our saddles, we pressed forward with pale cheeks, eyes flashing fire, teeth set firm, and revolvers clasped in our right hands. With the impetus of an avalanche, we charged forward through a storm of shot and shell, which sent many a comrade to his last account. While others whose horses were shot under them pressed forward on foot. The rebels could not stand the terrific assault and fled panic stricken from the field, and we turned our attention to capturing as many of them as we could. I pushed on with the rest, and skirting a piece of woods saw a reb rush out. Ordered him to halt, and as he paid no attention, fired a shot from my revolver which caused him to throw up his hands and surrender. Covering him with my revolver, I marched him back to camp, which I reached about 9 o'clock, and turned him over to the guard. The rest of the command were soon all in, and we laid down to sleep on the same ground we had held in the morning.

Such was the battle of Cedar Creek. We had whipped the rebel army under Early in great shape. He had been "early" in the morning and pushed

---

[16] Twenty-nine-year-old Pvt. Mortimer Andrews of Avery's hometown of Allegan.

[17] Pvt. Samuel W. Atkins of Watson, age twenty.

[18] Pvt. Vernon C. Goncher, whose name does not appear on the regimental roster.

[19] Sheridan, hearing of the raging battle, had dashed more than twenty miles from Winchester on his great war horse, Rienzi, prompting the writing of Thomas Buchanan Read's famous epic poem, "Sheridan's Ride." See James E. Taylor, *The James E. Taylor Sketchbook* (Dayton, Ohio: Morningside, 1989).

us, but was not so early at night, for we turned on him and gave him a terrible thrashing.[20]

The next morning we could see our work. The ground was literally covered with dead and wounded. Forty-nine pieces of captured artillery were parked at Sheridan's headquarters. Muskets by the cord were piled up, and we had captured a large number of prisoners. All the next day we chased the rebs.

Near Strasburg, we saw their hospital ground in a bit of woods. They had taken off arms and legs and left them on the ground, and some were still on their tables where the men had lain to undergo amputation. Along the roadside were broken wagons, broken gun carriages, dead mules with rope harness to draw with, and debris of all kinds. We followed as far as Woodstock, and then returned to Fishersville and went on picket. It was the biggest battle and most complete victory ever gained in the [Shenandoah] Valley, and was where Sheridan made his famous ride from Winchester, twenty miles away.

One thing I should have mentioned before this was a move we made up the valley a few days before the battle. We went as far as Staunton, and then fell back and burned everything in the shape of grain, hay, or other forage that we could find. One large mill was burned with a large quantity of wheat, which the rebs had garnered, and did not have time to move. Some barns were burned, in which large amounts of arms and shell had been stowed. This burning occupied all our time as we marched back, and extended over the whole width of the valley as far down as Fishersville.[21]

During our stay in camp, I had muster rolls to make, and also a report of our losses in men, horses and arms. On October 30th, 1864, I was assigned the duty of taking the entire regiment to water. Therefore, for a part of one day at least, I had command of the regiment.

[20] Early's shattered army fled, leaving little or no organized resistance in the Shenandoah Valley. Sheridan had caused an entire army to cease to exist with his decisive victory at Cedar Creek.
[21] This is the sad episode known as "The Burning," one of the few instances in American history where U.S. citizens made a concerted effort to destroy the homes and livelihoods of other American citizens in a systematic fashion. Virtually every farm and homestead in the Shenandoah Valley was burned in an effort to break the resistance of the populace. For a fine treatment of this sad episode, which lasted from 29 September to 8 October 1864, see John L. Heatwole, *The Burning: Sheridan in the Shenandoah Valley* (Charlottesville, Va.: Rockbridge Publishing, 1998).

⊷ 10 ⊷

The Fall and Winter
of 1864-65

"This was the iciest time I ever saw."

NOVEMBER 8TH, 1864, WAS ELECTION DAY, AND WE WERE ALLOWED TO VOTE
in the field. There was a tent put up for the judges of election, and the regiment was in line with arms in hand, as we expected the rebs would interfere,
so as to get Little Mc. elected, McClellan[1] and Lincoln were the candidates.
As each man voted, he returned to his place in the ranks, and thus the election passed off without disturbance. We expected this to be a close campaign, and thought if Lincoln was elected the war would be soon pushed to a
close. But if McClellan was elected on the peace platform, there was no
telling how long it would last. I had written home to my friends to vote for
Lincoln if they wanted to see the war ended, for if he was defeated, we would
not give up with our work only half done. We proposed to fight for peace,
not to crawl and beg for it. Lincoln was elected, and the war ended in less
than a year.

It may now be of interest to follow my diary for a few days to see the ever-
changing course of a regiment of cavalry. November 9th, we saddled up and

---

[1] Maj. Gen. George B. McClellan, the former commander of the Army of the Potomac, was the
Democratic nominee for the presidency, running on a peace platform. He was decisively
defeated by Lincoln, largely because of the soldier vote, which was overwhelmingly in the
president's favor.

unsaddled several times, expecting to have General Merritt inspect our regiment. He finally arrived and made a company inspection. On the 10th, we moved to within five miles of Winchester and went into camp. The 11th, moved camp a short distance and had some sharp skirmishing at the front. The 12th, we moved out to Newtown where we met the rebs.

While engaged with a party in front, we saw a heavy body on our right moving toward those in front, and supposed from their dark looking columns, that it was a portion of Custer's division moving down on the rebs. As they neared them, they struck into a trot, and we looked for a charge, but when almost on the rebel lines, they made a wheel, and changing front, swept down on our right front with carbines and revolvers in full play. We saw our mistake, but as many of them were dressed in blue, the mistake was natural. We repulsed their charge and held them, but their numbers were so much greater than ours, we finally retired, leaving them in possession of the field. We returned to camp where we remained until near night, when we again advanced toward the front.[2]

As we moved along, Frank and I were together, we discovered a bag, or grain sack just over the fence and dismounted and secured the prize which proved to be a large ham, and a large round box with small spice boxes inside. Frank took charge of the box, and I took the ham, strapping it on my saddle and carrying it until we were back in camp.

We moved out south of Newtown, where we again found the rebs disputing our way. Our lines were formed each side of the pike and we advanced to meet them, but found them so strongly posted that we could not push them, and therefore kept up a skirmish until about ten o'clock at night, when we again returned to camp. In this encounter we had several men killed and wounded in the regiment. Sergeant James[3] of Company H, was wounded and left on the field, and when we returned in the morning, he was dead; the surgeon said to all appearance he had frozen to death, as the night was very cold. Geo. Hodgetts[4] of Company I, was struck in the leg near the knee with

---

[2] Bvt. Maj. Gen. Alfred T. A. Torbert, Sheridan's chief of cavalry, personally commanded this expedition, which involved the entire mounted force of the Army of the Shenandoah. Torbert noted that his force defeated the cavalry divisions of Maj. Gens. Thomas L. Rosser and Lunsford L. Lomax, capturing 180 prisoners. He noted that "A portion of the First Division, Brevet Major-General Merritt commanding, moved out on the Valley pike and engaged the enemy's infantry about dark and fought them until about 10 o'clock." *O.R.*, vol. 43, part 1, p. 437.

[3] Sgt. Aaron B. James of Detroit, age twenty-four.

[4] Pvt. George Hodgetts, age twenty-one. Hodgetts was wounded in action twice and served out his entire term of service.

a musket ball, and lay on the ground until we were ready to move off when the ambulance came up to take in the wounded. John Burdick[5] and myself lifted him in and he begged us to leave him, it hurt him so, but we put him in and he was taken off, and away we went back to camp. I had a letter from him after the war thanking me for helping him.

One day, Lieutenant Lonsbury ordered me to make a spread eagle of one of the men for taking more than his share of rations. This was a severe punishment. The man was taken to a tree, a string tied around each thumb, and his arms stretched above his head with the thumbs tied to a limb overhead. There were several modes of punishing to keep and enforce discipline. One was to buck and gag; the soldier who underwent this punishment had his hands tied behind him, a stick put through his arms and legs, doubling him up pretty short, and another stick put in his mouth and tied in by passing a string back of his head. Another way was to make the soldier carry rail and march up and down a certain beat. To be put on guard two hours extra was also a really hard task, especially if one was very tired from a long march.

During the night, after the last skirmish described, my horse got loose and strayed off, so that I could not go out with the company. Therefore, I put in my time fixing up a tent for winter quarters. The regiment went out as far as Strasburg, but found no rebs. We then went to work to build stockades, or log pens. On top of which four of us put our tents together for a roof. Then we built a fireplace of stone and topped out with a stick chimney, which made quite a comfortable abode for the winter. Four of us in one bed made it rather close, but we were well drilled in the motion of right and left spoon; that is, each one turned over at the same time.

We were busy fixing up our quarters until November 21st, when we saddled up early and marched out to near Front Royal, where we went into camp in a piece of woods. It snowed hard, and was three or four inches deep on the ground. We cut down large trees and piled them up, making a fire large enough for one company to warm by. One man was hurt by a falling tree.[6]

The entire woods were brilliant with the fires, and although stormy and cold, the boys were very cheerful, and soon had tents up under which they could sleep. In the morning we went on picket until the next day, when we

---

[5] Pvt. John Q. Burdick of Kalamazoo, age twenty-six, was a replacement who had enlisted only in February 1864.

[6] While the 1st Division did this, Torbert led the 2d and 3d Divisions on a reconnaissance mission up the Shenandoah Valley, finally encountering the body of Early's force near Rude's Hill, nearly forty miles distant. After a brief skirmish intended to ascertain Early's strength, Torbert broke off the engagement and withdrew. *O.R.,* vol. 43, part 1, p. 437.

returned to our quarters. Just before this last move, Mort Andrews found my horse in another regiment so that I was again mounted. This horse was a large, splendid fellow, but he would wheel around very quickly every time I fired my revolver, and I could not hold him straight to the front, but he could jump a ditch in fine style.

November 24th, Boots and Saddles sounded suddenly, and we threw on our saddles and mounted in short order. Colonel Hastings led us out at a trot, and as soon as we struck the road we put our horses to a run for several miles, but could find nothing of any rebs, although they were reported by some train boys as being near and charging on them. Shaffer [Shaver] had run his mules for miles into camp. He, with other drivers, were out with teams after lumber and brick from old buildings for the officers to fix up their quarters, when the Johnnies made a dash for them, scaring them terribly. Finding nothing, we returned to camp.

Next day, not feeling well, I reported to the surgeon and got excused from duty and was off duty several days, but still attended to company business. Lonsbury had again taken charge, but I made all reports, which he signed as commissioned officer. I put in good time washing up my clothing, and getting cleaned up after a hard campaign. This washing makes me think of one Beniville Miller,[7] a recruit, who had a tent by himself. He was so dirty, no one would tent with him, and he was always hanging around the surgeons tent to get excused, but would never report sick to the sergeant before sick call blew. One day the doctor asked him what he wanted, he replied that he was sick. He was examined and found so dirty that they sent an order for me to detail a corporal and two men to scrub him. Accordingly, water was procured and the corporal proceeded to strip him. Goncher had the honor of executing this order, and was not tender about it either. He had the two men take horse brushes and scrub him nicely with soap and hot water. Then told him if he ever was found around the surgeon's tent again without reporting sick, I would have him scrubbed with cold water.

The 28th, the regiment went up the valley on a scout, but I remained in camp, being excused from duty. I will here state that at this time I found that I could hardly ride at spells, owing to a disease brought on by the hard service I had done. But I had kept steadily on duty until about this time, with the company on foot. There was part of the time I could ride, but as long as there was no particular need of it, I preferred to try and doctor up a little.

---

[7] This soldier does not appear on the regimental roster rolls.

Furloughs were being granted to some of the soldiers to go home for the first time since we left Michigan. I had several to make out for the boys. I therefore put in an application for one for myself. It had been said that if a man asked for a furlough, he would not get it, but I was determined to try, and accordingly wrote to President Lincoln asking him, as I knew of his granting furloughs. In a few days my letter was returned, endorsed by the President and referred to my commissioned officer, with a statement to me that it should be accompanied by a recommendation from my officer. Thus, the matter stood for a time, and we were yet to make a long march across the mountains.

The first half of December was spent in drill inspections, and picket duty, besides our regular camp duty, which was taking care of our horses and camp guard. Each day brought its line of duty for me as acting first sergeant.

Looking at the morals of the army, one could see the true condition of affairs during a stay in winter quarters. As far as my observation extended, I found the officers in a worse condition then the men. It might be, however, on account of the easy access they had to the commissary stores, which the men did not have.

An officer could obtain whiskey when the men could not, unless an officer signed an application or requisition for it, and unless the soldier could occasionally get a jug of Apple Jack, you would hardly ever see a drunken one. On the other hand, it was not uncommon to see a drunken officer. Of course I don't say, nor will I admit, that they would all drink, for some would not touch a drop; one of whom, as I said before, was Colonel Alger. I will not name those whom I have seen drunk, for it would not be to my purpose, but I will say they were comparatively few.

Card playing and gambling was quite a pastime with some of the officers, as well as men, but I believe if as large a body of men were brought together today from the community at large, no better, if as good morals would be seen than there was among the soldiers. And I believe from my own observations, that the soldiers that today are left from the ranks of that mighty army are more united, and have a more friendly and better feeling for one another, than any other class of men. And it is easily seen that the G.A.R. [Grand Army of the Republic], as an organization, is more free from contention and trouble then any other society known.

On December 19th, 1864, we saddled up for a long march, and were prepared for cold nights and wet weather. The first night we camped just south of Front Royal, on the side of a mountain facing the northwest. It was a bitter cold night, with just enough snow on the ground to cover the frozen earth.

And the northwest wind beating against us, would penetrate any covering we might have. All the fires we could build did us no good, only when we were close to them. We used to have in the regiment, a Negro called Mose, who was orderly for one of the officers. One of those cold nights while Sergeant White was sleeping as near the fire as he could comfortably get with his back to it, Mose crawled in between him and the fire. After a little while the chill awoke White, who, finding some object at his back, suddenly drew up his heel, which was armed with a sharp Mexican spur, and struck the sharp points into it, with the ejaculation "Get out of there," "Ise jist gwine massa; Ise jist gwine" said Mose, as he lit out double quick. The boys would sometimes get Mose to bunt heads with another one for sport. Their heads would whack together like two stones. It was amusing to see them; they would draw back like sheep, lower their heads, then come together with a rush. Which would seem as though it must demolish one or both, but they would experience no inconvenience from the bump.

On the 20th it stormed, but we moved on the 21st. We passed Little House where we found the rebs. We charged and drove them through the town, and held them until after dark, when we went into camp. Some of the boys went foraging, while others made fires and fixed up tents. Frank and I, with one or two others, built a large fire of rails, and then drove stakes about four feet high to which we fastened our tents in the shape of a wall on the side next the wind. Taking some corn stalks, which we found in a field near by, we made a hut over which we spread our blankets, and were quite well fixed.

During the night we were disturbed by John Madigan,[8] an Irishman, who had got some Apple Jack, and was drunk. He was all for fight with everyone, and was very noisy. After a little, he got up and went to another company where he made good deal of noise until he was knocked down, after which he was very still for a long spell, until he came to when he began to groan and swear, so that he had to have another treatment, finely [finally] he went to sleep and all was quiet until morning.

When we moved out again and found the rebs, but they quickly retired. This was the iciest time I ever saw; the snow had been tramped by the rebs the day before, and melted in the road, and had then frozen into glare ice. The horses slipped and slid, and many fell down, in some cases severely injuring their riders. The next day Custer's men captured two pieces of artillery from a party of rebs, whom they found in a mountain pass. Some of the rebs said

---

[8] This soldier also does not appear on the regimental roster rolls.

the battery was sent from Early to Sheridan by General Custer. We nearly always captured their artillery and this caused the remark.

We next marched to Robinson River, where a little over a year before, some of our boys had been taken prisoner. We went into camp in a pine wood. Where the trees were so thick that we could hardly ride our horses in between them, but we went in and fixed up our camp for the night. Breaking off the dry pine boughs, we made fires, and soon had our coffee cooked and were ready to sleep as tired soldiers do, on the cold ground. But we had the sheltering pines for a cover to break the cold wind.

December 24th, we passed James City and continued our march to near Culpeper, where we stayed all night. It was there that I made a famous short cake, of which I will give a recipe for the benefit of our modern cooks, and for those who may some day be similarly situated. I melted my lard and then took my flour and stirred it into the lard until it was thick; then mixed all the flour in that would mix, adding a little salt; then rolled or flattened with my hand and baked in the half of a canteen. I guarantee that a small piece of this short cake will go farther than any I have seen since. Some may ask where I got my lard and flour? A soldier never asks "where did you get," but always asks "is there any more where that came from?" I think, however, Frank could answer that question, as there was some foraging done that night.

We crossed the Rapidan and went into camp near Warrenton. On the march we took all the horses and cattle we found. On the 26th we were near Upperville, and our regiment went on picket. A splendid horse was found in a stable there, and as some of our men were about to go in to take it, a woman presented herself in their path with a revolver and said if anyone touched the horse she would shoot them. If it had been a man, they would have got the horse in spite of him, but, a woman was different, and they left it. I suppose they admired her grit. Passing Upperville, we moved on through Ashby's Gap and across the Shenandoah at Millwood, where we again camped for the night. On the 28th, we reached our old camp near Winchester, and gladly took up our old quarters. There we found Sergeant Weeks, White and Hill with several others, all of whom had just returned from rebel prisons. We were right glad to welcome them back again.

On December 31st, 1864, we mustered for pay. I assisted Weeks in making out the rolls. Weeks was about to be promoted to lieutenant and asked me to take his place as first sergeant, but I respectfully declined, as I preferred to remain as commissary, liking that position best.

The year 1864 was one of almost continued campaigning. Thousands of lives had been lost, but victory was ours as far as possible. Grant was hammering away at Petersburg, where he had corralled the rebel army of Virginia. At that point, every day brought its battle all winter. The troops were exposed to rebel fire, even in their entrenchments. In the valley, Sheridan had vanquished Early in several battles. Sherman was victorious in Tennessee.[9]

January 1st, 1865 found all quiet in camp, and we were preparing a New Year's dinner, of a goose sent us by friends in the north. There was a little trouble about it in this way; A box of goods had been received for the company, but not half enough to go around, so each mess was required to draw cuts to see who should have the goose. I was the one to draw for my tent, which contained myself, Frank, Mort Andrews, George Shupart and George Kanouse.

It happened that I drew the goose, and we set to work to prepare it for dinner. Soon grumbling was heard, and on making inquires, some were found, who in spite of the agreement, were dissatisfied and wanted the goose, claiming unfairness. I said, as far as I was concerned, I drew the goose, but it was just as fair as anyone had drawn, never the less, I would give up rather than have any hard feelings about it. But Frank said he should not give up, he would fight first; as it was ours honestly. Here the matter dropped, for the time, but it afterward was not forgotten and was thrown up sometimes. We had our share of such grumbles, and they were not worth minding. So we did not care farther about it.

Camp remained quiet until January 5th, when I received a furlough for twenty days. This made me feel pretty good, as I could now visit my family and friends in Michigan. Early on the 5th, I had my horse ready, and in company with several others, set out for Winchester, taking men along to lead our horses back; for this duty, Frank went with me, and to see me off for home. He sent a haversack well filled with trinkets for his mother, and I also carried one for my family. It was a cold, raw day to ride, but we arrived in Winchester in due time, and taking leave of Frank, I boarded the train for Harpers Ferry. It was not like taking the nice coaches we have now; the train consisted of box and stock cars, without seats. We crowded in and on anywhere to secure sitting or standing room. I took my place on top of a boxcar, and soon we were jolting along over the rough road from Winchester to Harpers Ferry. This road had been torn up so often as to be in bad condition.

[9] Maj. Gen. George H. Thomas, with whom Avery is mistaking Maj. Gen. William T. Sherman, had destroyed Gen. John B. Hood's Army of Tennessee at the Battle of Nashville on November 16, 1864.

During the day, the wind blew so hard as to take off my hat, and I had to go the balance of the way without it. We arrived in Harpers Ferry about two o'clock, and reported to the quartermaster for transportation. We had to wait so long that the train we were to take went off without a part of us, and we had to wait twelve hours for the next train. This found to be best for us however, as the first train met with an accident which might have been serious for us. We passed the time as best we could at a hotel where we got supper.

At two o'clock we took the train going west and were soon rushing along over the road toward Wheeling. During the darkness we passed Martinsburg, Hancock, and Cumberland, places I was very well acquainted with in the summer before, as I have before stated. When morning dawned, we were well on our way. We were now traveling in fairly comfortable coaches, and could see the romantic country from the car windows.

Arriving at Pittsburgh, we had to wait four hours until the train came, when we were soon aboard again, and, for the first time in over two years, in a northern state. Away from all care, or danger from rebs, but, if the rebs could not hinder us, the snow could, and blockaded us in a cut in southern Ohio. After getting out of this we had no more delays, until we arrived in Cleveland. Here we had to wait, so I took the opportunity to look over the city. After a short time, we were again on board, and after a few hours run, we pulled into Detroit on Saturday night, too late for trains going west. This was another vexatious stop. We went to the Soldiers Home, and attended church three times. We were up early Monday ready to start, and at eight o'clock got on board the westbound train for Grand Rapids.

As the train passed by the telegraph poles I counted the miles to see how fast we were going. The distance grew less and less, and at about 4:30, we reached Grand Rapids, and I was at the end of my railroad route; four long days on the trip from Winchester, and I was at last in the city near my home. As I stepped off the train, I felt light as air; I was soon to be home. I had yet five miles to go before I reached my wife's father's house, so I looked for a team going my way, but finding none, set out on foot. It was getting dark, and the snow, which had been deep, was melting, making the road bad for walking. I had heavy baggage to carry and puffed and panted. But I pressed on as fast as I could. Soon I came in sight of the light among the trees, and then was at the door. Without knocking, I opened the door and stepped in. My wife and little girl, and my wife's father, mother, brother and sister were all there to greet and welcome me. The first happy greetings over, I cast off my burdens and was at rest.

It was a very pleasant visit among my old friends and neighbors, but the time allowed me soon expired, and I again took leave of them and started back to the front. Although I stayed the full extent of my furlough, and was two days over due in camp, it was all right. It was very cold in the valley at that time, even colder than Michigan. The day following my return there was a detail for scouting, but I declined to go, as I was tired and it was too cold for me to ride off twenty or thirty miles. I remained in camp and wrote letters and took care of my horse. When the detachment came back, some had frozen feet, and some frozen fingers.

On January 31st, we drilled most of the day. And the next day had a Grand Review, in which the whole Cavalry Corps were on the ground, making a grand sight. Early in the morning the horses were nicely groomed, the equipment's all brushed up in good shape, the clothing neatly cleaned, the arms all bright, and the blankets rolled and strapped to the saddles. The companies were first viewed by the captain and colonel, and when all was ready, we fell into line and moved out into the field, looking over which we could see the large columns from all directions, as though preparing for a battle. As each regiment came into line, its guidon bearers rode out to the front and aligned themselves, and the troops rode forward and aligned by them, thus forming a perfect general alignment. "Officers, and non commissioned officers, to the front of your companies" was the order. And then "Prepare for inspection." Every sabre leaped from its scabbard and was brought to a carry, as the inspecting officer accompanied by the generals and staff rode along the front slowly, and carefully examining each horse, man, and sabre; passing thus the whole length of the front; they returned along the rear of the lines, thus making a thorough inspection of the men and their equipment's. The generals with their staff, and on that occasion, the general's wives, then dashed along in front of the entire lines, making a pleasant scene as they gaily rode along. The officers, with their bright uniforms and red sashes, and the ladies with their jaunty caps and long flowing habits.

They then took their position on a commanding point, and the order was given, "pass in review, by brigades, right wheel." The brigade wheeled into columns of brigade, and moved in heavy columns past the grand stand. Then each regiment marched by itself, making a column from three to four times as long as before; then marched by the stand by companies, the column stretching out for miles in length. The last was by fours, after which the regiments were marched to their quarters and dismissed to their stables and tents. It was tiresome, but grand. The day was pleasant, and all went well. The Cavalry Corps made a grand appearance.

About that time a review of the infantry took place. The first I ever witnessed, it was very nice, but they marched in light order and left their knapsacks in camp, which made a difference in their looks on parade. Their movements were perfect. There was perhaps a half dozen ladies at our cavalry review, among them, Mrs. Custer. The review was on a plain over which, in the July previous, the rebs moved around the flank of Crook, beating him back, and where Custer had put in his brigade at the proper time in the battle of September 19, 1864. Where Gabe Cole[10] captured a rebel flag and was wounded.

For a few days following the review, the weather was cold and stormy. The snow fell one night, February 7th, twelve inches deep, and the cold was intense. About that time, I was feeling rather unwell, and being excused from duty, I spent most of my time in my tent sewing. Everyone ought to know that a soldier could sew with more or less success, but I went a little farther than to mend my clothing. One day I took two ponchos and cut out a coat, sewed it together and had a good rubber coat. It was a new idea for the boys, and my work was in good demand at five dollars for each coat, which took me from one and a half to two days. I also cut pants out of heavy blankets, making good ones for fatigue duty, but they would not pass our inspection, for they were generally gray. Our jackets had such wide, stiff collars, as to cut a man's throat, and I used to cut them down about one half. Putting in extra pockets was another job I did, as many wanted them, and I was the only one, except Casper Raab,[11] who was a regular tailor. In this way, the days passed off very quickly, and our three years, which seemed so long to look forward to, were passing away.

For many days we kept hearing of a peace commission and talk of peace, and we did really indulge hopes that the rebs wanted to give up. But no idea of peace, on any terms but surrender, ever entered our heads. Although we desired to see the war ended, we proposed to fight it out until they gave up.

We were not like some of the faint hearts at the north who had taken no part in the struggle, but stood back trembling in the knees for fear of draft, and saying peace, peace. The army said are you really for peace? Will you throw down your arms and surrender? If you will do this we will stop shooting at you, if not we will keep on. Therefore you want a truce all right, if not,

---

[10] Cpl. Gabriel Cole of Salem. Cole was awarded the Congressional Medal of Honor for capturing the enemy battle flag at Third Winchester.

[11] Forty-eight-year-old Pvt. Casper Raab of Salem, who served out his entire term of service and was honorably discharged in June 1865.

keep your gray coats out of sight or we will put in extra buttonholes. This we said to the rebs in arms at our front. To those in our rear we said, we scorn you vipers, come our way and we will crush your heads under our heels, and to the soft hearted peace on army terms ones, we said, hide, hide your tender bodies under your beds and tremble. But the peace bubble burst like its soap sister, when the terms were made known what the rebs wanted, and all remained as before, busy preparations for war all over the country.

Although I was excused from duty, I still did my camp duty as commissary. A change was made in officers, Safford resigning, Lonsbury was promoted to captain of Company M, Sergeant Berdan to first lieutenant of Company I, and Weeks to second lieutenant of Company I. An incident also occurred which was considered an insult. One day a stranger, a young man, came to the company and reported himself for duty as lieutenant. He had never seen service, but had come as a substitute for some coward, for a thousand dollars had bought a commission as lieutenant, and was assigned to Company I. There were plenty of sergeants and privates who were capable of commanding the company, and to have a unserviceable substitute put over them, after they had served over two years at the front in the smoke of battle, was as I said, a rank insult. But he got enough, the boys made it so hot for him that he could not stay, and never saw or heard of him again.

Rain and snow, snow and rain, my diary says of winter in Virginia. February 14th, the cannons roared and boomed until we thought a fight was on, but it was only a salute fired on account of the fall of Wilmington.[12]

---

[12] Wilmington, North Carolina, the last remaining major Atlantic Ocean port available to the Confederates, finally fell in February 1865, after repeated Union efforts to capture it.

— 11 —

Illness Forces Avery to Miss
the End of the Civil War

"Finally there came a day of rejoicing and great joy. On Thursday, April 13, 1865, news was received that Lee had surrendered to Grant."

ON FEBRUARY 16TH, I WAS ORDERED TO THE HOSPITAL, AND AGAIN HAD TO leave the old company. I could not ride my horse or go on foot, and the surgeon's order was imperative, so packing up my personal effects, I turned in my sabre, revolver and horse, and getting into an ambulance was off, never to return to camp in the valley near Winchester.

Stopping at brigade hospital to report, I was sent on by Dr. Upjohn, the brigade surgeon, to Winchester, where I was taken to an old hotel called the Taylor, used as a hospital, and assigned to a large room by myself, in which there was a fireplace and one bed. This was uncommon, all the room to myself, and soon another patient was put in with me. My meals were brought to my room, and I settled down to take all the comfort I could, spending my time in reading and writing. Austin Andrews,[1] a member of my company, was also sick in the same hospital. Everything passed along quietly until February

---

[1] Thirty-five-year-old Pvt. Austin Andrews of Cheshire. Andrews recovered from his illness to complete his term of service. He was honorably discharged with the rest of the regiment on June 23, 1865.

24th, when the hospital assistants began packing up the stores and goods. And on the 25th, boarded the cars and left Winchester for Harpers Ferry. This was the fourth time that I had left Winchester. First on the skedaddle when Crook was defeated; second, when our cavalry moved out once to the north toward Charleston; third, when I was going home on furlough; and this time for the last. Winchester and the surrounding country has a great deal of interest for me to think and look back to. The memories of the Valley Campaign will always remain fresh with me.

When we arrived at Harpers Ferry, we found it impossible to cross the river on account of the high water. A heavy coal train had been run on the bridge to keep it from going down stream, and we were sent into a hospital to wait for the flood to subside.

On the following morning the bridge was found to be passable, and we were again ordered to take the train in the afternoon. Harpers Ferry is all on the west, or Virginia side of the river, and is situated along the low ground close to the water, except such as is built on the foot of the high hills, as they gradually rise for a short distance then break into steep bluffs in the rear of the burg. It is a small town, but is noted for being the point at which John Brown made his attempt to free the slaves. In the U.S. Arsenal, there his men procured arms for their work.[2]

During the war, the place was the objective point of crossing when the rebs made their raids into Maryland.[3] They could more easily cross here and have their flanks protected. As the mountain ranges covered their right and also their left.

The several gaps were easily held by a small force, and they could there-fore cross unmolested, except in front. And unless we had a pretty heavy force on the Maryland side, all they had to do was to slip past the foot of Bolivar Heights,[4] and cross at Berlin and swing around the works on Mary-land Heights.

---

[2] Avery is correct. In 1859 radical abolitionist John Brown led a small group of his followers in a raid on Harpers Ferry that he believed would cause the slaves to rise in rebellion. A force of U.S. Marines commanded by Col. Robert E. Lee captured Brown, and he was hanged after a treason trial.

[3] On each of the three major Confederate invasions of the North, Harpers Ferry, with its large arsenal, was a significant target of the invasion. During the 1862 Maryland Campaign, Lt. Gen. Thomas J. "Stonewall" Jackson captured the place, along with approximately ten thousand prisoners and the entire contents of the arsenal. It was quite an embarrassment for the Federal government.

[4] Bolivar Heights, to the west of the town, was a major Federal supply depot during Sheridan's 1864 Valley Campaign. As a result, it was strongly defended by an ample garrison.

The B&O Railroad crossed at the [Harpers] Ferry going from the west toward Baltimore and Washington, and also the road from Winchester and Staunton. At that time the town was in a fearful state of decay, and many buildings had been burned by shells and torch. The chimneys to the buildings were in southern style, one at each end and outside the building, from the ground up and at the base there was a large fireplace with an old crane on which to hang the kettles. Such cranes and hooks were in nearly every southern house, as stoves were then very rare in the south, as was everything modern.

The wagon road out of the town up the valley, ascends slowly for a long distance between the bluffs until many feet above the Ferry, and the railroad runs along the same slopes until it reaches the same elevated plain, where, after winding itself almost dizzy with the crooks and turns, it takes a fairly straight course for Winchester. As we left the old town, we crossed on the iron bridge that spans the Potomac, which river I had so often crossed on horseback, over bridges, through the water, on pontoons, or waded on foot, or crossed on railroads and steam boats. We crawled along the track, over the iron bridge, and under the bluffs which overhang the road on the Maryland side. Winding our way along like a huge serpent which throws fire and smoke from his nostrils. A few miles down the river we came to Point of Rocks, where, in the summer of '64, an old man sat in the shade of his house, peacefully smoking his pipe, when some rebs from the opposite shore wantonly fired upon him, riddling him with their murderous bullets.

Next we passed Berlin where we crossed on pontoons, when following up Lee's army in 1863 after the Gettysburg Campaign. Then we came to Sandy Hook, at the opening of Pleasant Valley, where I had spent many weary days in the hot July sun drilling with the musket. Leaving the river, our course was almost due east to the Monocacy River, where we took a branch from the main line and crossed the Monocacy at the point where General Lew Wallace was defeated in 1864 by a heavy body of rebs.[5] Moving on north a few miles, we reached Frederick City, a town well known to the Fifth Cavalry as well as to the whole brigade. For we were there fed by the citizens in June 1863, while we halted a few minutes in their streets.

Arriving there in the evening, we were taken to our destination in ambulances, and on our arrival were taken in charge by assistants and assigned good comfortable single beds. In the morning those of us who were able, went to the bath rooms and took a good wash. After which our breakfast was brought

---

[5] On July 6, 1864, Early's army defeated Maj. Gen. Lew Wallace at the Battle of Monocacy.

in by two attendants, who carried it in a large tin box, resembling an old fashioned tin oven. After breakfast we were required to take our beds again until the doctor examined us. Soon after a clerk came and took each man's name, together with his regiment and company. This he wrote on a card which he placed at the head of each bed. These cards were numbered, and duplicates entered in a book kept for the purpose. When the doctor came he examined each man, and his disease or wound was also put on the card and entered in the book. In this way, a perfect record was kept, and if properly attended to, a patient afterwards had no trouble in finding his record.

Now let us make the round of the ward with the doctor, and take a look at the patients and see in what condition they are. First, upon entering the ward, we commence at the right hand side and take that row of beds in regular order. The first two or three beds are occupied by convalescents who are now doing hospital duty, then comes a soldier who [is] about twenty two years of age, and by his bed is an elderly gray-haired gentleman who is his father, who has come from New York to assist in caring for his son, who has been dangerously sick with typhoid fever, and is still very low. Just look at his arm, take hold of it, you find the skin covers nothing but bone. I think this is the most annihilated person I ever saw, and as I afterward helped to take care of him, I found large bedsores, which were enough to kill a man of less stubborn will. But with good care and tender nursing, he pulled through, and was taken to his home in Tarry Town, New York, from which place he sent me a letter after the war.

Next we find a still younger boy with a gun shot wound in the arm, which was doing well and finely [finally] became sound, although a bad wound. Passing on we stand beside the bed of another young boy, and the doctor takes more than ordinary care to examine his wound, which is above the knee. Here we find the bone had been removed to the extent of three inches entirely cut away. Imagine a long gash cut in a leg, and the bone sawed off twice to remove a portion of shattered bone. Would you have the grit to do it, do you think you could even walk again?, you may think no, but this boy did. Although a very painful wound, he was cheerful and happy as anyone could be. I dressed his wound many times, and after the war he wrote me he could walk quite well with a cane.

Now reader, when you see a poor lame soldier, think of the poor boy with the bone cut out of his leg, and have a little pity for him. He exposed himself for you, and was crippled for life.

Here are one or two empty beds, the men have either been sent to the front, or are in the Veteran Reserve Corps, where many convalescents are detailed who cannot do duty at the front. Here is a bed with the card still in its place, but the man is absent. Where is he, the ward master says he is out on a pass. Now I must tell you of this man. He is an Irishman who goes out on pass, gets drunk and sometimes gets locked up. Probably this is where he is on this early morning, in the lockup. But we will pass over a few days, and while this man is under notice, speak of his manner while drunk. One night while I was on duty, he had been on pass in town and pretty drunk. Come to the ward, just at night, in real fighting, noisy condition. When it came time to go to bed, he did not propose to go. And the ward master had been having some trouble with him to keep him still.

But now as the ward master had retired to his home near town, and I was left in sole charge for the night, I did not propose to be troubled with him, and told him to get to bed and be still. He lay down a short time, then up he sprang and began to yell and holler. Now I have the least patience with a man who is drunk, of anything possible. Going to him as he sat on his bed, I took him by the collar and seat of the pants, lifting him like I would a small boy, I threw him on the bed, and with such force as to bump his head severely on the iron head piece. This was enough, Mr. Drunk never opened his mouth until morning. I think I knocked the whiskey out of his thick head. And he never made any more trouble in the ward.

At this late day, it will be impossible to remember all the cases of sick and wounded, as there were thirty-two beds in this ward. But a few I shall never forget. I see them as plain in my mind today, as I saw them in my eye at that time.

Therefore, we will pass on around to the opposite side and up near the middle of the row, when we find a young boy whose name is Clute. I think he was from Indiana. A rather stout build, but rather short. He was a very pale, almost white looking fellow. The doctors pronounced his trouble heart disease. He was soon discharged and went home.

The last one in the row, was a tall, well built man with heavy black whiskers, his name was Marston. He was an inveterate smoker, always with a pipe in his mouth, as he lay bolstered up in his bed. His was a terrible wound in the arm, just below the shoulder. It seemed enough to nearly take his arm off. The surgeons had cut and slashed in their experiments until one would think his arm was worthless, even if he should live. And still the ignorant rascals wanted to keep on cutting. One morning two of them came in to commence their torture on him again. He lay quietly smoking, and when he found out their business, he drew back his well arm and, "damn you if you touch me to cut my arm more, I shall strike you, you have tortured me enough." So they left him. He was removed to another ward soon, and when last I saw him, he said he could begin to use his hand a little.

Now in this case as in Woolsey's, the bone had been taken out for about two inches, still the prospect was he was going to be able to use it. If he had not bluffed the doctors off, they would have taken it off. So much for grit. Now in my experience in the hospital, I found that then, as now, the doctors' practice was in a great measure experimental, more than genuine knowledge of cases. The doctor of today, in many cases, looks you over, gives you medicine, and goes away. Calls again if the first don't do, give you another kind, until he happens to get the right one. It was the same then, many times a hospital steward would give medicine, and often they had no more knowledge of disease than the men they pretended to treat.

Now we will look at the make up of the ward, or barrack in which I found myself in the morning of March 7th, 1865. The interior of the building was long and narrow like a hall, with a row of beds on each side. And an alley between in which was placed two small coal stoves to warm the room. At the front end on the right hand was a bathroom, in which was a long iron vat over which were two gas pipes, one supplying hot, and the other cold water. The patient tempers the water to suit himself, then gets in the vat and takes a splendid bath, from which he comes out very much refreshed.

On the left of the door was the dish room, in which all the dishes used in the ward were washed. In the rear was a cloak, or clothes room, in which the soldiers stored their surplus clothing. Opposite was a room devoted entirely to the use of the female nurses, of which there was one in each barrack. The outside of the building was made of a wooded frame, sided with boards and battened. About four windows on each side gave light for the ward, and it was ventilated at the top of the roof in a similar manner to the ventilators in railroad coaches.

The hospital at Frederick, called the M. S. Hospital, was situated near the southern extremity of the city, and on the east side of the main street or Pike. The buildings were all built of board as described, and known as barrack A., B., etc. Situated nearly in a circle, there was quite a space in the center with a Liberty Pole, from which floated the Star Spangled Banner. Near the pole was a platform with seats, on which the band played every pleasant evening. The grounds were surrounded by a high board fence, at the entrance of which, and a little to the left, was a large stone building used as the surgeons headquarters. In this building, the female nurses also had their rooms. This stone house was built in Queen Anne's time as a protection against Indians, and other foes. It was quite long with a sort of wing projecting at each end, thus forming a complete work for cross fire at the only entrance. The windows were very high in the rear of the building so that they could not be easily reached. A balcony ran the entire length of the main building in the hollow square, with stairs to approach the upper stories. In the rear of this were the kitchens for the hospital.

In the lower story of this building was the dining room, in which all the convalescents went to get their meals, three times a day. The fare was rather slim, consisting of coffee, bread and meal, with soup once a week. Each man had a slice of bread, a cup of coffee, and a small piece of beef or other meat put at his place. I have after [often] seen men that were getting a good appetite after a long spell of sickness, go in to dinner, eat all their allowance, and when passing out, if they chanced to see a crust that some less hungry one had left, they would rush for it like a ravenous beast. Sometimes two or three would go for the same crust and the quickest was the best. Those who went there for their meals did not fare as well as those who could not go, and it often happened that some good friend in the ward would save what he could not eat for a hungry comrade when he returned from his meal, and it was eaten with a relish, and the kindness returned by giving him extra care. I have been given a good many extra meals in this way.

The rations were carried to the wards in a large tin oven, divided into compartments for each variety of food. This oven or box was carried by two assistants, and the rations dealt out for each patient according to orders given by the surgeon.

This carrying the trunk makes me remember one tall, slim man who was subject to fits, and I have seen him fall flat in a fit without a moment warning. This man's case shows what some recruiting officers would do for the sake of getting their compliment of men. He told me that he was subject to fits, but was accepted as a substitute, as was also the dirty fellow alluded to who was taken in the place of some coward. Many a man was accepted as a substitute, who would not have been taken as the original, and this laxness in accepting poor men filled our hospitals during the last few months to overflowing with poor, sick men, and homesick boys, who never saw the front, but got their big money as substitutes.[6]

The government should not have allowed any man to send another to take his bullets. Nor allow anyone to make money by excusing able men. I say this not because of my own knowledge, but from what can be often heard in con-

---

[6] When the Federal government implemented the draft in the fall of 1863, it allowed men to pay substitutes to go in their place. It became commonplace for men to accept payment for enlisting as a substitute, report, desert, and then join another regiment, accepting multiple payments. These scalawags made a cottage industry of cheating their fellow citizens.

versations among soldiers who claim to know of certain parties who got off by paying something.

There is one more explanation to make on this subject, which I know, and which was a shame because of its treatment of the soldier, who done his duty at the front. When the draft was put in force, the towns were allowed to raise, or contribute a certain amount to clear them from draft, by buying subs. Now each man who paid in a sum to clear himself, had his name on a list, and after the war, a tax was levied to pay back this amount, and the soldier was also taxed to pay his share. Mind you, the soldier went and fought three and four years at the front, and those subject to draft paid their money to stay at home, that is good so far as them, they had helped to put down the rebellion, and was at home in comfortable quarters. Then they tax the soldier to get their money back. This was wrong, for now they did not help to put down the rebellion, for the soldier had done all the work and paid them back their money. For where is the loyalty of such men, it all went out in that little sum.

Soon after reaching the hospital, I began to receive letters from home, at least twice each week, and I think I sent one as often as every second day. Even when on an active campaign I used to carry my portfolio and write every time I stopped, or that when a chance occurred. I had my mail ready to send, averaging not less than three each week. I had lots of time to write and read while in hospitals. The Christian Commission furnished plenty of literature, and besides, there was a reading room attached to the hospital, where one could get a variety of matter. The commission also furnished means of amusement, such as dominos, checkers, etc.

We were allowed a pass every day, and myself and Wm. Pailthorpe,[7] of Company K of my regiment, used to go out and roam over the fields and country feeling like free men. There was a large cherry tree we used to visit, where we would climb into the top and stay for hours eating cherries.

Another favorite resort was the reservoir, which furnished the town with water, brought under ground from a cold spring on the mountains, miles away across the beautiful Frederick Valley. There we would spend hour after hour, laying in the shade of the trees, reading and writing. Another jolly good fellow sometimes used to accompany us, whose name was F. H. Dinn, but as he had been shot in the foot, he could not walk as far as we could, and therefore, did not go on our long rambles. He had been wounded in a peculiar manner. One night while he was sitting in his tent warming his feet by the fire, and without boots on, some miscreant threw some cartridges down the chim-

---

[7] Pvt. William S. Pailthorpe of Vienna, age twenty-four. Pailthorpe was discharged from service on June 24, 1865, while still a patient at the hospital at Frederick.

ney, exploding them, and one struck his foot at the bottom, passing clean through, making a bad wound.

One day while I was at the reservoir alone, a party of young children from the school came and grouped under the shade of the trees. Opening their baskets, they proceeded to empty them of their contents, which proved to be a picnic dinner. Being rather hungry from small rations, I could not help wishing for some, as I saw them devour the dainty cakes and pie. As I was some little distance off, I could observe their movements without seeming rude.

Soon I saw that the little folks were taking some interest in me as I lay, apparently unconcerned. I saw their teacher speak to the group near her, and a little commotion with a plate, on which was an assortment of cake and pie, asking me pleasantly if I would not take it. I thanked the little one, and told her to thank the others for me, and proceeded to eat the nice offering. On one of our excursions into the country, we made a visit to the field in which we had camped during the first raid, or march through Frederick in 1863. Then we went out along the railroad to Monocacy River, where Wallace had his battle in 1864.

We visited the cemeteries and saw the graves of some noted men of olden times. Then we visited the cemetery where the dead soldiers were buried. A long trench holds them all. They are laid in a long tier beside each other, as fast as one died, he was placed in the row beside his comrade gone before. A board at the head gave his name, company and regiment. For rods the boards stood thickly in a row. We also went down town and bought little saws and files, with which to make rings and badges to designate our branch of the service. They were made of beef bones, which we picked up from the kitchen. We made them very nicely, and lettered them with colored sealing wax, making quite a beautiful piece of work.

I saw a most splendid ladies work box, made by one of the soldiers. It was composed of three hundred small bits of wood, walnut and maple, and cut in diamond shape. The workmanship was very fine, and the box was the finest I ever saw.

In these ways, the convalescents spent their time when off duty. Each had to take his turn at the work of caring for the sick, and thus, had to remain in a while each day, but at liberty most the time.

Finally there came a day of rejoicing and great joy. On Thursday, April 13, 1865, news was received that Lee had surrendered to Grant.[8] Cannons

---

[8] Lee surrendered the Army of Northern Virginia to Grant at Appomattox Court House on April 9, 1865. For a detailed study of the final campaign of the Civil War, see Christopher M. Calkins, *The Appomattox Campaign* (Conshohocken, Pa.: Combined Publishing, 1999).

boomed, flags were displayed, the streets were decorated, and the soldiers who were able to walk, marched in procession, those not able to walk, but who could ride, were carried in vehicles of some kind. In this way, the column moved until late at night, through brilliantly lighted streets, where all kinds of mottoes were displayed. Then we moved through dark streets where we could occasionally see a scowling face, as dark as the street. Those were the copperheaded sneaks hiding themselves in darkness.

In the main street we passed the house where the famous Barbara Fritchie displayed the Star Spangled Banner, as the rebel works passed by her window.[9] About ten o'clock at night, we marched into the hospital where we were served with an extra supper of cheese, crackers and tea, after which we retired to our wards and to bed, while the band still played patriotic tunes. We got to sleep and forgot, except in dreams, the splendor of our triumphal march, and the music of the band which in a very few hours was to be turned to a solemn dirge and funeral note, and our gay parade to marks of grief. The night passed on and the soldiers dreamed of peace and home. The war was nearly over and every one was glad, and the future looked bright and peaceful.

On Friday evening, April 14, 1865, President Lincoln was assassinated, and we received the news early the next morning, creating great excitement throughout the hospital and city. Flags were lowered to half mast; windows draped in mourning; anxious faces seen on all sides. Here and there you could see signs of exultation on the face of some sympathizer with rebellion. Some of the soldiers in town were met by things, calling themselves women, who spit in their faces. This was too much for soldiers to stand, and they came directly to the wards and told of it. There was great indignation expressed, and threats were made of burning the town.

Happily, the officers heard the complaints and placed heavy guards at the barrack doors and the gates, with loaded guns and bayonets. This was right, for otherwise, many a good loyal citizen would have suffered at the hands of an infuriated mob. Our female nurse in barrack E, whom the boys had always respected because she had cared for them kindly, was a Lincoln hater, and spoke carelessly of his death. She had to be removed and placed under guard, to save her from being mobbed. After this, she never returned to duty

---

[9] During the Confederate invasion of Maryland in September 1862, elderly Barbara Frietchie, a staunch Union woman, defied Stonewall Jackson's legions by proudly flying an American flag in front of her home, even though the Confederates occupied Frederick. Her bravery was documented by an epic poem.

at the hospital. Everyone was anxious to learn the particulars, and we soon heard that Lincoln was shot by an actor named Booth, who had escaped and was being hunted for in all directions.[10] The telegraph was watched close. Have they got him? Have they got him? was the question heard on every hand.

Our indignation was intensified by the news of the attempted assassination of Seward and others,[11] and we felt that the rebs were trying to gain by murder what they had lost on the battle field, or at least be revenged for their loss by taking the life of the President. When who would try to break up the Union and cause the death of thousands of soldiers, would not hesitate at the murdering of a hundred Presidents.

This was the nature of the southrans; murder was nothing to them. They had been brought up from childhood to be familiar with such acts. Slaves were killed without compunction, and they had become used to seeing them torn to pieces by dogs, whipped to death, or otherwise tortured.

At last the soldiers are ordered to be discharged as fast as possible. Booth has been captured, his accomplices are secured. He is taken nearly dead from a shot by a soldier, he dies and is buried, but few know where.[12] Johnston surrenders to Sherman, and the war is nearly over. Enlistments are stopped, and men are being discharged.

I write to my company for a descriptive list,[13] I got no answer. Days pass and still no reply. Now I learn the brigade has been ordered west.[14] Now while I am waiting for a description list, let us follow along with the company and see what they have been doing since I left them in February.

---

[10] John Wilkes Booth assassinated Lincoln at Ford's Theater in Washington, D.C., on April 13, 1865. Booth broke his leg while escaping and, after having his leg set by a local doctor, fled. An intensive manhunt eventually brought him to bay in a barn in rural Virginia, where he met his fate a few days later.

[11] Booth's plot included attempts on the lives of Grant, Secretary of State William Seward (who was knifed but survived), and Secretary of War Edwin M. Stanton.

[12] A Union cavalryman named Boston Corbett is credited with killing Booth. When Booth was finally brought to bay, he was trapped in a barn, which was set on fire. When Booth refused to surrender, Sgt. Corbett supposedly fired the fatal shot that killed the assassin. Corbett's is an interesting story. Unable to handle the pressure of his fame, he died a lonely alcoholic's death.

[13] A descriptive list was the record in the company's rolls describing the soldier's physical appearance. It was the means by which the authorities made sure that the proper soldier was being discharged.

[14] The Michigan Brigade, instead of being sent home, was sent west to fight Indians. Doing so caused a great hue and cry among the citizens of Michigan and wrecked the morale of the men, many of whom deserted rather than fight Indians in the desolate wastelands of the Northwest. While most were discharged in the fall of 1865, some did not get home until February 1866. See Longacre, *Custer's Wolverines,* pp. 279–94.

The 27th of February, 1865, the whole Cavalry Corps, with their long trains of wagons and artillery, took up the line of march up the Valley. All day the rattle of wheels, the rumble of artillery, and the clatter of horseshoes on the stoney pike to Woodstock could be heard without ceasing. The day was fine, the men in good spirits, the horses were in splendid trim, and all went merry as a marriage bell.

No rebs except a few guerillas were seen during the day. They went into camp near Woodstock the first night. Next day the column moved on to within a few miles of Harrisonburg, again going into camp. Now the red clay of Virginia was encountered, instead of a pike, which made traveling very heavy.

The third day the column passed Harrisonburg and on to Klines Mills beyond Mt. Crawford. During the next day march, Rosser's cavalry were found on one of the forks of the Shenandoah, where they endeavored to burn the bridge to prevent our men from crossing. A detachment of Custer's division came up, swam the river above and charged the rebs, driving them away and saving the bridge.

The column next moved on to Staunton, where they found Early's army prepared to fight. Custer again formed his men and charged the rebs, defeating them and capturing many prisoners. Early was driven through rain and mud to Waynesboro, and his army utterly broken up and rendered useless for further work in the [Shenandoah] Valley.[15] The prisoners and captured trains were all sent back to Winchester. The Cavalry Corps moved on, and were attacked by a small body of Rosser's cavalry, but the rebs were easily defeated, and almost all of them taken prisoners. Early was with this party, but escaped by swimming the South Anna River.

The canal and all the railroads north of the James River were now destroyed, and our army held, for the first time since the war began, all the country north of Richmond. The column moved on toward White House,[16] destroying on their way, all the rebel property to be found. Reaching White House, they found supplies waiting them, and soon apportioned them. They then moved on to the James River.

[15] The remnant of Early's army had spent the winter encamped near Waynesboro. Sheridan's cavalry, with Custer's division leading the charge, fell upon the bedraggled gray-clad veterans on March 1, 1865, routing them and driving them off in wild panic. Thus ended the Civil War in the Shenandoah Valley. For a detailed description of Sheridan's campaign, see Frederick C. Newhall, *With General Sheridan in Lee's Last Campaign* (Philadelphia: J. B. Lippincott, 1866) and Henry Edwin Tremain, *The Last Hours of Sheridan's Cavalry* (New York: Bonnell, Silver & Barrows, 1904).

[16] White House Landing on the Pamunkey River, a major Federal supply depot.

On this grand move, the work of the Michigan Brigade was along the James River Canal to Columbia, where it did splendid execution, destroying canal locks and railroads. My description of the moves of the brigade must be of a general character, as I have no data of any personal or special company adventure. But I will venture to assert from my knowledge of the company, that they did their duty, as only Michigan men knew how to do, and that their work was well done.

On March 27th, just one month after breaking camp in the [Shenandoah] Valley, they had accomplished all this labor, and went into camp in the rear of Grant's Army at Hancock Station, on Grant's left. On March 30th and 31st, the brigade took an active part in the battle of Five Forks, South Side Railroad April 2nd, Duck Pond Mill April 4th, Sailors Creek April 6th, and at Appomattox April 9th. At Appomattox, the brigade, after a severe fight, was in line of battle for a charge on the enemy, when a flag of truce appeared. The brigade was held still in line, ready to swoop down on the rebs, but it proved to be the last line formed for a charge by them in the war, for it was where Lee surrendered.[17]

During this campaign, Lieutenant Weeks,[18] while bravely leading on the company in battle, was struck by a ball, which caused the loss of part of his foot; Sergeant White won laurels for bravery; Bugler Gardner[19] won a brevet; Sergeant Batchelor did nobley, as also did Sergeants Smith,[20] Baldwin,[21] and all the corporals of whom I will especially mention, from information from my comrades, F. Miller, Goncher, Atkins,[22] Hawks,[23] and Cole.[24] Almost every man in our company proved himself a hero.

The brigade had made a splendid record. It had first met, and defeated the rebel cavalry at Littletown, Maryland;[25] next at Gettysburg, in that terrible three days fight, it had beaten back the heavy bodies of rebels on the right of

---

[17] In one paragraph, Avery has described the engagements of the final campaign of the war. See Calkins, *The Appomattox Campaign,* for a detailed narrative of these engagements.

[18] William C. Weeks of Allegan, one of the original sergeants of Company I, had been commissioned a lieutenant on February 1, 1865. He was wounded at Five Forks on 1 April and was honorably discharged because of this wound in July.

[19] Sgt. George N. Gardner of Ganges, bugler of Company I, was commissioned a lieutenant on April 14, 1865. Presumably this promotion is the brevet referred to by Avery. However, it was a full commission and not a brevet.

[20] Sgt. George H. Smith of Trowbridge.

[21] Sgt. Martin Baldwin of Allegan.

[22] Cpl. Samuel W. Atkins of Watson, age twenty-two.

[23] Cpl. Morgan B. Hawks of Allegan, age twenty-two.

[24] Cpl. Gabriel Cole of Salem, age thirty-four. Cole was wounded in action on April 6, 1865, three days before the surrender at Appomattox.

[25] This must refer to the fight at Hanover, Pennsylvania, on June 30, 1863.

our lines, thus saving our army, and insuring the defeat of Lee. It had come off victorious at Monterey Gap; Williamsport; Falling Waters; Boonsboro and Hagerstown. It had beaten back the right flank of Lee's army in the Wilderness; and still earlier, it had covered Meade's rear, with success against the heavy columns of Lee. It had given the rebs a terrible whipping at Brandy Station; it had fought at Cold Harbor with success in two heavy battles; it had beaten the rebs at Todds Tavern; burned nine days rations in the rear of Lee's army. It had fought and defeated the rebel cavalry at Yellow Tavern; Bottom's Bridge; and the White House; it had met and captured heavy bodies of rebs and horses at Trevilian Station. In the Valley it met the enemy often, and was always victorious; it was at the Battle of Winchester where Custer launched it against the rebel lines, just at the moment to insure success, sweeping the enemy from before it like chase before the wind; it charged at Cedar Creek, chasing the rebs for miles and miles; again at Woodstock; the James River Canal; Columbia; and all the way to Petersburg, and was in at the death struggle when Lee gave up the contest.

The world never saw a brighter record than this brigade had made during its three years of service. After the surrender of Lee, it went into camp a few days, and then moved into North Carolina,[26] from whence it marched to Washington, passing over the fields of its old conquests on its route, and arrived in Washington in time to take part in the grand review.[27]

In return for its noble work, it was sent to the far west to fight the Indians on the border. Instead of this, it should have been disbanded and sent home with honors. The Fifth was finally mustered out at Fort Leavenworth and sent home, arriving in Michigan on the first day of July, 1865. The men of the Sixth and Seventh Cavalry were treated still worse, being sent into Utah, where they were kept until March, 1866. When they were disbanded and left to pay their own way back to the States.[28]

---

[26] The Cavalry Corps was sent on an expedition toward Danville, Virginia, intended to cut off the remaining major Confederate army in the East, commanded by Gen. Joseph E. Johnston and located in North Carolina. However, Johnston surrendered before they could arrive, and the horse soldiers had a leisurely march back to camp. See Christopher M. Calkins, *The Danville Expedition of May and June 1865* (Danville, Va.: Blue & Gray Education Society, 1998).

[27] On May 23, 1865, the Army of the Potomac paraded through Washington, D.C., before President Andrew Johnson, Grant, Meade, Sherman, and a grateful American public. For the best description of the Grand Review, see Tremain, *The Last Hours of Sheridan's Cavalry,* pp. 495–551.

[28] The Michigan General Assembly had to enact special legislation to provide funds for these unfortunates to return home. It was a disgrace.

This was a great wrong, and if it was Pope[29] who caused it to be done, he should have been cashiered. If the government originated the order, it was very ungrateful for the noble work the brigade had done. As with the brigade, so it was with its noble commander in later years. The Administration was led, through a pack of worthless, jealous officers, to heap insult after insult upon the brave Custer, and I now say, his blood be upon their heads. They murdered him, with Indian bullets.[30] The brigade's work is done; Custer's work is done. The men of the brigade worshipped him; they worship him still. I have thus hastily followed the path of the brigade, all bright with valor to its end, and will return to my personal experience at the hospital.

As I said, I sent to the company for a descriptive list so that I might be discharged and sent home. There was no more work to do in the field, and each day we stayed in the hospital was so much more expense to the government. Besides this, inaction was not in keeping with members of the Michigan Brigade; we chafed under it; we asked to be allowed to walk to Washington to rejoin our companions, but we could not be allowed that boon; we must stay at Frederick until discharged. We finally discovered that the reason of our detention was that the surgeon in charge had the contract to furnish supplies for the hospital, and was making a good thing out of it; therefore, lots of time meant lots of money to him, and consequently, it was to his interest to keep us. We were allowed to go out however, and passed many long, hot days in the shade of the trees in the country.

I picked up a couple of fifty cent notes, on the bridge across the stream, which I had to cross. This was good, for I had drawn no pay for a long time and I could now buy some stamps. After this I was very careful to inspect the ground.

Making autograph albums in which the names of comrades were written, became a rage with us, and almost everyone had his album.

One night, hearing pounding in the rear of barrack E, we looked out and saw a light just behind the fence where workmen were busy at some kind of

---

[29] Maj. Gen. John Pope, commander of the Department of the West. Actually, the order originated with Pope's subordinate, Maj. Gen. Grenville E. Dodge, who saw an opportunity to use the veteran horse soldiers to put down an Indian uprising. For a detailed study of the plight of the 6th Michigan during this time, see Eric J. Wittenberg, ed., *One of Custer's Wolverines: The Civil War Letters of Bvt. Brig. Gen. James H. Kidd, Sixth Michigan Cavalry* (Kent, Ohio: Kent State University Press, 2000).

[30] Custer, of course, was killed in action while fighting Sioux and Comanche Indians at the Battle of Little Big Horn on June 25, 1876. There have been literally hundreds of books written on the unfortunate end met by Custer and nearly three hundred men of the 7th Cavalry.

work. As soon as daylight came, we found a tent had been put up, and a case of small pox was being treated there close to our ward. This was the third time I had been exposed to this disease and escaped. After a few days, a mustering officer was sent to muster out the men as fast as he could. He had to have several clerks, and I was detailed to help in his office. While there, I wrote out many descriptive lists for men to be discharged.

This was a good place, for all who worked in the office were allowed a side room for meals, and a bounteous supply of food of a good variety. The mustering officer, Captain Dietz, gave me a standing pass, as I had often to go to the train and express office to send off parcels or receive them. Many a poor sick fellow has brightened up when he saw me coming, after it was learned that I carried the discharges around to the boys. One day I went to barrack A to carry a discharge to a sick man, after calling his name several times, I was told he had died a day or two before.

In passing through a ward, I was greeted with "bring mine next, bring mine next," on all sides. The poor fellows had to wait their turn, and we worked on as fast as we could get the descriptive lists.

After waiting a sufficient length of time for a reply from my company, Pailthorpe, Dunn[31] and myself held a counsel, and it was decided that I should write to our State agent at Washington for information; accordingly, I wrote the agent of the way we were situated, and he, in due time, sent a reply that it should be attended to.

In a few days, a clerk from headquarters came into the ward, called my name, asked if I was the man who had written to the State Agent, and ordered me to report to headquarters. He also ordered Pailthorpe and Dunn to do the same. We obeyed orders, answered a few questions, and were dismissed. The next day we received our Spread Eagle[32] and were free men once more. We could go where we pleased, without asking any ones permission. Our Country was saved, and we had helped to save it. Peace was declared, and we were proud to have been soldiers. We had our discharges in our pockets and were ready to go home, but we had to get some pay first. We were sent to Baltimore to be paid off. The Sanitary Commission furnished each man with a clean suit of under clothing, and we benefited by their liberality.

[31] This soldier is not a member of the 5th Michigan.
[32] A slang term for discharge papers.

⇥ 12 ⇤

A Soldier Returns Home

"I have been a soldier, have tried to do my duty. Although broken in health, I am not sorry, I would not sell my experience for large sums of money."

ON THE MORNING OF JUNE 24, 1865, WE WERE UP EARLY AND DOWN TO THE depot long before time for the train to leave. The depot is on the main street of Frederick, running north and south. It was the only busy street in the town. Most of the other streets were dirty and filthy looking, such as you might expect to find in any town so reverently a slave holding town. There were two or three streets devoted entirely to resorts of crime, and many a soldier had been ruined in those places. Not only gambling, but places where women are to be found, who take away their money and their manhood, giving in return, ruin and disgrace.

The colored population of the city were so numerous, that at a certain hour on Sunday you would think it was all Negroes, when coming from church of which they had their own, the street would be literally packed with them. Each evening it would seem that the whole city was on the streets, as the walks were crowded with all classes of humanity. Rich and poor, black and white, all mingled and jostled each other as they passed and passed again. It seemed a continuous stream with its currents running up and down, so as to make it fairly bubble. All styles of dresses were to be seen, and among them a good spattering of blue coats.

One very pleasant street was Church Street, which was broad and thickly lined with shade trees. On this street were several churches whose bells would chime for hours on each Sunday. One church had a dozen bells, all in chime, making very nice music. On one side of the street the shade trees were all basswood, called in the south, linden wood. At the time I passed them, they were in blossom, making the air almost sickening with their sweet perfume. I think the most beautiful shade trees were the soft maple. In a grove of these stood the schoolhouse. Maryland is a noted fruit country, and near the town were large peach orchards. Apples were abundant, and a person riding along the country roads could drive up to the trees anywhere, and pick cherries.

Taking one more look to the west, we see once more the dim peaks of the Blue Ridge, enveloped in smoke as though the battle clouds still hang over them. Almost directly to the west we see the towering top of Maryland Heights, always guarding Harpers Ferry. As you look beyond those smokey hills, you might imagine that you could hear the guns at Antietam just to the right, or the volleys of musketry as our Michigan 17th Infantry charged up South Mountain. You could imagine John Brown just over at the Ferry. Away still farther to the north lies Gettysburg, sleeping in peace. Casting the eye to the left, your vision covers (although you cannot see,) Pleasant Valley, Sandy Hook and Point of Rocks where the old people were inhumanely shot by reb bushwhackers. A little to the left you see Sugar Loaf Mountain, beyond which, as far as the eye can reach is Washington, forty miles distance. The country across which you look is the beautiful Frederick Valley.

As I stand and look across the fertile plain and over those smokey ridges I can, in my mind, see all the paths, which along with my company, I have marched in the heat of a midday sun, and under cover of the cool night, as we followed in the track of the retreating rebs. Twisting and turning through mountain passes, or moving over the straight, smooth, limestone pike. A pity 'tis that such a country should be torn and destroyed by an enemies guns, or its soil be reddened by the blood of friends.

But Antietam and Gettysburg had been seethed and scorched, and soaked in the fire and blood of friend and foe.

Frederick we leave you, all thy beauty and thy ugliness we leave behind. You will to us only dwell in the memory of the past. Farewell, the train is here on which we take our seats, and are whirled away toward Baltimore. On our way we see to us a novel sight, we call it a skirmish line. It is a long line of young Negroes raking hay in a field nearby.

Now again we pass over the Monocacy River and strike the main line of the B&O Railroad. Moving swiftly on, we pass the Relay House at the Washington Junction, and are soon in sight of the Chesapeake Bay. Gliding along the side of the bay, we then curve into the city of Baltimore. This time without fear of molestation, and without arms. Still we here of many robberies of soldiers in this dark looking hole of a city, where the worst characters the world ever knew congregates and watch for prey and plunder. Here we are told of a soldier that had just been discharged and paid off, being robbed of all his money by two miserable comrades, who pretended to be soldiers.

On reporting to the paymaster, we were told that we should have to wait until next day. So having several hours of daylight, we took a turn through the city to see what manner of thing it was.

Traversing through some low, dirty streets, in which could be seen as low, dirty creatures in the guise of human form. The streets were so narrow, that the tall brick blocks seemed to almost touch at the top.

We soon open into a broader street, on each side of which were solid blocks of business houses, and the street was fairly clean. But one objection I take to southern streets, is the cess drains from the kitchens, which are open and run across the sidewalk into the ditch, or gutter at the side of the street.

I have seen well dressed ladies walk along those streets with their long trains sweeping the walks, never raising them over those drains, but letting them drag through the filth and pass on unconcerned. Now this would look terrible dirty to a northern lady, but I suppose it is all in use. On we went, regardless of time or distance, until we reached the top of a high elevation on which was Washington's Monument. We paid twenty-five cents each, and went up this tower where we had an extended view of the city, as well as Chesapeake Bay.

This part of Baltimore is very pretty, and its streets are well laid out and well shaded. As it was getting near night and we had seen all of Baltimore we cared for, we returned to the post office in which was the paymaster's office. This was a large building surrounding an open court, around which extended a wide hallway, or walk over, which was a veranda to correspond, approached by stairs from the lower floor. The lower floor of this building was mostly an open space, in which refreshments were sold. The post office was on the lower floor, but all the other government offices were on the second floor. Here we spent the night loafing around as best we could, waiting for our turn. At length, morning came and the day was passing away, and yet our turn came not. About mid-day we received notice that we would have to go to Washington, again we were disappointed.

Let the reader now follow us to Washington over this now more than interesting route, as it is the last time we ever expect to visit the National Capitol. Taking the first train south from Baltimore, we soon reach and pass the Relay House, the Junction of the Washington branch of the B&O Railroad. Near here is where Butler went into camp with his troops in 1861. From which point he watched the proceeding of the rebel element, which threatened to mob our troops the second time.

Here the country is quite rough and broken, but flattens out into a level plain as you pass on south. At Annapolis Junction it is low and level. Here another branch of the B&O Railroad runs to Annapolis.

It is but a short distance to the capitol of Maryland, at which place the Naval School is situated.[1] All of this country over which we are now passing is Revolutionary, historical ground. Here the British and Americans moved alternately, and continually for nearly eight years, [with] Baltimore being one of the principal points of contention.

At Baltimore and Annapolis some of the most enterprising and daring privateers have been filed out, during the wars with Foreign Nations, that ever sailed from American Ports. All those things we remember, as we gaze off toward the broad Atlantic, just behind the trees and bluffs along the coast. But we glide along swiftly, and as we pass other scenes take the place of those we leave behind.

Ever varying, ever changing, the landscape seems to fly to the rear, rolling around and massing in heavy columns as if to annihilate some unseen foe, from which we were swiftly flying.

On, on we move over the plain, only broken here and there by some rivulet, or light range of hills, until we near the great city. When the face of the country begins to show the rougher aspect, and soon the frowning elevations on which are hundreds of guns seems to bid defiance to all foes that may approach from this direction.

We are now approaching the defenses of Washington. Some of those heavy works I have visited early in the war, when guards paced night and day, with never ceasing vigilance on its towering ramparts.

Those heavy cannon belched out fire, smoke and hail as the rebs advanced from this side in 1864. When they expected to find but a handful of convalescents to defend the city, but they struck against an unseen rock, for the old Sixth Corps was there. It had arrived just in time, and the rebs withdrew in disgust.[2]

---

[1] By Naval School, Avery refers to the United States Naval Academy, located on Chesapeake Bay in Annapolis.

[2] Avery refers to the skirmish at Fort Stevens, in Silver Spring, Maryland, that marked the high point of the final Confederate invasion of the north. This skirmish occurred on July 12, 1864.

But we are now in Georgetown, the northern position of the city of Washington. We pass the freight and stock depot, where we unshipped our horses in 1862 as we arrived from Michigan, and from where we proceeded to camp on East Capitol Hill. Now we are at the passenger depot, and step off the train. Again we tread the streets of Washington.

No provost guard could now march us off to prison, for we had a paper in our pockets that would pass us anywhere in the United States. This is a privilege we have fought three years for, and we have won.

All who carry the Spread Eagle are free, made so by their own hand. Who would not be proud of this. With our sabres, we did hew our path to freedom.

We have come to the Capitol to receive our pay, without which we cannot buy our bread. We have fought years for our country for a small sum, the value of from four to five dollars in gold. Where the Government paid the gold for bonds, it paid the soldier greenbacks. That took three dollars to make one in gold. All the more did we want our pay, for we could buy only thirty-three and one-third cents worth of goods with each dollar.

Now all kinds of merchandise was high, even up to gold prices, therefore our dollar, or the soldiers dollar, would buy but a very small amount of goods. Yet this was good, we had hewn out the greenback with the sword, and it would pay our bills if we had enough. But look at the rebs, they had lost, and their paper was worth just enough to light a cigar or pipe. They had failed, their swords were dull, they could not make their money good. Their fighting was in vain. They had no money, they had no credit. They had to have a pardon to pass, then, we had our discharges.

Going to the state agent's office, we laid our case before him. He at once proceeded to business, going with us to the paymaster's office, making all plain before that officer. But now, as the day was far advanced, the paymaster said we would have to wait until next day. The state agent now gave us each a ticket entitling us to food and lodging, while we stay at the Michigan Soldiers Home, where we went and got our supper, lodging, breakfast and dinner. While taking a walk to look once more at this beautiful, dirty, clean, homely, aristocratic, low-born, elevated scum of a foreign and domestic Capitol of the United States. Here is where our noble senators and representatives spend their time on the people's money. Smoking, drinking, gambling, dancing, doing little work, but much blowing. Here a few make laws binding millions of people, sometimes good, often poor, without care of their constituents. After one of those dishonorable honors get elected to congress, what does he care about those who sent him. He is their master, not they his, as they should be.

He says he represents the people, but let me say right here, he represents just the mind of one man. And that all are of this class, for they are not, as our records show the work of some noble, high-minded honorable men in congress, but there is to many of the other kind.

But as I was going to say, while walking out for exercise, and to take a last look of Washington, I saw the first woman drunk that I had ever seen. Even so beastly drunk as to require a policeman to keep her from falling down. Falling; if she had not fallen, I can't say what it is to fall, but what I wish to say is, to keep her from lying down like a beast on the street. But here in Washington it is fashionable to drink, women as well as men drink. Many aristocratic receptions are marked by drinking, and thick and maudlin voices, and fumes of tobacco and wine. I did not intend to write of the vices or virtues of public or private parties, but the air we breathe in this place is corruption, and as long as we are in this city, we can't help but speak of it, as we cast a last glance over the splendid blocks and poor cottages.

Now after passing one night here, we will soon be away. We reported early at the office of the paymaster, but still had to wait some time. Finally, we were called in, paid off in full with commutations for rations and traveling expenses home.

Taking the first train out, we were soon on our way toward Baltimore again. As we were leaving the city, we cast one more glance back over the spires and Dome, and were whirled away from the city of Washington forever, for ought we knew.

Arriving at Baltimore just at night, we went to a place called the Soldiers Rest, where we tried to get some sleep. Now if soldiers could not rest here, no one could. But alas, you might as well be in some other hot place and have ten thousand imps pricking you with their pitchforks. This was a large, two-story brick building, in the upper story were bunks built in tiers, one above another, without straw or bedding, not even blankets.

The other boys could not stand it, so they went down and spent the night lying on the walk beneath. I thought it would be nice to lie by the open window. Pulling a bench up close to the window, I took my position on it, and went to sleep. But I woke up in the early evening feeling a terrible itching and burning. In fact, I felt as though my clothing was alive, and busy trying to prick holes in me with the point of every thread. Now I got hold of one nob, it is a big knot in my garments. No, it bursts, it is a big, fat, bed bug. Whew, I am literally covered with the big, fat bugs. They crawl, they bite, they stink. The room is hot, I sweat, I itch, I burn, I grab my blankets and down I go to the walk, shaking off the bugs as best I can. Redbacks are worse then greybacks, soldiers rest indeed! No soldier but a dead one could rest in that building on such a night, and I do believe they would raise a dead one. But lying on a brick walk under the starry skies, with the breeze gently fanning the leaves on the trees near by, I think I got some rest.

The following morning we were again on the train moving out of Baltimore, and leaving those fearful burglars and night raiders behind to torment some other poor soldier, who might be misled by the word rest.

Good-bye Baltimore, you are to us as a thing of the past, but thy bugs, we shall long remember. Now we approach the broad Susquehanna River, pass over its long bridge and into Harrisburg. Here we have to wait a couple of hours for the train to move on. At this place, again we three walk out to look at this city by daylight, but our time is limited, and we don't wish to stop over, we have been in southern climes long enough. While waiting for the train, a rough looking chap came along and asked me if I did not wish to buy some clothing, saying he could show me where I could get clothing very cheap. Telling him I did not wish to buy until I got into Michigan. I tried to evade talking any more with him. Soon he approached again, and renewed the subject. Now I told him I knew my own business, and could buy clothing to suit myself. As I had no more money than I wished, I did not propose to let anyone get hold of me or my pocketbook.

In this man you will at once recognize the professional stool pigeon, or decoy. Somewhere in the city is a place where perhaps a small stock of clothing may be kept as a blind, to make a show of respectability. In another room you will find a bar, or worse still perhaps, a nicely fitted room, where you may be invited to sit down at your ease, pending a purchase of a suit, and where you may, if you wish, try on a suit without being observed. Next, if you are a pretty good-natured simple kind of a fellow, you are asked to take a friendly drink. As the proprietor is a great friend to the soldier, and wishes to give you a good bargain, and treat you nicely besides. Now beware, if you are keen, you will remember the man sent to solicit your patronage, and you will take all things together and make out a very suspicious case before you.

If you are thoughtless and don't remember the opening of this adventure, you take the glass offered you, thinking it to be offered in sympathy of your being a soldier, and all in good part. Now you thoughtlessly put the glass to your lips, and down goes the poison. Poison at all times, no matter how pure, but this time you are drugged. Your senses soon are gone, this is what is wanted of you. You are next robbed of your money, led into another part of the city, and left to come to your senses, as best you may, or taken in hand by an officer and put in the lock-up. In either case, your money is gone, and you have no way by which you can locate the place where you were robbed. For if you do at last find the place, you can prove nothing if you bring an officer. The place will be declared to be a respectable business, and the dealer will threaten you with arrest if you don't leave. What will you do, you were found drunk, and what is a drunkard's word worth?

Although it looked small, I always said I would never treat anyone, or allow anyone to treat me, that is to strong drink. Now you have the secret of so many robberies of soldiers on their way home. Through drink, some were boldly attacked and robbed in the streets, but the most of them through their lack of spirit to say no. In the first place then, don't be fooled by any decoy, and in the last place, let the devil's firewater alone. I will say right here for the benefit of the young men of today, I have seen the effects of drink, and I would not trust my life with the best man living if he drinks. No one who drinks is a man, nor will he ever be a man. He willfully pours down stuff that immediately takes away all the man, and leaves him forever a beast, and worse still, a devil.

No excuse is there for any man, or boy for drinking, not even the least parcel. I see no difference in a man who puts a weapon in his pocket saying "I will kill someone," than his putting down whiskey and saying "I will kill someone."

A few minutes more we wait for another train to take us along still further toward home. Soon the train draws up to the depot and we look for our car which we suppose to be as before, a second class smoking car. The conductor, hearing our remarks says "here boys, get right into this car, 'tis the best we can do, but I am sorry 'tis not still better." We were surprised, and supposed he had made a mistake, as we stepped on the car, and entering the door, found we were in a first class car in which were ladies and gentlemen. But it was all right, that conductor took soldiers to be gentlemen, although dressed in their old, worn uniforms. Now this was a luxury which we had not been accustomed to for a long three years.

Box and stock cars had been our portion, when being transported from place to place in the army. Now we were again swiftly traveling homeward, crossing the Allegheny River, and approaching the Ohio River, where we crossed at Bearwood, moving on to Belaire. We took the Cleveland, Columbus, and Pittsburgh Railroad. We were flying along through Ohio at the top of our speed. And as we gaily move along, let us recall some of the conversation carried on by the boys, Pailthorpe and Dunn. Finding that I had never been on water, and as our route lay across Lake Erie, the boys were chaffing me as they thought, because they expected to see me seasick, and they would have some fun after. As we were riding along, they would remark the fun of having a seasick comrade.

Crossing Lake Erie by steamship, the boys discouraged, as I did not become sick. We arrived in Detroit early morning at the wharf.

"Soldiers, right this way, breakfast is all ready," was the greeting. We were led by a gentleman up a flight of stairs from the wharf, where we were ushered into a large hall, all set with tables of nice food and steaming coffee. We took our places at the tables, and while doing justice to the good things set before us, we glance around the room. The whole building is decorated with mottoes, flags, and other patriotic devices in honor of the soldiers now coming home every day from the war.

Bidding my companions good-bye, I left the dining hall and set out to find a place where I could procure a suit of clothing. Entering a clothing store, I was soon being shown a large assortment, from which I selected a suit, which pleased me in style and quality.

After settling my bill, I went into another store where I purchased a nice dress for each my wife and little girl, in memory of Detroit, where I had spent many a day in camp duty and drill in 1862.

I now learned that my regiment were expected in town this day from the west where they had been disbanded. But on thinking the matter over, I saw it would keep me in Detroit until night, by missing the morning train west. And it would do me no particular good. So I concluded to start directly on first train for Grand Rapids. Reporting at the depot, I found the train ready, and stepping aboard, the train soon moved out of town.

I afterward found that Ellis had found my good friend Williams (the soldier's duty had proved too severe for Captain Williams, who got sick, resigned in May 1863, and afterward raised a regiment of infantry, the 28th Michigan), in Detroit, and had spent part of the day looking for me. But I was fast moving away from them, and was at such a distance that no recall could reach me. The regiment did reach the city the same day, and were paid off and sent home.

Now as I transverse again those long bands of iron, which fly from under the rear wheels of the fast moving train, again I count the miles on the poles as they fly past. I find I am nearing house, yes swiftly, surely, nearing home.

Five o'clock again finds me in Grand Rapids, where I step off the train. This time not into the snow, but into the hot, dusty air at the depot at the close of a very warm day, the thirtieth day of June, 1865. Again I set out on foot, through the city and out on Grandville Avenue toward the house of my father-in-law, Mr. Dillenback, in the township of Wyoming. Where I arrived this time, just before dark. I found that my wife was, at this time, at our home in Hopkins. Early in the morning I set out again for home. Walking out to the old plank road, I waited for the stage going south. Which soon made its appearance, over the hill north of Plaster Creek, rattling along over the rough and uneven plank.

As the old stage came rolling along I called it to halt, and climbed in and took my seat with other passengers.

Again the driver whipped up, and we bounced along toward Wayland, where I was to leave the stage route and travel home on foot. Getting a little acquainted with the people in the stage, I found one, a sister of one of the member's of Company L, of my regiment from Kalamazoo. Her brother had been killed just before the close of the war.

If I remember rightly, his name was Lusk.[3] And another was a soldier who lived in Dorr, and like myself, was returning home. The others were strangers from a distance.

After pounding over the terrible rough road through Dorr and Leighton, we arrived in due time at Wayland. Here I was surprised to find quite a nice thriving business town, where, when I went away three years before, there were but a few buildings.

Calling at the post office for mail for home, and to talk a few moments with the postmaster, T. Van, with whom I had been acquainted before the war, and also with Sheriff White, an old friend, I set out for home.

I now had only four miles to travel to reach my home, and I rapidly paced off the distance. Recalling to my mind, the many times I had walked the same road through mud and wet to get news from the war in its early stages.

Over this same road too, my wife had walked to Wayland, time after time during the war to get her letters from me, and to send me word from home.

Those were surely dark days when our dear friends were looking anxiously for news from us, not knowing what that news would be. For many it would come from a strange hand saying your husband, or your brother is dead, killed in battle at the front, or died of disease in the hospital, or equally as bad, is a prisoner of war.

But now I near my little home, I can see it in the distance, a smoke is issuing from the chimney, yes, they are there, someone is there. Now I see my little girl

---

[3] There were two soldiers named Lusk in Company L of the 5th Michigan. Cpl. George W. Lusk of Oshtemo was mustered out of service at Fort Leavenworth with the rest of the regiment in June 1865. Cpl. John C. Lusk of Alamo was discharged on a surgeon's certificate of disability in May 1865. Perhaps Avery was confused as to the reason for this man's leaving the service.

playing about the door. She looks up, claps her little hands, "Oh ma, here comes pa!" and I tell you, I was quickly there! Yes, I am home now, the war is over, we are reunited, and I have come home to the little home which I left three long years before to be a soldier.

I have been a soldier, have tried to do my duty. Although broken in health, I am not sorry, I would not sell my experience for large sums of money.

In this home at least, there was joy and gladness. House, home, at last home to stay, no more war. All peace, peace . . .

THE GRAND ARMY OF THE REPUBLIC

On April 6th, 1866, the first post of the Grand Army of the Republic was created. The Grand Army of the Republic, made up of all the old members of the different regiments all over the United States. This is indeed, a Grand Army. Organized to perpetuate the memory of those gone before, by decorating their graves once each year. And for the extension of brotherly aide to all its feeble and broken comrades, and to administer such comforts and aid to the widows of its fallen comrades, as many require its aide.

Such is indeed a Grand Army, and its campfires now burn brightly over thousands of hills, and in many vales throughout the Union. Those surviving comrades have been instrumental in saving today. The loyal people everywhere have great reason to be thankful and kind to those who gather once more with their bright uniforms to pay their respects to the dead. And this work had kindled in the hearts of many of our citizens a desire to take part in the ceremonies, and to perpetuate the memory of those dead heroes from generation to generation. And this beautiful duty will be continued so long as our country stands as a nation. Long after the last soldier is laid to rest will his friends march in solemn procession, and strew his grave with sweet flowers. This now is a National rite (on May 5th, 1868, the date of May 30th, 1868, was assigned as Memorial Day), and will continue to increase in favor as the years pass by. And as a soldier drops out, his place will be filled by some friend.

The Campaigns of the 5th Michigan Cavalry

THE 5TH MICHIGAN CAVALRY WAS MUSTERED INTO SERVICE FOR A THREE-year term of service at Camp Banks in Detroit, Michigan, on October 13, 1862. Prominent former judge and lumberman Joseph Tarr Copeland organized it. The regiment was immediately ordered to Washington, D.C. Its original commander was Copeland, who served as the regiment's colonel until November 1862, when he was promoted to brigadier general. In February 1863, Col. Russell A. Alger was transferred from the 6th Michigan Cavalry to assume command of the 5th Michigan. When Alger resigned his commission in the fall of 1864, Smith Hastings was promoted to colonel and took command of the regiment. On December 4, 1862, the new regiment left Detroit and traveled to Washington, where it encamped on East Capitol Hill, located in the northeast quadrant of the city.

From the time of its arrival until June 1864, the regiment served with Brig. Gen. Julius Stahel's independent division of cavalry, assigned to the defenses of Washington, D.C. In June 1863, it was assigned to the Cavalry Corps, Army of the Potomac, where it served until the summer of 1864. There, it served as the 2d Brigade, 3d Division, under command of Brig. Gen. Judson Kilpatrick. In 1864 it became 2d Brigade, 1st Division, under command of Brig. Gen. A. T. A. Torbert. In August 1864 Maj. Gen. Philip H. Sheridan was given command of the newly formed Army of the Shenandoah. From August 1864 until March 1865, the 6th Michigan served in the 1st Division of the Cavalry Corps of the Army of the Shenandoah. From March 1865 to June 1865, the regiment served in the 1st Division of the Cavalry Corps of the Army of the Potomac. In June 1865, the Michigan Brigade, including the 5th Michigan Cavalry, was assigned to the District of the Plains, until it was mustered out of the service in November 1865.

At all times, the regiment was armed with sabers and repeating weapons. Along with the 6th Michigan, the 5th Michigan was one of two units armed with Spencer repeating rifles in 1863. In 1864 it traded in the Spencer rifles for Spencer repeating carbines. Throughout its tenure of service, it was proficient in fighting dismounted, making good use of its repeating weapons.

The following is an itinerary of the raids and battles in which the 5th Michigan Cavalry participated. Routine reconnaissances and scouting missions are not included in this list.

1863

December 1862–February 1863: On duty at Camp Copeland on East Capitol Hill, in the defenses of Washington, D.C.

February 27–28: Scout from Centreville to Falmouth, Virginia.

March–April: Expedition to Freedom Hill, Virginia.

March 26: Expedition to Fairfax Courthouse, Virginia.

March 27: On picket duty near Chantilly, Virginia.

April 3–8: Expedition to the Loudoun Valley of Virginia, to pursue Capt. John S. Mosby's raiders.

April 13: Skirmish at Hauxhurst Mills, Virginia. The regiment remained on picket duty until June 20, when it crossed the Potomac River into Maryland and joined the Army of the Potomac's Cavalry Corps.

June 4: Stationed on Lawyer's Road, near Fairfax Courthouse and Frying Pan, Virginia.

June 25: Ordered to join Army of the Potomac in the field.

June 27: Reconnaissance up the Catoctin Valley in Maryland.

June 28: Occupation of Gettysburg, Pennsylvania.

June 30: Battle at Hanover, Pennsylvania.

July 2: Battle at Hunterstown, Pennsylvania.

July 3: Battle at Gettysburg, Pennsylvania.

July 4: Battle at Monterey Pass, Pennsylvania.

July 5: Battle at Smithsburg, Maryland.

July 6: Engagements at Hagerstown and Williamsport, Maryland.

July 9: Battle at Boonsboro, Maryland.

July 12: Battle at Hagerstown, Maryland.

July 14: Affair at Falling Waters, Maryland.

July 17: Skirmish at Snicker's Gap, Virginia.

July 21: Engagement at Ashby's Gap, Virginia.

July 24: Engagement at Battle Mountain, Virginia.

August 1–8: Expedition from Warrenton Junction between Bull Run and Blue Ridge Mountains.

August 24: Skirmish at King George Courthouse, Virginia.

August 25: Skirmish at Hartwood Church, Virginia.

September 1–3: Expedition to Port Conway, Virginia.

September 1: Engagement at Port Conway, Virginia.

September 13–17: Advance from the Rappahannock River to the Rapidan River.

September 13: Battle at Culpeper Courthouse, Virginia.

September 14: Engagement at Raccoon Ford, Virginia.

September 16: Engagement at Somerville Ford, Virginia.

September 21–23: Reconnaissance across the Rapidan River.

September 21: Battle of Jack's Shop (Madison Courthouse), Virginia.

September 22: Engagement at Liberty Mills, Virginia.

September 23: Engagement at Robertson's Ford, Virginia.

September 30: Skirmish at Woodville, Virginia.

October 8–22: Meade's Bristoe Station Campaign.

October 8–10: Occupation of James City, Virginia.

October 10: Engagement at James City, Virginia.

October 11: Battle at Brandy Station, Virginia.

October 12: Skirmish at Hartwood Church, Virginia.

October 14: Skirmishes at Grove Church and Gainesville, Virginia.

October 17–18: Stationed at Groveton, Virginia.

October 19: Battle at Buckland Mills, Virginia (the "Buckland Races").

November 7–8: Advance to line of the Rappahannock River.

November 7: Engagement at Stevensburg, Virginia.

November 22–23: Expedition to Morton's Ford, Virginia.

November 26–December 2: Meade's Mine Run Campaign.

November 26: Skirmish at Morton's Ford on the Rapidan River.

November 26–27: Skirmish at Raccoon Ford on the Rapidan River.

December 1: The regiment went into winter encampment at Brandy Station, Virginia. It remained on picket duty there along the Rapidan and Rappahannock Rivers until May 4, 1864.

1864

February 6–7: Demonstration on the Rapidan River.

February 28–March 4: Kilpatrick's Raid on Richmond.

March 1: Fortification of Richmond and skirmish at Brooks's Turnpike, Virginia.

March 3: Detachment sent to Tunstall's Station, Virginia.

March 5–May 2: The regiment engaged in picket duty along the Rappahannock River until the beginning of General Grant's spring campaign.

May 3–June 25: Grant's Overland Campaign from the Rapidan to the James River.

May 5–6: Skirmishes at Todd's Tavern, Virginia.

May 6: Engagements at Brock Road and the Furnaces, Virginia.

May 6–7: The Battle of the Wilderness, Virginia.

May 7–8: Battle of Todd's Tavern, Virginia.

May 9–24: Sheridan's Richmond Raid.

May 9: Engagement at Beaver Dam Station, Virginia.

May 11: Battle of Yellow Tavern, Virginia.

May 12: Engagement at Meadow Bridge, Virginia.

May 19: Expedition to Bottom's Bridge, Virginia.

May 20: Skirmish at Milford Station, Virginia.

May 21: Engagement at Hanover Courthouse, Virginia.

May 26–28: On line of the Pamunkey River.

May 27: Engagement at Hanovertown, Virginia.

May 28: Battle of Hawes Shop, Virginia.

May 28–31: On line of the Totopomoy River.

May 30: Engagements at Old Church and Mattadequin Creek, Virginia.

May 30–31: Battle of Cold Harbor, Virginia.

May 31: Skirmish at Bottom's Bridge, Virginia.

May 31–June 1: Engagements at Bethesda Church and Cold Harbor, Virginia.

June 7–25: Sheridan's Trevilian Raid.

June 11–12: Battle of Trevilian Station, Virginia.

June 21: Skirmish at Black Creek or Tunstall's Station, Virginia.

June 21: Skirmish at White House Landing or St. Peter's Church, Virginia.

June 23: Skirmish at Jones's Bridge, Virginia.

June 25–August 1: On picket duty with the Army of the Potomac near Petersburg, Virginia.

July 27–29: Demonstration north of the James River.

July 27–28: Battle of Deep Bottom, Virginia.

August 1: Ordered to Washington, D.C., and assigned to the Cavalry Corps, Army of the Shenandoah.

August 7–November 28: Sheridan's Shenandoah Valley Campaign.

August 10: Skirmish at Berryville Pike, Virginia.

August 11: Skirmish at Tell Gate, near White Post and Winchester.

August 12: Engagement at Winchester, Virginia.

August 16: Engagement at Front Royal, Virginia.

August 19: Skirmish at Snicker's Gap Pike, Virginia.

August 19: Skirmish at Berryville, Virginia.

August 21: Skirmish at Summit Point, Virginia.

August 25: Skirmishes at Kearneysville and Shepherdstown, Virginia.

August 28–29: Expedition to Smithfield, Virginia.

August 29: Engagements at Leetown and Smithfield.

August 29: Skirmish at Smithfield Crossing, Opequon Creek, Virginia.

September 3–4: Engagement at Berryville, Virginia.

September 15: Skirmish at Locke's Ford, Opequon Creek, Virginia.

September 19: Battle of the Opequon—Third Battle of Winchester, Virginia.

September 21: Battle of Fisher's Hill, Virginia.

September 22: Skirmish at Milford, Virginia.

September 24: Skirmish at Luray, Virginia.

September 26–28: Battle of Port Republic, Virginia.

October 2: Skirmish at Mt. Crawford, Virginia.

October: Participated in the destruction of the Shenandoah Valley known as "The Burning."

October 9: Battle of Tom's Brook, Virginia, also known as "The Woodstock Races."

October 19: Battle of Cedar Creek, Virginia.

November 11: Skirmish near Kernstown, Virginia.

November 12: Engagement at Newtown, Virginia.

November 18: Engagement in Loudoun County, Virginia.

November 22: Engagement at Rood's Hill, Virginia.

November 28–December 3: Expedition into Loudoun and Faquier Counties.

December 8–28: Sheridan's Raid to Gordonsville, Virginia.

December 21: Skirmish at Madison Courthouse, Virginia.

December 22: Skirmish at Liberty Mills, Virginia.

December 23: Engagement at Jack's Shop, near Gordonsville, Virginia.

December 29: The regiment went into winter quarters near Winchester, Virginia, where it remained on picket duty until February 28, 1865.

1865

February 13–17: Expedition to Little Fort Valley, Virginia.

February 27–March 25: Sheridan's Expedition from Winchester into Central Virginia.

March 1: Battle of Waynesboro, Virginia.

March 2: Occupation of Staunton and Waynesboro, Virginia.

March 8: Engagement at Duguidsville, Virginia.

March 10: Regiment marches to Petersburg, Virginia, to rejoin Army of the Potomac's Cavalry Corps.

March 28–April 9: Appomattox Campaign.

March 30–31: Battle of Dinwiddie Courthouse, Virginia.

April 1: Battle of Five Forks, Virginia.

April 2: Skirmish at Scott's Cross Roads on the South Side Railroad.

April 4: Skirmish at Tabernacle Church or Beaver Pond Creek, Virginia.

April 6: Battle of Sailor's Creek, Virginia.

April 8: Battle of Appomattox Station, Virginia.

April 9: Surrender of Army of Northern Virginia at Appomattox Court House, Virginia.

April 23–29: Expedition to Danville, Virginia.

May 15–22: March to Washington, D.C.

May 23: Participated in the Grand Review of the Army of the Potomac.

June 1: Moved to Fort Leavenworth, Kansas.

June 23: Regiment mustered out. Veterans and recruits transferred to 1st Michigan Cavalry. The 5th Michigan Cavalry mustered 1,866 officers and men. During its term of service, it lost 101 men and officers killed in action and another 24 who died of wounds suffered in battle, for a total of 125. A total of 69 more members of the regiment died while prisoners of war. Further, another 109 died of disease during the course of the war, and another 150 were discharged for disability, for total dead and wounded numbering 453. There are no statistics available for the number of members of the regiment wounded or taken prisoner during the course of the war. The 5th Michigan Cavalry left behind a rich legacy as a hard fighting regiment with good leadership.

Bibliography

PRIMARY SOURCES

Newspapers
National Tribune
New York Times
Wayland, Michigan *Saturday Globe*

Manuscript Sources
Gettysburg National Military Park Library, Gettysburg, Pennsylvania:
 Luther S. Trowbridge Letters
Historical Society of Pennsylvania, Philadelphia:
 Simon Gratz Collection
Michigan State Archives, Lansing, Michigan:
 Adjutant General's Reports
Monroe County Library System, Monroe, Michigan:
 Robert Frost Collection of Custeriana
The National Archives, Washington, D.C.:
 James Henry Avery Service Records
 James Henry Avery Pension Records, RG 15
 Lewis Herner Consolidated Service and Pension Files
University of Michigan, Bentley Historical Library, Ann Arbor, Michigan:
 Victor E. Comte Papers
 James H. Kidd Papers
Waldo Library, Western Michigan University, Kalamazoo, Michigan:
 William Ball Papers
 Albert and Byron Fisher Letters
 Joseph Gillett Letters
 Edwin Harvey Letters

Bibliography

William H. Rockwell Letters
Henry W. Stewart Letters
Francis Wright Letters

Articles and Separate Book Chapters

Bigelow, J. Allen. "Custer's Michigan Cavalry Brigade." *National Tribune,* 24 July 1919.

Butler, Matthew C. "The Cavalry Fight at Trevilian Station." In *Battles and Leaders of the Civil War,* edited by Robert U. Johnson and Clarence C. Buel, volume 4, pp. 237–39. New York: Century Publishing Co., 1884–1904.

Carpenter, Louis H. "Sheridan's Expedition around Richmond May 9–25, 1864." *Journal of the United States Cavalry Association* 1 (1888): 300–324.

Cole, A. V. "In the Raid to Richmond." *National Tribune,* 30 June 1910.

Harris, Moses. "The Union Cavalry." *War Papers Read Before the Commandery of the State of Wisconsin, Military Order of the Loyal Legion of the United States* 1 (1891): 340–73.

Harris, Samuel. "Major General George A. Custer—Stories Told around the Campfire of the Michigan Brigade of Cavalry." *Illinois Central Magazine* 3 (December 1914): 14–20.

Hastings, S. H. "The Cavalry in 1863: A Difference of Opinion—The Third Division's Escape From Lee." *Philadelphia Weekly Times,* 18 October 1879.

Imboden, John D. "The Confederate Retreat from Gettysburg." In *Battles and Leaders of the Civil War,* edited by Robert U. Johnson and Clarence C. Buel, volume 3, pp. 420–28. New York: Century Publishing Co., 1884–1904.

Isham, Asa B. "The Cavalry of the Army of the Potomac." *Sketches of War History, 1861–1865: Papers Prepared for the Ohio Commandery of the Military Order of the Loyal Legion of the United States* 5 (1903): 301–27.

———. "Through the Wilderness to Richmond." *Sketches of War History, 1861–1865: Papers Prepared for the Ohio Commandery of the Military Order of the Loyal Legion of the United States* 1 (1888): 198–217.

Kempster, Walter. "The Cavalry at Gettysburg." *War Papers: Read Before the Commandery of the State of Wisconsin, Military Order of the Loyal Legion of the United States* 4 (1896): 429–43.

Kidd, James H. "Address of General James H. Kidd, at the Dedication of Michigan Monuments on the Battle Field of Gettysburg, June 12, 1889." *Journal of the U. S. Cavalry Association* 4 (1891): 41–63.

Kilpatrick, Judson. "Lee's Campaign in October, '63: Wise in Conception, But in Execution a Failure. Major McClellan Reviewed." *Philadelphia Weekly Times,* date unknown.

Klement, Frank L., ed. "Edwin B. Bigelow: A Michigan Sergeant in the Civil War," *Michigan History* 38 (1954): 193–252.

Lowden, J. K. "A Gallant Record: Michigan's 5th Cav. in the Latter Period the War." In three parts, *National Tribune,* 16, 23, and 30 July 1896.

McClellan, Henry B. "The Campaign of 1863: The Cavalry Operations at and about Brandy Station in October. A Reply to General Kilpatrick." *Philadelphia Weekly Times,* 7 February 1880.

———. "With Stuart in October, '63: A Campaign Brimful of Successful Service and Stirring Incidents." *Philadelphia Weekly Times,* 7 June 1879.

Merritt, Wesley. "Sheridan in the Shenandoah Valley." In *Battles and Leaders of the Civil War,* edited by Robert U. Johnson and Clarence C. Buel, volume 4, pp. 345–61. New York: Century Publishing Co., 1884–1904.

Munford, Thomas T. "Operations Under Rosser." *Southern Historical Society Papers* 13 (1896): 133–44.

Newhall, Frederick C. "The Cavalry in 1863: Colonel Newhall Made Some Important Corrections of General Kilpatrick's History." *Philadelphia Weekly Times,* 30 August 1879.

Rice, Allan. "A Letter from a Young Michigan Cavalryman." *America's Civil War* 10 (March 1997): 74–79.

Rodenbough, Theophilus F. "Sheridan's Richmond Raid." In *Battles and Leaders of the Civil War,* edited by Robert U. Johnson and Clarence C. Buel, volume 4, pp. 188–93. New York: Century Publishing Co., 1884–1904.

———. "Sheridan's Trevilian Raid," In *Battles and Leaders of the Civil War,* edited by Robert U. Johnson and Clarence C. Buel, volume 4, pp. 233–36. New York: Century Publishing Co., 1884–1904.

Trowbridge, Luther S. "Operations of the Cavalry in the Gettysburg Campaign." *Michigan War Papers, Military Order of the Loyal Legion of the United States* 1 (October 6, 1888): 7, 8.

Books

Agassiz, George R., ed. *Meade's Headquarters 1863–1865: Letters of Colonel Theodore C. Lyman from the Wilderness to Appomattox.* Boston: Atlantic Press, 1922.

Allen, Stanton P. *Down in Dixie: Life in a Cavalry Regiment in the War Days from the Wilderness to Appomattox.* Boston: D. Lothrop & Co., 1888.

Carroll, John M., ed. *Custer in the Civil War: His Unfinished Memoirs.* San Rafael, Calif.: Presidio Press, 1977.

Chamberlain, Joshua L. *The Passing of the Armies.* New York: G. P. Putnam's Sons, 1915.

Cooper, David M. *Obituary Discourse on Occasion of the Death of Noah Henry Ferry.* New York: John F. Trow, 1863.

Custer, Elizabeth Bacon. *The Civil War Memoirs of Elizabeth Bacon Custer.* Edited by Arlene Reynolds. Austin, Tex.: University of Texas Press, 1994.

Doubleday, Abner. *Chancellorsville and Gettysburg.* New York: Charles Scribner's Sons, 1882.

Ford, Worthington C., ed. *A Cycle of Adams Letters 1861–1865.* 2 vols. Boston: Houghton-Mifflin, 1920.

Glazier, Willard. *Three Years in the Federal Cavalry.* New York: R. H. Ferguson & Co., 1870.

Grant, Ulysses S. *Personal Memoirs of Ulysses S. Grant.* 2 vols. New York: Charles L. Webster & Co., 1886.

Hagemann, E. R., ed. *Fighting Rebels and Redskins: Experiences in Army Life of Colonel George B. Sanford, 1861–1892.* Norman, Okla.: University of Oklahoma Press, 1969.

Harris, Samuel. *A Curious Way of Getting Rid of a Cowardly Captain.* Chicago: Press of Adolph Selz, n.d.

———. *A Story of the War of the Rebellion: Why I Was Not Hung.* Chicago: privately published, 1895.

———. *In a Raid With the Fifth Michigan Cavalry.* Chicago: Press of Adolph Selz, n.d.

———. *Michigan Brigade of Cavalry at the Battle of Gettysburg, July 3, 1863, Under Command of Brig. Gen. Geo. A. Custer.* Cass City, Mich.: Annual Reunion, Co. A, 5th Michigan Cavalry, 1894.

———. *On the Picketline, Thankful.* Chicago: Press of Adolph Selz, n.d.

———. *Personal Reminiscences of Samuel Harris.* Chicago: Rogerson Press, 1897.

History of the Eighteenth Regiment of Cavalry, Pennsylvania Volunteers (163rd Regiment of the Line), 1862–1865. New York: Publication Committee 18th Pennsylvania Cavalry, 1909.

Humphreys, Andrew A. *The Virginia Campaign of 1864 and 1865.* 2 vols. New York: Charles Scribner's Sons, 1883.

In Memoriam: John Hammond. Chicago: P. F. Pettibone & Co., 1890.

Isham, Asa B. *An Historical Sketch of the Seventh Regiment Michigan Volunteer Cavalry from Its Organization, in 1862, to Its Muster-Out, in 1865.* New York: Town Topics Publishing, 1893.

Kidd, James H. *Historical Sketch of General Custer.* Monroe, Mich.: Monroe County Library System, 1978.

———. *The Michigan Cavalry Brigade in the Wilderness.* Detroit: Winn & Hammond, 1890.

———. *Personal Recollections of a Cavalryman in Custer's Michigan Brigade.* Ionia, Mich.: Sentinel Printing, 1908.

Lanman, Charles. *The Red Book of Michigan: A Civil, Military and Biographical History.* Detroit: E. B. Smith & Co., 1871.

Lee, William O., comp. *Personal and Historical Sketches and Facial History of and by Members of the Seventh Michigan Volunteer Cavalry, 1862–1865.* Detroit: Ralston-Stroup Printing, 1904.

McDonald, William N. *A History of the Laurel Brigade.* Baltimore: Sun Job Printing Office, 1907.

Merrington, Marguerite, ed. *The Custer Story: The Life and Letters of General George A. Custer and His Wife Elizabeth.* New York: Devin-Adair Co., 1950.

Michigan at Gettysburg: Proceedings Incident to the Dedication of the Michigan Monuments upon the Battlefield at Gettysburg, June 12th, 1889. Detroit: Winn & Hammond Printers and Binders, 1889.

Moore, James, M.D. *Kilpatrick and Our Cavalry: Comprising a Sketch of the Life of General Kilpatrick.* New York: W. J. Widdleton, 1865.

Mosby, John S. *The Memoirs of Colonel John S. Mosby.* New York: Little, Brown & Co., 1917.

———. *Stuart's Cavalry in the Gettysburg Campaign.* New York: Moffat, Yard & Co., 1908.

Newhall, Frederick C. *With General Sheridan in Lee's Last Campaign.* Philadelphia: J. B. Lippincott, 1866.

Nevins, Allan, ed. *A Diary of Battle: The Personal Journals of Colonel Charles S. Wainwright, 1861–1865.* 1962. Reprint. Gettysburg, Pa.: Stan Clark Military Books, 1990.

Pond, George E. *The Shenandoah Valley in 1864.* New York: Charles Scribner's Sons, 1883.

Record Fifth Michigan Cavalry, Civil War, 1861–1865. Kalamazoo, Mich.: Ihling Bros. & Everard, 1905.

Record First Michigan Cavalry, Civil War, 1861–1865. Kalamazoo, Mich.: Ihling Bros. & Everard, 1905.

Record Seventh Michigan Cavalry, Civil War, 1861–1865. Kalamazoo, Mich.: Ihling Bros. & Everard, 1905.

Record Sixth Michigan Cavalry, Civil War, 1861–1865. Kalamazoo, Mich.: Ihling Bros. & Everard, 1905.

Robertson, John, comp. *Michigan in the War.* Lansing, Mich.: W. S. George & Co., 1882.

Rosser, Thomas L. *Riding With Rosser.* S. Roger Keller, ed. Shippensburg, Pa: Burd Street Press, 1997.

Schaff, Morris. *The Battle of the Wilderness.* Boston: Houghton-Mifflin, 1910.

Sheridan, Philip H. *Personal Memoirs of P. H. Sheridan, General, United States Army.* 2 vols. New York: Charles L. Webster & Co., 1888.

Sumner, Merlin E., comp. *The Diary of Cyrus B. Comstock.* Dayton, Ohio.: Morningside House, 1987.

Supplement to the Official Records of the Union and Confederate Armies. 100 vols. in 3 series. Wilmington, N.C.: Broadfoot Publishing, 1990.

Taylor, James E. *The James E. Taylor Sketchbook.* Dayton, Ohio.: Morningside, 1989.

Tremain, Henry Edwin. *The Last Hours of Sheridan's Cavalry.* New York: Bonnell, Silver & Barrows, 1904.

Wallace, Robert C. *A Few Memories of a Long Life.* Fairfield, Wash.: Ye Galleon Press, 1988.

The War of the Rebellion: A Compilation of the Official Records of the Union and Confederate Armies. 128 vols. in 3 series. Washington, D.C.: Government Printing Office, 1880–1901.

Wells, Edward L. *Hampton & His Cavalry in '64.* Richmond, Va.: B. F. Johnson Publishing Co., 1899.

Wilson, James Harrison. *Under the Old Flag: Recollections of Military Operations in the War for the Union, the Spanish War, the Boxer Rebellion, Etc.* 2 vols. New York: D. Appleton, 1912.

Wittenberg, Eric J., ed. *One of Custer's Wolverines: The Civil War Letters of Bvt. Brig. Gen. James H. Kidd, Sixth Michigan Cavalry.* Kent, Ohio.: Kent State University Press, 2000.

SECONDARY SOURCES

Articles and Separate Book Chapters

Black, Linda J. "Gettysburg's Preview of War: Early's June 26, 1863 Raid." *Gettysburg: Articles of Lasting Historical Interest* 3 (July 1990): 3–8.

Bush, Garry L. "Sixth Michigan Cavalry at Falling Waters: The End of the Gettysburg Campaign." *Gettysburg: Articles of Lasting Historical Interest* 9 (July 1993): 109–16.

Ellis, Richard N. "Volunteer Soldiers in the West, 1865." *Military Affairs* 34 (1970): 53–55.

Fagan, Roberta E. "Custer at Front Royal: 'A Horror of the War'?" In *Custer and His Times: Book Three,* edited by Gregory J. W. Urwin and Roberta E. Fagan, pp. 17–81. Conway, Ark: University of Arkansas, 1987.

Klingensmith, Harold A. "A Cavalry Regiment's First Campaign: The 18th Pennsylvania at Gettysburg." *Gettysburg: Articles of Lasting Historical Interest* 20 (December 1998): 51–74.

Krick, Robert E. L. "Stuart's Last Ride: A Confederate View of Sheridan's Raid." In *The Spotsylvania Campaign,* edited by Gary W. Gallagher, pp. 127–69. Chapel Hill, N.C.: University of North Carolina Press, 1998.

Krolick, Marshall D. "Forgotten Field: The Cavalry Battle East of Gettysburg on July 3, 1863." *Gettysburg: Articles of Lasting Historical Interest* 4 (January 1991): 75–88.

Lloyd, Harlan Page. "The Battle of Waynesboro." In *The Custer Reader,* edited by Paul Andrew Hutton, pp. 69–82. Lincoln, Neb.: University of Nebraska Press, 1992.

Longacre, Edward G. "Judson Kilpatrick." *Civil War Times Illustrated* 10 (1971): 10–12.

———. "Sir Percy Wyndham." *Civil War Times Illustrated* 8 (1968): 12–14.

McKinney, Francis F. "Michigan Cavalry in the Civil War." *Michigan Alumnus Quarterly Review* 43 (1957): 136–46.

Monaghan, Jay. "Custer's 'Last Stand'—Trevilian Station, 1864." *Civil War History* 8 (1962): 245–58.

Ramage, James A. "Mosby in the Valley." *North & South* 3, No. 1 (November 1999): 10–22.

Shevchuk, Paul. "The Battle of Hunterstown, Pennsylvania, July 2, 1863." *Gettysburg: Articles of Lasting Historical Interest* 1 (July 1989): pp. 93–104.

Urwin, Gregory J. W. "'Come On You Wolverines!': Custer's Michigan Cavalry Brigade." *Military Images* 7, No. 1 (July-August 1985): 7–15.

———. "Custer—The Civil War Years." In *The Custer Reader,* edited by Paul Andrew Hutton, pp. 7–32. Lincoln, Neb.: University of Nebraska Press, 1992.

Wittenberg, Eric J. "This Was a Night Never to Be Forgotten: The Midnight Fight in the Monterey Pass, July 4–5, 1863." *North and South* 2, No. 6 (August 1999): 44–54.

———. "Ulric Dahlgren in the Gettysburg Campaign." *Gettysburg: Articles of Lasting Historical Interest* 23 (December 1999).

Books

Bearss, Ed, and Chris Calkins. *The Battle of Five Forks.* Lynchburg, Va.: H. E. Howard Co., 1985.

Calkins, Christopher M. *The Appomattox Campaign.* Conshohocken, Pa.: Combined Publishing, 1999.

———. *The Danville Expedition of May and June 1865.* Danville, Va.: Blue & Gray Education Society, 1998.

Carter, Samuel III. *The Last Cavaliers: Confederate and Union Cavalry in the Civil War.* New York: St. Martin's Press, 1979.

Catton, Bruce. *The Coming Fury.* Garden City, N.Y.: Doubleday & Co., 1961.

Coddington, Edwin B. *The Gettysburg Campaign: A Study in Command.* New York: Charles Scribner's Sons, 1968.

Fishel, Edwin C. *The Secret War for the Union: The Untold Story of Military Intelligence in the Civil War.* Boston: Houghton-Mifflin, 1996.

Freeman, Douglas Southall. *R. E. Lee: A Biography.* 4 vols. New York: Charles Scribner's Sons, 1934.

Graham, Martin F., and George F. Skoch. *Mine Run: A Campaign of Lost Opportunities, October 21, 1863–May 1, 1864.* Lynchburg, Va.: H. E. Howard Co., 1987.

Hafen, LeRoy R., and Ann W. Hafen, eds. *Powder River Campaigns of 1865.* Glendale, Calif.: Arthur H. Clarke Co., 1961.

Heatwole, John L. *The Burning: Sheridan in the Shenandoah Valley.* Charlottesville, Va.: Rockbridge Publishing, 1998.

Heitman, Francis E. *Historical Register and Dictionary of the United States Army.* 2 vols. Washington, D.C.: Government Printing Office, 1903.

Henderson, William D. *The Road to Bristoe Station: Campaigning With Lee and Meade, August 1–October 20, 1863.* Lynchburg, Va.: H. E. Howard Co., 1987.

Historical Publication Committee. *Prelude to Gettysburg: Encounter at Hanover.* Hanover, Pa.: Hanover Chamber of Commerce, 1963.

Hunt, Roger D., and Jack R. Brown. *Brevet Brigadier Generals in Blue.* Gaithersburg, Md.: Olde Soldier Books, 1990.

Hutton, Andrew Paul, ed. *The Custer Reader.* Lincoln, Neb.: University of Nebraska Press, 1992.

Jones, Virgil Carrington. *Ranger Mosby.* Chapel Hill, N.C.: University of North Carolina Press, 1944.

Judge, Joseph. *Season of Fire: The Confederate Strike on Washington.* Lexington, Va.: Rockbridge Publishing, 1994.

Keen, Hugh C., and Horace Mewborn. *43rd Battalion Virginia Cavalry: Mosby's Command.* Lynchburg, Va.: H. E. Howard Co., 1993.

Kinsley, D. A. *Favor the Bold—Custer, The Civil War Years.* New York: Promontory Press, 1967.

Longacre, Edward G. *Army of Amateurs: General Benjamin F. Butler and the Army of the James, 1863–1865.* Mechanicsburg, Pa.: Stackpole Books, 1997.

———. *The Cavalry at Gettysburg. A Tactical Study of Mounted Operations during the Civil War's Pivotal Campaign, 9 June–14 July, 1863.* Rutherford, N.J.: Fairleigh-Dickinson University Press, 1986.

———. *Custer and His Wolverines: The Michigan Cavalry Brigade 1861–1865.* Conshohocken, Pa.: Combined Books, 1997.

Mahr, Theodore C. *The Battle of Cedar Creek: Showdown in the Shenandoah, October 1–30, 1864.* Lynchburg, Va.: H. E. Howard Co., 1992.

May, George S. *Writing on Michigan and the Civil War by Michigan Residents from 1960 to October, 1962.* Lansing, Mich.: Michigan Civil War Centennial Observance Commission, 1962.

Morgan, James A. III. *Always Ready, Always Willing: Battery M, Second U.S. Artillery.* Gaithersburg, Md.: Olde Soldier Books, n.d.

Morris, Roy B. Jr. *Sheridan: The Life and Wars of General Phil Sheridan.* New York: Crown Publishers, 1992.

Nye, Wilbur S. *Here Come the Rebels!* Baton Rouge, La.: Louisiana State University Press, 1965.

O'Neill, Robert F. Jr. *The Cavalry Fights at Aldie, Middleburg and Upperville: Small but Important Riots, June 10–27, 1863.* Lynchburg, Va.: H. E. Howard Co., 1993.

Pfanz, Harry W. *Gettysburg: Culp's Hill and Cemetery Hill.* Chapel Hill, N.C.: University of North Carolina Press, 1993.

Rhea, Gordon C. *The Battles for Spotsylvania Court House and the Road to Yellow Tavern, May 7–12, 1864.* Baton Rouge, La.: Louisiana State University Press, 1997.

———. *The Battle of the Wilderness, May 5–6, 1864.* Baton Rouge, La.: Louisiana State University Press, 1994.

Sears, Stephen W. *Landscape Turned Red: The Battle of Antietam.* New York: Ticknor & Fields, 1983.

———. *To the Gates of Richmond: The Peninsula Campaign.* New York: Ticknor & Fields, 1992.

Stackpole, Edward J. *Sheridan in the Shenandoah.* Harrisburg, Pa.: Stackpole Books, 1992.

Starr, Stephen Z. *The Union Cavalry in the Civil War.* 3 vols. Baton Rouge, La.: Louisiana State University Press, 1979–1984.

Swank, Walbrook D. *Battle of Trevilian Station: The Civil War's Greatest and Bloodiest All Cavalry Battle.* Shippensburg, Pa.: Burd Street Press, 1994.

Urwin, Gregory J. W. *Custer Victorious: The Civil War Battles of General George Armstrong Custer.* Rutherford, N.J.: Associated University Presses, 1983.

Warner, Ezra J. *Generals in Blue: Lives of the Union Commanders.* Baton Rouge, La.: Louisiana State University Press, 1964.

Wert, Jeffrey D. *Custer: The Controversial Life of George Armstrong Custer.* New York: Simon & Schuster, 1996.

———. *From Winchester to Cedar Creek: The Shenandoah Campaign of 1864.* Carlisle, Pa.: South Mountain Press, 1987.

———. *Mosby's Rangers: The True Adventures of the Most Famous Command of the Civil War.* New York: Simon & Schuster, 1990.

Wittenberg, Eric J. *Gettysburg's Forgotten Cavalry Actions.* Gettysburg, Pa.: Thomas Publications, 1998.

Index

Company M, 114, 132
Cook, Henry, 12
Cook, John, 12
Copeland, Joseph Tarr, 1–2, 3, 12, 161
"Copeland's Mounted Rifles," 3
Croff, Orlanda, 13
Crook, George, 101, 102, 134
Crosby, Lawrence L., 12
Culpeper, VA, 49, 50, 55, 127, 163
Cumberland, MD, 103, 104
Cummings, David, 12
Custer, George Armstrong, 61, 77,
    126–127, 131, 146
  battle strategy, 26
  at Beaver Dam Station, 69–70
  at Brandy Station, 51–52
  at Cedar Creek, 116
  death, 147
  at Gettysburg, PA, 1, 32, 35, 37
  at Meadow Bridge, 73
  at Old Church, 81
  orders retreat at Buckland Mills, 54
  at Tom's Brook, 112–114
  at Waynesboro, VA, 144
  at Yellow Tavern, 72
Custer, Mrs. Elizabeth B., 131

Dake, Crawley P., 47
Dallman, Henry, 13
Dalrymple, Benj. S., 13
Danville, VA, 166
Deep Bottom, VA, 164
description list, 143, 148
deserters, 57, 117
Detroit, MI, 3, 4, 9–16, 157
D&GH Railroad, 14
Dietz, Captain, 148
Dinn, F.H., 140–141
Dinwiddie Courthouse, VA, 166
discharge papers, 148
discipline, 123
District of the Plains, 161–162
Drury, George, 13
Drury, William, 13, 50
Duck Pond Mill, 145
Duguidsville, VA, 166

Dunker Church, 106
Dunn, William H., 13, 37, 148, 156
Dutcher, George M., 12, 19, 31–32
Dyre brothers, 83
Dyre, James, 13, 60
Dyre, Robert, 13
Dyre, Russell, 13
Dyre, Seth, 13
dysentery, 48

Earle, George W., 12, 73
Early, Jubal, 118–119, 127, 128, 144
East Capitol Hill, Washington, 19–20,
    161
Eaton, O.P., 13, 40, 94
Edwards, Arthur, 12
Edwards Ferry, VA, 27, 98
Edwards, Wm., 13
18th Connecticut Infantry, 99
Eighth Infantry Corps, 116
elections, 15, 121
Ellis's Ford, 92, 157
Ely's Ford, 65
Emmitsburg, PA, 31, 38
Emmons, Abiul, 13, 60
enlistment stopped, 143

Fairfax Courthouse, VA, 162
Fair Oaks, VA, 74
Falling Waters, MD, 43–44, 146, 163
Falmouth, VA, 22, 44, 54, 162
Faquier County, VA, 124, 165
Ferry, Noah, 4, 37
Ferry, Thomas, 4
Fifth Corps, 116
Fifth Michigan Cavalry, 1, 2, 24, 51, 72,
    73, 157
  assignment to Army of the Shenan-
    doah, 165
  at Banks Barracks, 10–16
  camp at Brandy Station, 163
  Camp Copeland, 19–20
  "Copeland's Mounted Rifles," 1, 3
  at Fort Leavenworth, KS, 166
  Grand Reviews, 130, 146, 166
  march to the front, 16–19, 166

Trowbridge, Luther S., 12, 37
Troy, Ohio, 4
Tunstall's Station, VA, 164

uniforms, 131
  Johnnies in blue, 91, 122
  red cravats, 1
Upjohn, Dr., 133
Upperville, VA, 45, 127
U.S. Arsenal, 134

Van, T, 158
Veteran Reserve Corps, 136–137
Virginia Central Railroad, 69, 86
Virginia/Maryland Pennsylvania Theater map, 23
Virginia/Maryland Theater, 62
voting in the field, 119

Wallace, Lew, 135, 141
Warner, E.A., 13
Warner, Edward A., 20
Warner, Henry, 13
War of the Rebellion, 82
War of the Revolution, 82
Warrenton Junction, VA, 22, 47–48, 163
Warrenton Junction Union hospital, 5, 48, 49
Warrenton, VA, 127
Washington, D.C., 70, 107, 135, 146, 150
  on the homeward trip, 151–154
  raided by Army of the Valley, 97
Washington, George (infantry man), 98
Washington, President George, 22, 87
Wasson, Homer, 13, 59
Wayland, MI, 5, 6, 15, 158
Waynesboro, VA, 144, 166
weapons
  cavalry issue, 18, 162
  infantry issue, 97

inspections, 61, 63
Jackass Batteries, 104
loss of in Winchester, 104
Weber, Peter, 43
Weeks, William C., 12, 40, 50, 57, 127
  captured at Richmond, 60
  personal attributes, 41
  wounded at Five Forks, 145
Werner, Henry, 72
White House Landing, VA, 76, 144, 146, 164
White Oak Swamp, VA, 74
White Post, VA, 165
White's Ford, 55
White, William E., 12, 50, 60, 126, 127, 145
Williamsport, MD, 39–40, 146, 162
Williamsport Pike, 41, 43
Williams, William B., 8–9, 12, 19, 31–32, 157
Wilmington, NC, 132
Wilson, James H., 114
Wilson, John P., 12
Winchester, VA, 5, 101, 128, 134, 135, 165, 166
  battle of, 146
  camp, 127, 165
  picket south of, 100
  third battle of, 107, 108, 131, 165
Wolverines, 1–2, 81
Woodstock Races, The. See Tom's Brook, Battle of
Woodstock, VA, 144
Woodville, VA, 163
Woolsey (boy from Tarrytown), 136

Yankee Doodle, 51, 58
Yellow Tavern, VA, Battle of, 70–72, 146, 164
  map, 71
York, PA, 31, 32

About the Compiler

KARLA JEAN HUSBY OF MARYSVILLE, WASHINGTON, IS THE GREAT-GREAT-granddaughter of James Henry Avery. She has been interested in history, and especially family history, for many years. Her grandmother, Lois Clay, introduced her to the writings of Henry Avery, and Karla spent a number of years compiling Henry's writings into the memoir that appears today. Her diligence in compiling this memoir was a key factor in bringing Henry Avery's story to light.

About the Editor

ERIC J. WITTENBERG IS A PRACTICING ATTORNEY IN COLUMBUS, OHIO. A native of southeastern Pennsylvania, he was educated at Dickinson College and the University of Pittsburgh School of Law. Mr. Wittenberg has spent years studying the actions of the Federal cavalry and is the author of numerous articles on the role of Army of the Potomac's Cavalry Corps. His first book, *Gettysburg's Forgotten Cavalry Actions,* won the third annual Bachelder-Coddington Literary Award as the best work on the Battle of Gettysburg of 1998. He has written two other books on the role of the Michigan Cavalry Brigade, is completing the first book-length study of Sheridan's June 1864 Trevilian Raid, and will be the coauthor of *Rush's Lancers: The Story of the Sixth Pennsylvania Cavalry,* a new regimental history of one of the Civil War's finest mounted units. He is a founding member of the Civil War Cavalry Association and serves on the board of directors of that group.